Edexcel International GCSE

Physics

International GCSE Physics is a challenge, that's for sure. Luckily, we've squeezed all the facts, theory and practical skills you'll need into this brilliant CGP book!

What's more, there are plenty of exam-style questions for every section, plus a full set of practice papers that'll really put your Physics knowledge to the test.

It's great for the Physics parts of Edexcel's International GCSE Science Double Award too — if you're studying this course, you'll only need to learn the Paper 1 topics.

Complete
Revision & Practice

Everything you need to pass t

Name ...Stella P-M...

Form ...VRy...

St Paul's Girls' School   W6 7BS

Contents

Throughout this book you'll see grade stamps like these:

These grade stamps help to show how difficult the questions are.

Remember — to get a top grade you need to be able to answer **all** the questions, not just the hardest ones.

Section 5 — Solids, Liquids and Gases

Section 6 — Magnetism and Electromagnetism

Section 7 — Radioactivity and Particles

Section 8 — Astrophysics

Describing Experiments

Practice Exams

Published by CGP

From original material by Paddy Gannon.

Editors: Luke Bennett, Mary Falkner and Caroline Purvis.

Contributor: Jason Howell.

ISBN: 978 1 78908 084 1

With thanks to Glenn Rogers for the proofreading.

With thanks to Ana Pungartnik for the copyright research.

Data used to construct stopping distance diagram on page 17 from the Highway Code.
Contains public sector information licensed under the Open Government Licence v3.0.
http://www.nationalarchives.gov.uk/doc/open-government-licence/version/3/

Data used to construct stopping distance table on page 173 from the Highway Code.
Contains public sector information licensed under the Open Government Licence v3.0.
http://www.nationalarchives.gov.uk/doc/open-government-licence/version/3/

Graph on page 192 contains public sector information licensed under the Open Government Licence v3.0.
http://www.nationalarchives.gov.uk/doc/open-government-licence/version/3/

Printed by Elanders Ltd, Newcastle upon Tyne.
Clipart from Corel®

Based on the classic CGP style created by Richard Parsons.

Speed and Velocity

2

Speed and velocity are similar, but in physics they're not quite the same...

Speed and Velocity are Both How Fast You're Going

1) Speed and velocity both simply say how fast you're going, and both are measured in m/s (or km/h or mph). But there is a subtle difference between them which you need to know:

> Speed is just how fast you're going (e.g. 30 mph or 20 m/s) with no regard to the direction.

> Velocity, however, must also have the direction specified, e.g. 30 mph north or 20 m/s, 060°.

2) This means you can have objects travelling at a constant speed with a changing velocity.

3) This happens when the object is changing direction whilst staying at the same speed.

Speed, Distance and Time — the Formula

For any object, the distance moved, (average) speed, and time taken are related by this formula:

You'd use the same formula to calculate velocity.

$$\text{Average Speed} = \frac{\text{Distance moved}}{\text{Time taken}}$$

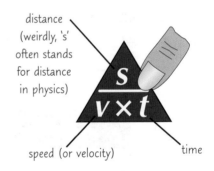

distance (weirdly, 's' often stands for distance in physics)

$$\frac{s}{v \times t}$$

speed (or velocity)   time

(If you're not sure how to use formula triangles, have a look inside the back cover.)

Example: A cat skulks 20 m in 35 s.
  Find: a) its average speed,
       b) how long it takes to skulk 75 m.

Answer: Using the formula triangle:
  a) $v = s/t = 20/35 = 0.57$ m/s (to 2 d.p.)
  b) $t = s/v = 75/0.57 = 132$ s = 2 min 12 s

Objects that are changing direction have a changing velocity...

...even if they're travelling at a steady speed. It's easy to get speed and velocity mixed up — they both tell you how fast something's going and even have the same units. So get the difference clear in you mind.

Acceleration

Acceleration is the rate of change of velocity. There are a couple of useful formulas for calculating acceleration on this page. Using them might take you a while at first, but over time you should get faster.

Acceleration is How Quickly Velocity is Changing

1) Acceleration is not the same as velocity or speed. Acceleration is how quickly the velocity is changing.

> The formulas for acceleration on this page only work when the acceleration is constant (uniform).

2) This change in velocity can be a change in speed or a change in direction or both. You only have to worry about the change in speed bit for calculations.

3) The unit of acceleration is m/s². Not m/s, which is velocity, but m/s².

4) There are two formulas you need to know:

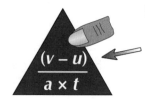

Here 'v' is the final velocity and 'u' is the initial velocity.

① $$\text{Acceleration} = \frac{\text{Change in Velocity}}{\text{Time taken}}$$

A negative value for acceleration means something is slowing down (decelerating).

There's a slightly tricky thing with this formula — the '$(v - u)$' means working out the 'change in velocity', rather than just putting a simple value for velocity or speed in.

> Example: A skulking cat accelerates from 2 m/s to 6 m/s in 5.6 s. Find its acceleration.
> Answer: Using the formula triangle: $a = (v - u) \div t = (6 - 2) \div 5.6$
> $= 4 \div 5.6 = 0.71$ m/s²

② $$v^2 = u^2 + 2as$$

Here 'v' is the final velocity, 'u' is the initial velocity, and 's' is the distance travelled while accelerating.

> Example: A van travelling at 23 m/s starts decelerating uniformly at 2.0 m/s² as it heads towards a built-up area 112 m away. What will its speed be when it reaches the built-up area?
> Answer:
> 1) Put the numbers in — remember a is negative because it's a deceleration.
> $v^2 = u^2 + (2 \times a \times s)$
> $= 23^2 + (2 \times -2.0 \times 112) = 81$
> 2) Finally, square root the whole thing.
> $v = \sqrt{81} = 9$ m/s

Make sure you're comfortable rearranging equations...

You'll need to be able to rearrange all types of formulas in your exam. Make sure you can deal with the ones that don't fit into a formula triangle (like $v^2 = u^2 + 2as$) as well as the ones that do.

Distance-Time Graphs

Distance-time (D-T) graphs tell you how fast an object is moving and how far it's travelled.
Simple as that really. Make sure you get them straight in your head before turning over...

Distance-Time Graphs Tell You How Far Something has Travelled

The different parts of a distance-time graph describe the motion of an object:

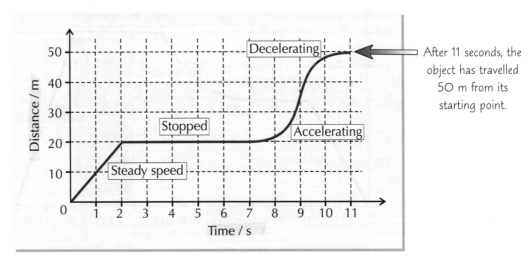

After 11 seconds, the object has travelled 50 m from its starting point.

1) The gradient (slope) at any point gives the speed of the object.

2) Flat sections are where it's stopped.

3) A steeper graph means it's going faster.

4) Curves represent acceleration.

5) A curve getting steeper means it's speeding up (increasing gradient).

6) A levelling off curve means it's slowing down (decreasing gradient).

Calculating Speed from a Distance-Time Graph

To calculate the speed from a distance-time graph, just work out the gradient:

In the above graph, the speed of the first section (between 0 and 2 s) is:

$$\text{Speed} = \text{gradient} = \frac{\text{vertical}}{\text{horizontal}} = \frac{20}{2} = 10 \text{ m/s}$$

Don't forget that you have to use the scales of the axes to work out the gradient. Don't measure in cm!

You can also calculate the average speed of an object over a period of time by dividing the total distance travelled by the time it takes to travel that distance.
For example, the average speed over the whole journey is 50 ÷ 11 = 4.5 m/s (to 2 s.f.)

Read the axes of any graph you get given carefully...

EXAM TIP Make sure you don't get confused between distance-time graphs and velocity-time graphs (which are coming up next). They do look quite similar, but they tell you different things...

Velocity-Time Graphs

Velocity-time (V-T) graphs show you how the velocity of an object changes over time. Simple as that really.

Velocity-Time Graphs can have a Positive or Negative Gradient

How an object's velocity changes over time can be plotted on a velocity-time graph.

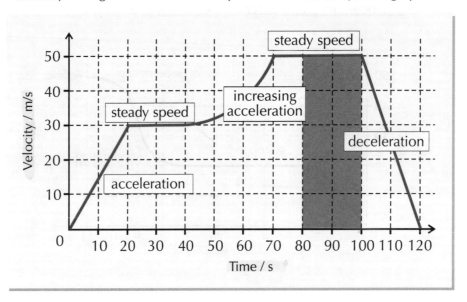

1) Gradient = acceleration.

2) Flat sections represent steady speed.

3) The steeper the graph, the greater the acceleration or deceleration.

4) Uphill sections (/) are acceleration.

5) Downhill sections (\) are deceleration.

6) The area under any part of the graph is equal to the distance travelled in that time interval.

7) A curve means changing acceleration.

Finding Acceleration, Speed or Distance from a V-T Graph

1) The acceleration represented by the first section of the graph is:

$$\text{Acceleration} = \text{gradient} = \frac{\text{vertical}}{\text{horizontal}} = \frac{30}{20} = 1.5 \text{ m/s}^2$$

2) The speed at any point is simply found by reading the value off the velocity axis.
3) The distance travelled in any time interval is equal to the area under the graph.

> The distance travelled between $t = 80$ s and $t = 100$ s is
> equal to the shaded area, which is 50 m/s × 20 s = 1000 m

Mass, Weight and Gravity

It might seem a bit odd, but it's true — <u>mass</u> and <u>weight</u> are not the same thing.
The difference between them is all thanks to the force of <u>gravity</u>...

Gravity is the Force of Attraction Between All Masses

<u>Gravity</u> attracts <u>all</u> masses, but you only notice it when one of the masses is <u>really big</u>, e.g. a planet.
Anything near a planet or star is <u>attracted</u> to it <u>very strongly</u>. This has <u>three</u> important effects:

1) On the surface of a planet, it makes all things <u>accelerate</u> towards the <u>ground</u>
   (all with the <u>same</u> acceleration, g, which is about <u>10 m/s^2</u> on Earth).
2) It gives everything a <u>weight</u>.
3) It keeps <u>planets</u>, <u>moons</u> and <u>satellites</u> in their <u>orbits</u>. The orbit is a <u>balance</u> between the
   <u>forward</u> motion of the object and the force of gravity pulling it <u>inwards</u> (see page 145).

Weight and Mass are Not the Same

To understand this you must <u>learn all these facts</u> about <u>mass and weight</u>:

1) <u>Mass</u> is just the <u>amount of 'stuff'</u> in an object.
   For any given object this will have the same value <u>anywhere</u> in the universe.
2) <u>Weight</u> is caused by the <u>pull</u> of gravity. In most questions the <u>weight</u> of an object is just
   the <u>force</u> of gravity pulling it towards the centre of the <u>Earth</u>.
3) An object has the <u>same</u> mass whether it's on <u>Earth</u> or on the <u>Moon</u> — but its <u>weight</u> will be <u>different</u>.
   A 1 kg mass will <u>weigh less</u> on the Moon (about 1.6 N) than it does on <u>Earth</u>
   (about 10 N), simply because the <u>force</u> of gravity pulling on it is <u>less</u>.
4) Weight is a <u>force</u> measured in <u>newtons</u>. It's measured using a <u>spring balance</u>
   or <u>newton meter</u>. <u>Mass</u> is <u>not</u> a force. It's measured in <u>kilograms</u> with
   a <u>mass balance</u> (an old-fashioned pair of balancing scales).

The Very Important Formula Relating Mass, Weight and Gravity

weight = mass × gravitational field strength $W = m \times g$

1) Remember, weight and mass are <u>not the same</u>. Mass is in <u>kilograms</u> (kg), weight is in <u>newtons</u> (N).
2) The letter "g" represents the <u>strength</u> of the gravity and its value is <u>different</u> for <u>different planets</u>.
   <u>On Earth $g \approx 10$ N/kg</u>. <u>On the Moon</u>, where the gravity is weaker, g is only about 1.6 N/kg.
3) This formula is <u>very easy</u> to use:

> <u>Example:</u> What is the <u>weight</u>, in newtons, of a <u>5 kg mass</u>, both on <u>Earth</u> and on the <u>Moon</u>?
> <u>Answer:</u> Use the formula $W = m \times g$.
> On Earth: $W = 5 \times 10 = 50$ N (The weight of the 5 kg mass is 50 N.)
> On the Moon: $W = 5 \times 1.6 = 8$ N (The weight of the 5 kg mass is 8 N.)

Weight is dependent on gravity — mass is not...

In everyday life, people tend to talk about their body "<u>weight</u>" in <u>kg</u> — but that's actually their body <u>mass</u>.

Warm-Up & Exam Questions

It's time to take a break and check how much of the information on the previous few pages has gone in. The warm-up questions will help get those brain cogs up to speed before you tackle the exam questions.

Warm-Up Questions

1) How are speed and velocity different?
2) Samuel runs 125 metres at an average speed of 6.50 m/s. How long does this take Samuel?
3) What are the units of acceleration?
4) What is represented by the gradient of a velocity-time graph?
5) What are the units of mass? And of weight?

Exam Questions

1   A cyclist travels 1500 m from his house to his local shops in 300 seconds.

   (a)   Calculate the cyclist's average speed in m/s during his journey.

   [2 marks]

   (b)   On the return home, the cyclist accelerates from 2.0 m/s with a steady acceleration of 2.4 m/s². Calculate the time in seconds that it takes the cyclist to reach a speed of 10 m/s.

   [3 marks]

2   A student is measuring gravitational field strength, *g*, in a classroom experiment. He takes an object with a mass of 2.0 kg and suspends it from a newton meter held in his hand. He takes multiple readings of the object's weight and calculates an average value of 19.6 N.

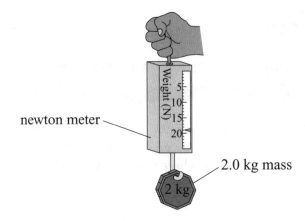

   (a)   (i) State the equation linking weight, mass and gravitational field strength.

   [1 mark]

   (ii) Calculate the gravitational field strength in the student's classroom and give the unit.

   [3 marks]

   (b)   The Moon's gravity is weaker than the Earth's. State how the student's measurement of the object's weight would differ if he performed the same experiment on the Moon. Explain your answer.

   [2 marks]

Exam Questions

3 A tractor ploughing a field accelerates at 2 m/s² for 10 metres, after which its speed is 7 m/s. Calculate the tractor's speed in m/s before it started accelerating.

[3 marks]

4 A student walked from her home to a sports centre for a football training session. Below is a distance-time graph for her journey.

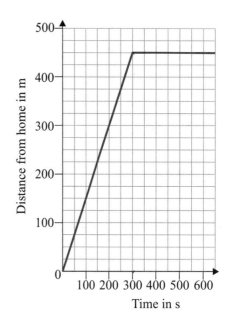

(a) Use the graph to find the time in seconds that it took for the student to reach the sports centre.

[1 mark]

(b) State whether the student walked to the sports centre at a steady speed. Explain how you know.

[2 marks]

(c) Use the graph to calculate the student's average speed in m/s as she walked to the sports centre.

[3 marks]

(d) The student returns home in a car after training. During the journey, the car constantly accelerates for 10 s to overtake another vehicle and then travels at a constant speed for a further 30 s.

Sketch a velocity-time graph to show the motion of the car during this time.

[3 marks]

5 The diagram shows a velocity-time graph for a car during a section of a journey.

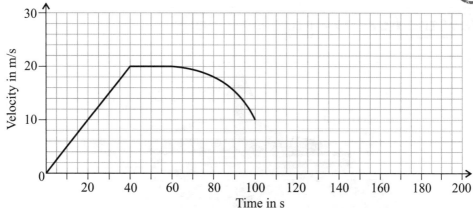

(a) Describe the motion of the car between 60 and 100 seconds.

[2 marks]

(b) Calculate the distance travelled by the car in metres between 40 and 60 seconds.

[3 marks]

(c) Calculate the acceleration of the car in m/s between 0 and 40 seconds.

[3 marks]

(d) After 100 seconds, the car accelerates steadily for 40 seconds until it reaches a steady velocity of 30 m/s, which it maintains for 60 seconds. Copy and complete the graph to show this motion.

[2 marks]

Forces

Forces are your friends — without them, you'd never get anywhere, and movement would be impossible.

There are Loads of **Different Types** of **Force**

A force is simply a push or a pull. There are lots of different types of force you need to know about:

1) Gravity or weight (see page 5) — close to a planet this acts straight downwards.

2) Reaction force — acts perpendicular to a surface and away from it (so if the surface is horizontal, the reaction force acts straight upwards).

3) Electrostatic force between two charged objects. The direction depends on the type of the charge (like charges repel, opposite charges attract) — see page 45.

4) Thrust — e.g. push or pull due to an engine or rocket speeding something up.

5) Drag or air resistance or friction which is slowing the thing down.

6) Lift — e.g. due to an aeroplane wing.

7) Tension in a rope or cable.

You Can **Draw** the **Forces** Acting on a Body

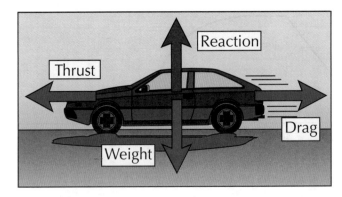

1) Chances are, there are loads of forces acting on you right now that you don't even know about. You don't notice them because they all balance out.

2) Any object with a weight feels a reaction force back from the surface it's on. Otherwise it would just keep falling.

3) When an object moves in a fluid (air, water etc.) it feels drag in the opposite direction to its motion.

All forces are just a push or a pull

Learn all of the different types of force listed above, and make sure you understand what they mean. You can test yourself by trying to come up with examples of each type of force in action.

Friction

Friction is found nearly everywhere, <u>slowing down</u> and <u>stopping</u> moving objects.

Friction is Always There to **Slow Things Down**

1) If an object has <u>no force</u> propelling it along, it will always <u>slow down and stop</u> because of <u>friction</u> (unless you're <u>in space</u> where there's no friction). Friction is a <u>force</u> that <u>opposes motion</u>.

2) To travel at a <u>steady speed</u>, things always need a <u>driving force</u> to <u>counteract</u> the friction.

3) Friction occurs in <u>three main ways</u>:

a) Friction Between **Solid Surfaces** Which Are **Gripping**

This is known as <u>static friction</u>.

b) Friction Between **Solid Surfaces Which Are Sliding Past Each Other**

This is known as <u>sliding friction</u>.

You can <u>reduce</u> both these types of friction by putting a <u>lubricant</u> like <u>oil</u> or <u>grease</u> between the surfaces. Friction between <u>solids</u> can often cause <u>wear</u> of the two <u>surfaces</u> in contact.

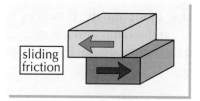

c) **Resistance** or **"Drag"** from **Fluids** (Liquids or Gases, e.g. Air)

1) The most important factor <u>by far</u> in <u>reducing drag in fluids</u> is keeping the shape of the object <u>streamlined</u>, like sports cars or boat hulls.

- Lorries and caravans have "<u>deflectors</u>" on them to make them more streamlined and reduce drag.
- <u>Roof boxes</u> on cars spoil their streamlined shape and so slow them down.

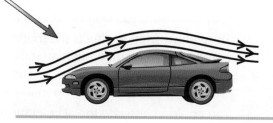

2) For a given thrust, the <u>higher</u> the <u>drag</u>, the <u>lower</u> the <u>top speed</u> of the car.

3) The <u>opposite extreme</u> to a sports car is a <u>parachute</u> which is about as <u>high drag</u> as you can get — which is, of course, <u>the whole idea</u>.

4) In a <u>fluid</u>, <u>friction always increases as the speed increases</u> — see page 16.

Motion is always opposed by friction (unless you're in a vacuum)
You can't move without <u>counteracting friction</u>. But it can be <u>useful</u>, e.g. if you need to <u>slow something down</u>.

 **Investigating Motion**

You can **Investigate** the Motion of a **Toy Car** on a **Ramp**

1) Set up your <u>apparatus</u> like in the diagram below, holding the car still just before the first light gate.

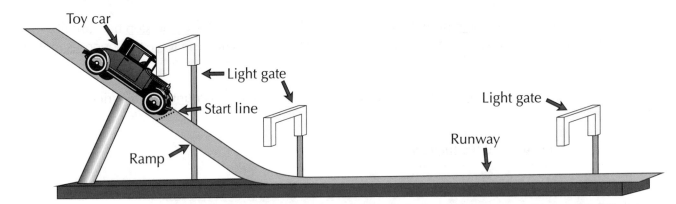

2) Mark a <u>line</u> on the ramp — this is to make sure the car starts from the <u>same point</u> each time.

3) Measure the <u>distance</u> between each light gate — you'll need this to find the car's <u>average speed</u>.

4) <u>Let go</u> of the car just before the light gate so that it starts to roll down the slope.

5) The light gates should be connected to a <u>computer</u>. When the car passes through each <u>light gate</u>, a beam of light is broken and a <u>time</u> is recorded by <u>data-logging software</u>.

Using light gates means you don't get any timing errors as a result of a person reacting slowly. If you don't have light gates, you could use a stopwatch with a lap function.

6) <u>Repeat</u> this experiment several times and get an <u>average time</u> it takes for the car to reach each light gate.

7) Using these times and the distances between light gates you can find the <u>average speed</u> of the car on the ramp and the average speed of the car on the runway — just divide the <u>distance between the light gates</u> by the average <u>time taken</u> for the car to travel between gates (see page 1).

You Could **Play Around** with the **Experimental Set-up**

You could change <u>different things</u> in this <u>experiment</u> to investigate <u>other factors</u> that might affect the car's motion. Just make sure that if you do change something, every other part of the experiment stays <u>the same</u>.

1) You could try seeing if the <u>mass</u> of the car affects its average speed — just load weights onto it (but make sure you don't overload it so that the wheel axles grind).

2) To see how <u>friction</u> affects the motion of the car you could try placing different materials on the ramp. If you do this, make sure they're laid <u>flat</u> and they don't change the <u>angle</u> of the ramp in any way.

3) You could investigate the <u>acceleration</u> of the car due to gravity by starting it off higher up the ramp and seeing how this affects its <u>average speed</u> between the gates.

4) You could change the <u>angle</u> of the ramp to see how that affects the car's speed down the slope.

5) You could even try it with <u>different cars</u> — see how the size, shape and weight of the car affects how fast it goes down the ramp.

You'd expect more streamlined cars to go quicker — see p.9.

Only change the independent variable...

...e.g. if you're investigating the <u>effect</u> of the angle of the slope on the car's motion, make sure that's the <u>only</u> thing that changes. <u>Control</u> the other <u>variables</u> (like the distance travelled along the ramp).

Warm-Up & Exam Questions

OK, questions can be a drag — but they'll really help you see how much you've taken in, so go on...

Warm-Up Questions

1) Give the name of the force that pulls objects towards the centre of the Earth.
2) What are electrostatic forces?
3) What is static friction?
4) Suggest how putting bikes on the roof of a car would affect its top speed.

Exam Questions

1 The diagram below shows a truck moving forwards at a steady speed. The thrust (driving force) acting on the truck is shown.

Grade **4-6**

thrust

   (a)   (i) As the truck moves, it experiences resistance from drag and friction. State the direction in which the resistance acts.

[1 mark]

        (ii) Describe how the speed of the truck affects the resistance force it experiences.

[1 mark]

   (b) Name **one** more force that acts on the truck and state the direction in which it acts.

[2 marks]

| PRACTICAL |

2 A student wants to carry out an experiment to investigate the motion of a trolley down a ramp. His textbook suggests setting up his apparatus as shown in the diagram.

Grade **4-6**

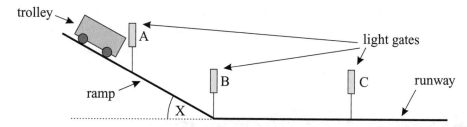

trolley — A — light gates — B — C — runway — ramp — X

   (a) Describe how he could use this apparatus to find the acceleration of the trolley down the ramp.

[6 marks]

   (b) The student decides to investigate how the distance the trolley travels down the ramp and the angle of the ramp (X) affect the trolley's speed at the bottom of the ramp. He changes both the angle of the ramp and the distance of the trolley along the ramp each time he repeats the experiment. He uses light gates to measure the trolley's speed at the bottom.

       The student concludes that as the angle of the ramp decreases, the speed of the trolley increases. Explain why he cannot conclude this from his data and suggest how he could improve his method.

[3 marks]

The Three Laws of Motion

In the 1660s, a chap called <u>Isaac Newton</u> worked out <u>three laws of motion</u>. Here are the first <u>two</u>.

First Law — **Balanced Forces** Mean **No Change** in **Velocity**

So long as the forces on an object are all <u>balanced</u>, then it'll just <u>stay still</u>, or else if it's already moving it'll just carry on at the <u>same velocity</u>.

1) When a train or car or bus or anything else is <u>moving</u> at a <u>constant velocity</u> then the <u>forces</u> on it must be <u>balanced</u>.
2) Never let yourself entertain the <u>idea</u> that things need a constant overall force to <u>keep</u> them moving.
3) To keep going at a <u>steady speed</u>, there must be <u>zero resultant force</u> — and don't you forget it.

steady speed

Second Law — A **Resultant Force** Means **Acceleration**

If there is an <u>unbalanced force</u>, then the object will <u>accelerate</u> in that direction.

1) The <u>overall unbalanced force</u> is often called the <u>resultant force</u>.
2) An <u>unbalanced</u> (or resultant) force will always produce <u>acceleration</u> (or deceleration).
3) This "<u>acceleration</u>" can take <u>five</u> different forms:
   - <u>starting</u>,
   - <u>stopping</u>,
   - <u>speeding up</u>,
   - <u>slowing down</u>,
   - <u>changing direction</u>.
4) On a force diagram, the <u>arrows</u> will be <u>unequal</u>.

accelerating

<u>Don't ever say</u>: "If something's moving there must be an overall resultant force acting on it". You get <u>steady</u> speed from <u>balanced</u> forces. If there's an <u>overall</u> force it will always <u>accelerate</u>.

Resultant Force = Mass × Acceleration

The three points below are probably pretty obvious:
1) The bigger the <u>force</u>, the <u>greater</u> the <u>acceleration</u> or <u>deceleration</u>.
2) The bigger the <u>mass</u>, the <u>smaller the acceleration</u>.
3) To get a <u>big</u> mass to accelerate <u>as fast</u> as a <u>small</u> mass it needs a <u>bigger</u> force. Just think about pushing <u>heavy</u> trolleys and it should all make sense.

In a nutshell, any <u>resultant force</u> will produce <u>acceleration</u>, and this is the <u>formula</u> for it:

Force = mass × acceleration

$F = ma$

m = mass a = acceleration
F is always the resultant force

The Three Laws of Motion

You can use Newton's second law to find an object's <u>acceleration</u>. All you need to know is the object's <u>mass</u> and the <u>resultant force</u> acting on it. You might have to rearrange the equation first though...

Resultant Force is Really Important — Especially for "F = ma"

1) The notion of <u>resultant force</u> is a really important one for you to get your head round. It's not especially tricky — it's just that it seems to get kind of <u>ignored</u>.

2) In most <u>real</u> situations there are at least <u>two forces</u> acting on an object along any direction. The <u>overall</u> effect of these forces will decide the <u>motion</u> of the object — whether it will <u>accelerate</u>, <u>decelerate</u> or stay at a <u>steady speed</u>.

3) If the forces act along the same line, the "<u>overall effect</u>" is found by just <u>adding or subtracting</u> them (see next page). The overall force you get is called the <u>resultant force</u>. When you use the <u>formula</u> "<u>F = ma</u>", F must always be the <u>resultant force</u>.

> <u>Example:</u> A car of mass of <u>1750 kg</u> has an engine which provides a resultant driving force of <u>5200 N</u>. Find the car's <u>acceleration</u>.
>
> <u>Answer:</u> First draw a <u>force diagram</u> for the car — this will make the situation easier to understand:
>
> Apply "<u>F = ma</u>" using the formula triangle:
>
> $$a = F/m$$
> $$= 5200 \div 1750$$
> $$= 3.0 \text{ m/s}^2 \text{ (2 s.f.)}$$
>
> 5200 N   acceleration   1750 kg

The Third Law — Reaction Forces

> If object A <u>exerts a force</u> on object B then object B exerts <u>an equal and opposite force</u> on object A.

This is Newton's third law of motion.

1) That means if you <u>push</u> something, say a shopping trolley, the trolley will <u>push back</u> against you, <u>just as hard</u>.

2) And as soon as you <u>stop</u> pushing, <u>so does the trolley</u>.

3) So far so good. The slightly tricky thing to get your head round is this — if the forces are always equal, <u>how does anything ever go anywhere</u>? The important thing to remember is that the two forces are acting on <u>different objects</u>. Think about a pair of ice skaters:

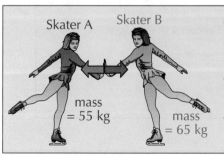

Skater A   Skater B   mass = 55 kg   mass = 65 kg

- When skater A pushes on skater B (the '<u>action</u>' force), she feels an equal and opposite force from skater B's hand (the '<u>reaction</u>' force).
- Both skaters feel the <u>same sized force</u>, in <u>opposite directions</u>, and so accelerate away from each other.
- Skater A will be <u>accelerated</u> more than skater B, though, because she has a <u>smaller mass</u> — remember <u>F = ma</u>.

4) It's the same sort of thing when you go <u>swimming</u>. You <u>push</u> back against the <u>water</u> with your arms and legs, and the water pushes you forwards with an <u>equal-sized force</u> in the <u>opposite direction</u>.

Paper 2

Combining Forces

When you're talking about the forces acting on an object, it's not enough to just talk about the <u>size</u> of each force. You need to know their <u>direction</u> too so you know which way the object will accelerate.

Vectors Have Size and Direction — Scalars Only Have Size

1) When there are <u>multiple forces</u> acting on an object, it's often useful to know the <u>resultant force</u> acting on the object (see previous page). To do this you need to know the <u>size</u> of all the <u>different forces</u> acting on the object and their <u>direction</u>.

In diagrams, vector quantities are usually represented by arrows.

2) Force is a <u>vector quantity</u> — vector quantities have a <u>size</u> and a <u>direction</u>.

3) Lots of <u>physical quantities</u> are vector quantities:

> <u>Vector quantities</u>: force, velocity, acceleration, momentum, etc.

4) Some physical quantities <u>only</u> have size and <u>no direction</u>. These are called <u>scalar quantities</u>:

> <u>Scalar quantities</u>: mass, temperature, time, length, etc.

To Work Out Resultant Force You Need To Combine Vectors

<u>Example:</u> What's the <u>resultant force</u> of a <u>220 N force north</u>, a <u>180 N force south</u> and a <u>90 N force south</u>?

<u>Answer:</u> Start by choosing a direction as the positive — let's say north. This means you <u>add</u> any forces in the north direction and <u>subtract</u> any forces in the south direction.

Resultant force = 220 – 180 – 90 = –50 N, so 50 N south.

<u>Example:</u> The jets on a plane are producing a <u>thrust</u> of <u>22 000 N east</u>, and the <u>friction</u> from the air is <u>8000 N west</u> at this speed.

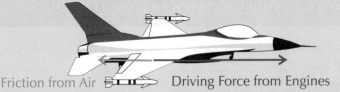

Friction from Air   Driving Force from Engines

a) What is the <u>resultant force</u> acting on the plane?

b) Find the <u>acceleration</u> of the plane in part a) if it has a mass of <u>10 000 kg</u>.

<u>Answer:</u>

a) Draw the vectors <u>end to end</u>:

Engine thrust   +   Friction   =   Resultant Force 14 000 N east
22 000 N east   8000 N west

b) Rearrange $F = ma$ to give:

$a = F \div m = 14\ 000 \div 10\ 000 = 1.4$ m/s^2

The resultant force — one force with the same result as many

You'll most often encounter a <u>resultant force</u> as the <u>difference</u> between some kind of <u>driving force</u> and a <u>resistive force</u>, acting in <u>opposite</u> directions along the <u>same line</u>. For example, driving force and friction.

Warm-Up & Exam Questions

I won't force you to do these questions, but there's no better way for you to prepare for your exams...

Warm-Up Questions

1) What is Newton's first law of motion?
2) If two forces are acting in the same direction, how do you find the resultant force?
3) State whether each of the following is a scalar or vector quantity:
   a) mass   b) velocity   c) force   d) time

Exam Questions

1   A camper van has a mass of 2500 kg. It is being driven along a straight, level road at a constant speed of 20 m/s.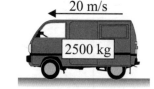

   (a)   A wind blows straight at the front of the van with a force of 200 N, causing it to slow down. Calculate the van's deceleration in m/s^2.

                                                   [2 marks]

   (b)   The van begins travelling at a steady speed before colliding with a stationary traffic cone that has a mass of 10 kg. The traffic cone accelerates at 29 m/s^2 in the direction of the van's motion.

      (i) Calculate the force in N applied to the traffic cone by the van.

PAPER 2   *[2 marks]*

      (ii) State the size of the force in N applied by the cone to the van during the collision.

                                                   [1 mark]

      (iii) Calculate the deceleration of the van in m/s^2 during the collision. Assume all of the force applied by the cone to the van causes the deceleration.

                                                   [2 marks]

2   The figure below shows two hot air balloons, labelled with the forces acting on them.

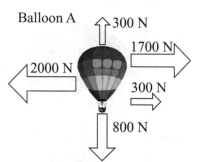

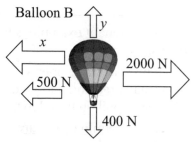

Balloon A   300 N   1700 N   2000 N   300 N   800 N

Balloon B y x 2000 N   500 N   400 N

   (a)   Calculate the resultant force in N acting on balloon A.

                                                   [2 marks]

   (b)   The resultant force acting on balloon B is zero.
      (i) Calculate the size of force y in N.

                                                   [1 mark]

      (ii) Calculate the size of force x in N.

                                                   [1 mark]

Terminal Velocity

If an object <u>falls</u> for long enough before it hits the ground, it will reach its <u>maximum</u>, or <u>terminal</u>, <u>velocity</u>.

Moving Objects Can Reach a Terminal Velocity

Frictional forces <u>increase</u> with <u>speed</u> — but only up to a <u>certain point</u>.

1) When an object first starts to fall, it has <u>much more</u> force <u>accelerating</u> it than <u>resistance</u> slowing it down.

2) As its <u>velocity</u> increases, the resistance <u>builds up</u>.

3) This resistance force gradually <u>reduces</u> the <u>acceleration</u> until eventually the <u>resistance force</u> is <u>equal</u> to the <u>accelerating force</u>. At this point, the object won't be able to accelerate any more. It will have reached its maximum velocity or <u>terminal velocity</u>.

This whole terminal velocity thing is explained by Newton's laws of motion (see page 12).

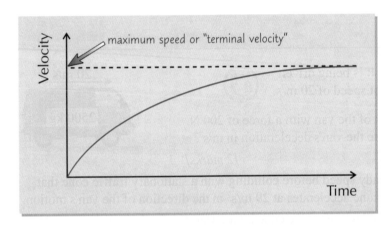

It's a bit like when you (very carefully) put your hand out of the window of a car as it moves along. At low speeds, you hardly notice the air pushing against your hand. But as the car goes faster, the air pushes your hand backwards much harder.

Shape and Area Affect the Terminal Velocity of Falling Objects

1) The <u>accelerating force</u> acting on <u>all falling objects</u> is <u>gravity</u> and it would make them all accelerate at the <u>same rate</u>, if it wasn't for <u>air resistance</u>.

2) To prove this, on the Moon, where there's <u>no air</u>, a hammer and a feather dropped simultaneously will <u>hit the ground together</u>.

3) However, on Earth, <u>air resistance</u> causes things to fall at <u>different speeds</u>, and the <u>terminal velocity</u> of any object is determined by its <u>drag</u> compared to its <u>weight</u>. The drag depends on its <u>shape and area</u>.

- The most important example is the <u>human skydiver</u>.
- Without his parachute open he has quite a <u>small area</u> and a force equal to his <u>weight</u> pulling him down.
- He reaches a <u>terminal velocity</u> of about <u>120 mph</u>.
- But with the parachute <u>open</u>, there's much more <u>air resistance</u> (at any given speed) and still only the same force pulling him down.
- This means his <u>terminal velocity</u> comes right down to about <u>15 mph</u>, which is a <u>safe speed</u> to hit the ground at.

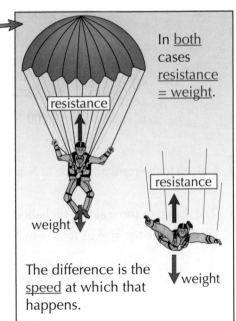

In <u>both</u> cases <u>resistance = weight</u>.

The difference is the <u>speed</u> at which that happens.

Stopping Distances

Looking at things simply — if you <u>need to stop</u> in a <u>given distance</u>, then the <u>faster</u> you're going, the <u>bigger braking force</u> you'll need. But in real life there are lots of <u>other factors</u> involved...

Many Factors Affect Your Total Stopping Distance

1) The stopping distance of a car is the distance covered in the time between the driver <u>first spotting</u> a hazard and the car coming to a <u>complete stop</u>. (They're pretty keen on this in exam questions, so make sure you <u>learn it</u>.)

2) The distance it takes to stop a car is divided into the <u>thinking distance</u> and the <u>braking distance</u>.

> Stopping Distance = Thinking Distance + Braking Distance

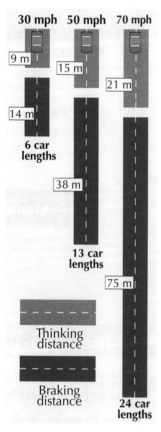

1) Thinking Distance

> "The distance the car travels in the time between the driver noticing the hazard and applying the brakes."

It's affected by <u>two main factors</u>:

a) <u>How fast you're going</u> — whatever your reaction time, the <u>faster</u> you're going, the <u>further</u> you'll go.

b) <u>Your reaction time</u> — this is affected by things like <u>tiredness</u>, <u>drugs</u>, <u>alcohol</u> and <u>old age</u>. <u>Inexperience</u> can also affect your <u>reaction time</u>.

2) Braking Distance

> "The distance the car travels during its deceleration whilst the brakes are being applied."

The figures above for typical stopping distances are from the Highway Code.

It's affected by <u>four main factors</u>:

a) <u>How fast you're going</u> — the <u>faster</u> you're going the <u>further</u> it takes to stop.

b) <u>The mass of the vehicle</u> — with the <u>same</u> brakes, the <u>larger the mass</u> of a vehicle, the <u>longer it takes to stop</u>. A car won't stop as quickly when it's full of people and towing a caravan.

c) <u>How good the brakes are</u> — brakes must be checked and maintained <u>regularly</u>. Worn or faulty brakes may let you down <u>catastrophically</u> just when you need them the <u>most</u>, i.e. in an <u>emergency</u>.

d) <u>How good the grip is</u> — this depends on <u>three things</u>:
   1) <u>road surface</u>,
   2) <u>weather</u> conditions,
   3) <u>tyres</u>.

> To avoid an accident, drivers need to leave <u>enough space</u> between their car and the one in front so that if they have to stop suddenly they can do so <u>safely</u>. 'Enough space' means the <u>stopping distance</u> for whatever speed they're going at. <u>Speed limits</u> are important because <u>speed</u> affects <u>stopping distance</u> so much.

Bad visibility can also be a major factor in accidents — lashing rain, thick fog, bright oncoming lights, etc. might mean that a driver doesn't notice a hazard until they're quite close to it — so they have a much shorter distance available to stop in.

Momentum and Collisions

A <u>large</u> rugby player running very <u>fast</u> is going to be a lot <u>harder to stop</u> than a small one out for a Sunday afternoon stroll — that's <u>momentum</u> for you.

Momentum = Mass × Velocity

1) The <u>greater</u> the <u>mass</u> of an object and the <u>greater</u> its <u>velocity</u>,the <u>more momentum</u> the object has.

2) Momentum is a <u>vector</u> quantity (see page 14) — it has size <u>and</u> direction (like <u>velocity</u>, but not speed).

Momentum (kg m/s) = Mass (kg) × Velocity (m/s)

p is the symbol for momentum.

Momentum **Before** = Momentum **After**

<u>Momentum is conserved</u> when no external forces act — the total momentum <u>after</u> is the <u>same</u> as it was <u>before</u>.

Example: Two skaters approach each other, <u>collide</u> and <u>move off together</u> as shown. At what <u>velocity</u> do they move after the collision?

Answer:
1) Choose which direction is <u>positive</u> — in this example, I'm going to say '<u>positive</u>' means '<u>to the right</u>'.

2) <u>Total momentum before</u> collision
= Ed's momentum + Jo's momentum
= {80 × 2} + {60 × (−1.5)}
= <u>70 kg m/s</u>

3) <u>Total momentum after</u> collision
= momentum of Ed and Jo together
= <u>140 × v</u>

4) So 140v = 70,
i.e. v = 0.5 m/s to the right

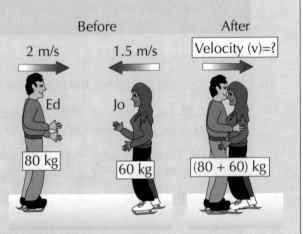

Momentum questions may need you to analyse a scenario...

Make sure you <u>read</u> any momentum questions <u>carefully</u>. You need to identify what the <u>objects</u> and <u>momentum</u> were <u>before the interaction</u>, and what they are <u>after the interaction</u>. The question may not be a scenario you're familiar with, so you'll need to work out what's going on.

Momentum and Collisions

Momentum is <u>conserved</u> in collisions, when external forces aren't acting. But when a <u>force</u> does <u>act</u> on an object it causes its <u>momentum to change</u>. <u>Bigger</u> forces cause <u>faster</u> momentum changes.

Forces Cause Changes in Momentum

1) When a <u>force</u> acts on an object, it causes a <u>change</u> in momentum.

$$\text{force (N)} = \frac{\text{change in momentum (kg m/s)}}{\text{time (s)}} \quad \text{or} \quad F = \frac{(mv - mu)}{t}$$

<u>Example</u> : A gun fires a bullet as shown.
     a) At what <u>speed</u> does the gun move <u>backwards</u>?
     b) Find the <u>force</u> exerted on the gun if it is <u>accelerated</u> for <u>0.1 seconds</u>.

velocity of gun (v) = ?
velocity of bullet = 150 m/s
mass of bullet = 0.01 kg
mass of gun = 1 kg

After firing

<u>Answer</u>:   a) Choose which direction is <u>positive</u> —
I'll use '<u>to the right</u>' as 'positive'.
<u>Total momentum before</u> firing = <u>0 kgm/s</u>
<u>Total momentum after</u> firing
= bullet's momentum + gun's momentum
= $(0.01 \times 150) + (1 \times v) = \underline{1.5 + v}$
So $1.5 + v = 0$, i.e. $v = -1.5$ m/s.
So the gun moves backwards at 1.5 m/s. ← This is the gun's recoil.

     b) <u>Momentum</u> of gun <u>before</u> firing = mu = 1×0 = <u>0 kg m/s</u>
<u>Momentum</u> of gun <u>after</u> firing = mv = 1×-1.5 = <u>−1.5 kg m/s</u>
<u>Force</u> = $\dfrac{mv - mu}{t} = \dfrac{-1.5 - 0}{0.1} = -15$ N

By Newton's third law, this means the force on the bullet must be 15 N in the opposite direction.

2) A <u>larger</u> force means a <u>faster</u> change of momentum (and so a greater <u>acceleration</u>).

3) Likewise, if someone's momentum changes <u>very quickly</u> (like in a <u>car crash</u>), the <u>forces</u> on the body will be very <u>large</u>, and more likely to cause <u>injury</u>.

4) This is why cars are designed to slow people down over a <u>longer time</u> when they crash — the longer it takes for a change in <u>momentum</u>, the <u>smaller</u> the <u>force</u> (and the <u>less severe</u> injuries are likely to be).

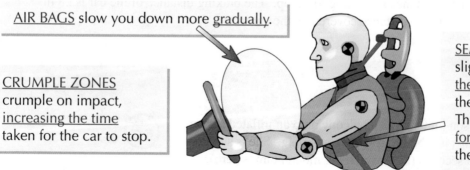

<u>AIR BAGS</u> slow you down more <u>gradually</u>.

<u>CRUMPLE ZONES</u> crumple on impact, <u>increasing the time</u> taken for the car to stop.

<u>SEAT BELTS</u> stretch slightly, <u>increasing the time</u> taken for the wearer to stop. This <u>reduces the forces</u> acting on the chest.

A slower change in momentum means smaller forces...

You might get asked to <u>explain</u> how <u>safety features prevent injury</u> in your exam, so make sure you can.

Paper 2

Warm-Up & Exam Questions

Don't stop now — tackle these questions, then go on to the next section while you've got the momentum.

Warm-Up Questions

1) When does a falling object reach terminal velocity?
2) Explain why a car takes longer to stop when it's full of passengers.
   State two additional factors that increase stopping distance.
3) What does "conservation of momentum" mean?

Exam Questions

1   The stopping distance of a car is the distance covered in the time between the driver first spotting a hazard and the car coming to a complete stop.

  (a) (i) What name is given to the distance travelled by a car between
            the driver first spotting a hazard and the driver applying the brakes?

[1 mark]

      (ii) Give **two** factors that can affect this distance.

[2 marks]

  (b) (i) What is meant by the **braking distance** of a car?

[1 mark]

      (ii) Give **two** factors that can affect this distance.

[2 marks]

2   A person is driving a car in heavy rain.

  (a) State and explain **one** way in which heavy rain can increase a car's stopping distance.

[2 marks]

  (b) Suggest **one** way a driver can decrease their stopping distance if driving in heavy rain.

[1 mark]

  (c) The driver sees a deer and stops the car. The car covers a distance of 37 m between the driver
      spotting the deer and the car coming to a stop. The braking distance of the car is 28 m.
      Calculate the thinking distance covered by the car in m.

[2 marks]

PAPER 2

3   A 65 kg stuntperson jumps from a balcony onto an inflated airbag.
   Her speed is 14 m/s just before she hits the airbag. She is stopped
   in a period of 1.3 seconds (after which her momentum is zero).

  (a) (i) State the equation linking momentum, mass and velocity.

[1 mark]

Exam Questions

(ii) Calculate the momentum of the stuntperson just before she hits the airbag and give the unit.

[3 marks]

(b) (i) State the equation linking force, change in momentum and time taken.

[1 mark]

(ii) Calculate the average force in N acting on the stuntperson as she is stopped by the airbag.

[2 marks]

PAPER 2

4   A skater with a mass of 60 kg is moving at 5.0 m/s.
He skates past a bag and picks it up from the floor,
causing him to slow down to 4.8 m/s.

Calculate the mass of the bag.
Assume there are no frictional forces.

[5 marks]

PAPER 2

5   In a demolition derby, cars drive around an arena and crash into each other.

(a)   One car has a mass of 650 kg and a velocity of 15 m/s.
Calculate the momentum of the car in kg m/s.

[2 marks]

(b)   The car collides head-on with another car of mass 750 kg moving in the opposite direction.
The two cars stick together. Calculate the combined velocity of the two cars in m/s
immediately after the crash if the other car was travelling at 10 m/s before the collision.

[4 marks]

(c)   The cars have crumple zones at the front of the car that crumple on impact.
Explain how a crumple zone reduces the forces acting on a driver during a collision.

[2 marks]

6   A student is studying the forces acting on objects falling at terminal velocity.

The student takes two balls of the same size but with different weights and drops them off a
high balcony. Which of the two balls will have a lower terminal velocity? Explain your answer.

[3 marks]

Turning Effects

When <u>forces</u> act around a fixed point called a <u>pivot</u> they have <u>turning effects</u> called <u>moments</u>. We use these effects all the time in everyday life — e.g. when we use door handles or <u>spanners</u>...

A **Moment** is the **Turning Effect** of a Force

$$\text{Moment (Nm)} = \underline{\text{Force}}\text{ (N)} \times \frac{\text{Perpendicular }\underline{\text{distance}}\text{ (m)}}{\text{between line of action and pivot}}$$

1) The <u>force</u> on a spanner causes a <u>turning effect</u> or <u>moment</u> on the nut. A <u>larger</u> force would mean a <u>larger</u> moment.

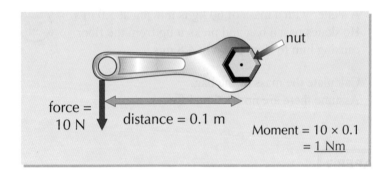

force = 10 N   distance = 0.1 m   nut

Moment = 10 × 0.1 = <u>1 Nm</u>

2) Using a longer spanner, the same force can exert a <u>larger</u> moment because the <u>distance</u> from the pivot is <u>greater</u>.

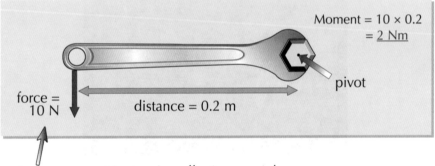

Moment = 10 × 0.2 = <u>2 Nm</u>

force = 10 N   distance = 0.2 m   pivot

3) To get the <u>maximum</u> moment (or turning effect) you need to push at <u>right angles</u> (perpendicular) to the spanner.

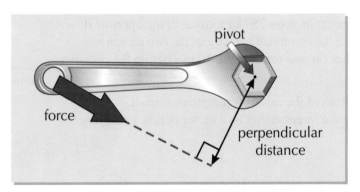

pivot

force

perpendicular distance

4) Pushing at <u>any other angle</u> means a smaller moment because the <u>perpendicular</u> distance between the line of action and the pivot is <u>smaller</u>.

The moment of a force = force × distance...

Think of the <u>extra force</u> you need to use to open a door by pushing it near the hinge compared to pushing by the handle — the <u>distance from the pivot</u> is less, so you need <u>more force</u> to get the <u>same moment</u>.

Centre of Gravity

The <u>weight</u> of an object can be thought to act through a <u>point</u> called its <u>centre of gravity</u>.

The **Centre of Gravity** Hangs **Below** the **Point of Suspension**

1) You can think of the <u>centre of gravity</u> of an object as the point through which the <u>weight</u> of the object acts.

2) A freely suspended object will <u>swing</u> until its centre of gravity is <u>vertically below</u> the <u>point of suspension</u>.

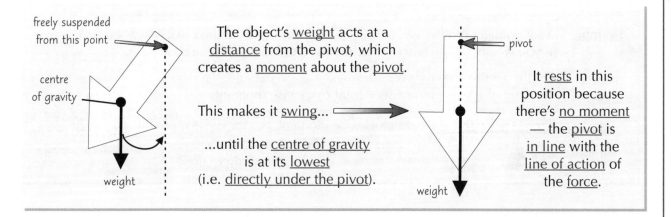

freely suspended from this point

centre of gravity

weight

The object's <u>weight</u> acts at a <u>distance</u> from the pivot, which creates a <u>moment</u> about the <u>pivot</u>.

This makes it <u>swing</u>...

...until the <u>centre of gravity</u> is at its <u>lowest</u> (i.e. <u>directly under the pivot</u>).

pivot

It <u>rests</u> in this position because there's <u>no moment</u> — the <u>pivot</u> is <u>in line</u> with the <u>line of action</u> of the <u>force</u>.

weight

3) This means you can find the <u>centre of gravity</u> of any flat shape like this:

1) Suspend the shape and a <u>plumb line</u> from the same point, and wait until they <u>stop moving</u>.

2) <u>Draw</u> a line along the plumb line.

3) Do the same thing again, but suspend the shape from a <u>different</u> pivot point.

4) The centre of gravity is where your two lines <u>cross</u>.

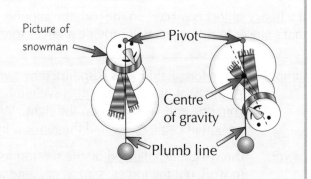

Picture of snowman

Pivot

Centre of gravity

Plumb line

4) But you don't need to go to all that trouble for <u>simple</u> shapes. You can quickly guess where the centre of gravity is by looking for <u>lines of symmetry</u>.

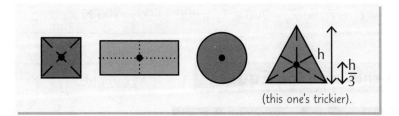

(this one's trickier).

A suspended object swings until its centre of gravity is below the pivot

So there you go — now you know how to <u>find</u> the <u>centre of gravity</u> of any <u>irregularly-shaped</u> object in a few easy steps. Remember: for simple shapes, the centre of gravity is where the lines of symmetry cross.

Paper 2

Paper 2

Principle of Moments

Once you can calculate moments, you can work out if a <u>seesaw is balanced</u>. Useful thing, Physics.

A Question of **Balance** — Are the **Moments Equal?**

The <u>principle of moments</u> says:

> If an object is balanced then:
> Total <u>Anticlockwise</u> Moments = Total <u>Clockwise</u> Moments

You can use this idea to help solve problems where forces are acting on a <u>balanced object</u>.

<u>Example:</u>   Your younger brother weighs <u>300 N</u> and sits <u>2 m</u> from the pivot of a seesaw.
If you weigh <u>700 N</u>, where should you sit to balance the seesaw?

<u>Answer:</u>   For the seesaw to <u>balance</u>:
Total <u>anticlockwise</u> moments = total <u>clockwise</u> moments

anticlockwise moment = clockwise moment
$300 \times 2 = 700 \times y$
$y = 0.86$ m (to 2 s.f.)

Ignore the weight of the seesaw — its centre of mass is on the pivot, so it doesn't have a turning effect.

2 m, y
300 N, 700 N

Forces are **Not Always Equal** Across All **Supports**

1) If a <u>light rod</u> is being supported at <u>both ends</u>, the <u>upwards force</u> provided by each support <u>won't</u> always be the <u>same</u>.

2) If a <u>heavy object</u> is placed on the rod, the support that's <u>closer</u> to the object will provide a <u>larger force</u>.

"Light" means you can ignore the weight in your calculations. In general, if they don't tell you the weight, you can ignore it.

<u>Example:</u>   A <u>6 m long light rod</u> is suspended by <u>two cables</u> (<u>A</u> and <u>B</u>) at its ends. A <u>900 N</u> weight is placed <u>4 m</u> <u>from one end</u>, as shown on the right. Work out the <u>tension</u> in <u>cable A</u>, T_A, and the <u>tension</u> in <u>cable B</u>, T_B.

T_A T_B
A   B
2 m   4 m
900 N

<u>Answer:</u>   The weight is <u>balanced</u> by the tension forces in the cables. To work out the forces, start at one end and treat that end as a <u>pivot</u>, so you can work out the <u>upward force</u> at the other end:

<u>clockwise moment</u> around B = <u>anticlockwise moment</u> around B
$T_A \times 6 = 900 \times 4$, so $T_A = 3600/6 = 600$ N

Then you can work out the force in B as we know the <u>vertical forces balance</u>:
900 N $= T_A + T_B$, so $T_B = 900 - T_A = 900 - 600 = 300$ N

And if the Moments are **Not Equal...**

> If the Total <u>Anticlockwise</u> Moments
> <u>do not equal</u> the Total <u>Clockwise</u> Moments,
> there will be a <u>Resultant Moment</u>

...so the object will <u>turn</u>.

<u>Example:</u>

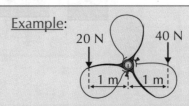

20 N   40 N
1 m   1 m

clockwise moments = $40 \times 1 = 40$ Nm
anticlockwise moments = $20 \times 1 = 20$ Nm
So the propellor will turn <u>clockwise</u>.

Paper 2

Paper 2

Hooke's Law

Applying a <u>force</u> to an object can cause it to change shape temporarily... or even permanently.

Hooke's Law Says that Extension is Proportional to Force

1) The length of an <u>unstretched</u> metal wire is called its <u>natural length</u>, *l*.

2) If a metal <u>wire</u> (see right) is supported at the top and then a <u>weight</u> attached to the bottom, it <u>stretches</u>. The weight pulls down with force *F*, producing an equal and opposite force at the support.

3) This will also happen to <u>helical springs</u> and any object that will stretch without immediately snapping or deforming.

4) Robert Hooke discovered in 1676 that the <u>extension</u> of a stretched wire is <u>proportional</u> to the <u>load</u>, or <u>force</u>. This relationship is now called Hooke's law.

5) A metal spring (or other object) will also obey Hooke's law if a pair of <u>opposite forces</u> are applied to each end.

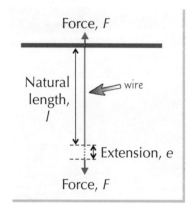

You Can Investigate Hooke's Law with a Spring

PRACTICAL

1) Set up the apparatus as shown below. Make sure you have plenty of extra masses, and measure the <u>weight</u> of each (with a balance).

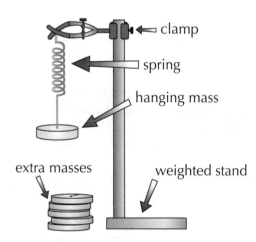

2) Measure the <u>length</u> of the spring (e.g. with an <u>accurate</u> mm ruler) when <u>no load</u> is applied. Ensure the ruler is <u>vertical</u> (e.g. with a set square) and measure the spring at <u>eye level</u>. (This is the spring's <u>natural length</u>.)

3) Add one mass at a time and allow the spring to come to <u>rest</u>, then measure the new <u>length</u> of the spring. The <u>extension</u> is the change in length from the original length. Adding a marker to the top and bottom of the spring might make measuring lengths easier. <u>Repeat</u> this process until you have enough measurements (no fewer than 6).

4) Once you're done, <u>repeat</u> the experiment and calculate an <u>average</u> value for the length of the spring for each applied weight.

5) Plot your results on a <u>graph</u> — show <u>force</u> (i.e. the total <u>weight</u>) on the <u>vertical axis</u> and the <u>total extension</u> on the <u>horizontal axis</u>. You should find that the same increase in the <u>weight</u> on the end of the spring always leads to the same increase in <u>extension</u> — this is Hooke's law in action.

6) <u>Repeat</u> the experiment using a <u>metal wire</u> or a <u>rubber band</u> instead of the spring.

Hooke's Law

If you stretch a spring too far, Hooke's law <u>won't apply</u> and it <u>won't</u> go back to its <u>original shape</u>.

Hooke's Law **Stops Working** when the **Force** is Great Enough

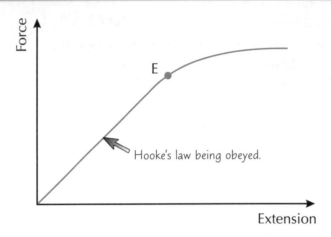

Hooke's law being obeyed.

1) There's a <u>limit</u> to the force you can apply for Hooke's law to stay true. The graph above shows <u>force against extension</u> for a typical <u>metal wire</u>.

2) The <u>first part</u> of the graph shows <u>Hooke's law</u> being <u>obeyed</u> — there's a <u>straight-line relationship</u> between force and extension.

3) When the force becomes great enough, the graph starts to <u>curve</u>.

4) The point <u>marked E</u> on the graph is called the <u>elastic limit</u>. If you <u>increase</u> the force <u>past</u> the elastic limit, the material will be <u>permanently stretched</u>. When all the force is removed, the material will be <u>longer</u> than at the start.

5) Some materials, like <u>rubber</u>, only obey Hooke's law for really <u>small extensions</u>.

A Material Can Return to its **Original Shape** After an **Elastic** Deformation

1) If a material returns to its <u>original shape</u> once the forces are removed, it displays <u>elastic behaviour</u>.

2) Metals display elastic behaviour as long as <u>Hooke's law</u> is obeyed.

If the force-extension graph is linear, Hooke's law holds true...

...and this means that the <u>deformation is elastic</u> (so you know that the deformed material can <u>return</u> to its original shape from that amount of extension). As soon as the graph <u>starts to curve</u>, you know that the material has been stretched <u>past</u> its <u>elastic limit</u> — so it will no longer spring back into its original shape.

Warm-Up & Exam Questions

Time for questions — the warm-up ones will ease you in, but the exam ones should stretch you...

Warm-Up Questions

1) Briefly describe how you could find the centre of gravity of an irregular flat shape.

2) True or false? The shorter the perpendicular distance between the line of action of a force and the pivot, the greater the moment of the force.

3) What does it mean if a material displays "elastic behaviour"?

Exam Questions

1 A student investigates how a spring extends when a force is applied to it. *Grade 4-6*

His results are shown in the graph to the right.

(a) Describe the relationship between force and extension up to a force of 5 N.

[1 mark]

(b) An identical spring is pulled with a force of 7.5 N. The elastic limit of the spring is 7.2 N. State and explain whether or not the spring will return to its original shape.

[1 mark]

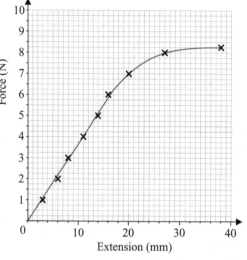

PAPER 2

2 A door has a horizontal door handle. To open the door, its handle needs to be rotated clockwise. *Grade 6-7* Pictures A, B, C and D show equal forces being exerted on the handle. State which picture shows the largest moment on the handle. Explain your answer.

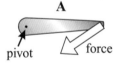 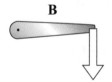

A   B   C   D

pivot force

[2 marks]

PAPER 2

3 The diagram shows three weights on a light plank, resting on a pivot. Weight A is 2 N and *Grade 7-9* sits 20 cm to the left of the pivot. Weight B exerts an anticlockwise moment of 0.8 Nm.

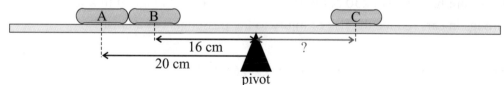

A   B   C

16 cm ?

20 cm

pivot

(a) Calculate the anticlockwise moment in Nm exerted by weight A.

[3 marks]

(b) The system is currently balanced. Weight C has a weight of 8 N. Calculate the distance of weight C from the pivot in metres.

[4 marks]

Revision Questions for Section 1

That was a wild ride through forces and motion but thankfully that's all for <u>Section 1</u>. Time to <u>test</u> yourself.
- Try these questions and <u>tick off each one</u> when you <u>get it right</u>.
- When you've done <u>all the questions</u> under a heading and are <u>completely happy</u> with it, tick it off.

Speed, Distance and Time (p.1-4) ☑
1) What's the relationship between the average speed, distance moved and time for a moving object?
2) *How long would a robot take to reach 2.7 m/s from rest if it had an acceleration of 0.5 m/s²?
3) What does a straight, horizontal line show on a distance-time graph?
4) What does a straight, horizontal line show on a velocity-time graph?
5) How can you find the acceleration of an object from its velocity-time graph?
6) How could you find the distance travelled by an object from its velocity-time graph?

Mass, Weight and Gravity (p.5) ☑
7) What's the force that acts between all masses called?
8) What's the difference between mass and weight?
9) *The value of *g* on the moon is 1.6 N/kg. How much would a mass of 60 kg weigh on the Moon?

Forces (p.8-10) ☑
10) In what direction does friction always act?
11) Describe a simple experiment you could carry out to investigate the motion of a toy car.

Newton's Laws of Motion and Combining Forces (p.12-14) ☑
12) What will happen to the velocity of a moving object if there is an unbalanced force on it?
13) What's the relationship between force, mass and acceleration?
14) What is Newton's third law of motion?
15) What's the difference between a vector quantity and a scalar quantity?
16) *What's the resultant force on a train with a driving force of 19 000 N and a drag of 13 500 N?

Terminal Velocity, Stopping Distances and Momentum (p.16-19) ☑
17) Why does a falling object reach a terminal velocity?
18) Which two distances do you add to find the stopping distance of a car?
19) What's the relationship between momentum, mass and velocity?
20) *What's the mass of a car that has a momentum of 14 700 kg m/s when moving at 15 m/s?
21) *A car's brakes apply a force of 230 N for 10 seconds. Find its change in momentum.
22) How do airbags in cars reduce the risk of injury to the passengers in a crash?

Turning Forces, Moments and Hooke's Law (p.22-26) ☑
23) *Find the moment produced by a 5 N force acting at a perpendicular distance of 1.3 m from a pivot.
24) What name is given to the point through which all of an object's weight acts?
25) *A light rod is hung from two cables, one at each end. The rod is 1 m long. A mass is placed on the rod 25 cm from the left-hand end. Which cable will provide the largest supporting force?
26) Describe a simple experiment you could use to investigate Hooke's law using a metal wire.

*Answers on page 206.

Circuits — The Basics

Electricity's a pretty important topic in Physics. First up, some <u>definitions</u> and <u>symbols</u> to learn...

The **Properties** of a **Circuit**

Current

<u>Current</u> is the rate of <u>flow</u> of <u>charge</u> round the circuit. <u>Electrons</u> usually carry the charge — they're <u>negatively charged</u> particles. Current will <u>only flow</u> through a component if there is a <u>voltage</u> across that component. Current is measured in <u>amperes</u>, <u>A</u>.

Or 'amps' for short.

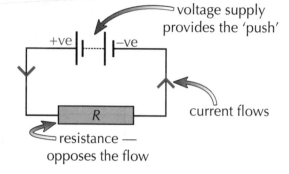

voltage supply provides the 'push'

+ve   −ve

current flows

resistance — opposes the flow

Voltage

<u>Voltage</u> is what drives the current round the circuit. Kind of like "<u>electrical pressure</u>". You may also see it called <u>potential difference</u> (or p.d.). Voltage is measured in <u>volts</u>, <u>V</u>.

Resistance

<u>Resistance</u> is anything in the circuit which <u>slows the flow down</u>. If you add <u>more components</u> to the circuit (one after the other) there will be a <u>higher overall resistance</u>. Resistance is measured in <u>ohms</u>, <u>Ω</u>.

There's a <u>balance</u>. The <u>voltage</u> is trying to <u>push</u> the current round the circuit, and the <u>resistance</u> is <u>opposing</u> it — the <u>relative sizes</u> of the voltage and resistance decide <u>how big</u> the current will be:

> If you <u>increase the voltage</u> — then <u>more current</u> will flow.
> If you <u>increase the resistance</u> — then <u>less current</u> will flow
> (or <u>more voltage</u> will be needed to keep the <u>same current</u> flowing).

Circuit Symbols You Should **Know**:

You <u>will</u> need these for the <u>exam</u> — so learn them <u>now</u>.

cell	battery	power supply	switch open	switch closed	earth/ground
filament lamp	LED	loudspeaker	microphone	electric bell	motor
fixed resistor	variable resistor	ammeter	voltmeter	diode	LDR
heater	generator	fuse/ circuit breaker	thermistor	transformer	relay

Circuits — The Basics

The standard test circuit is really useful — you can use it to find the current that's flowing through a component in a circuit, as well as the voltage that's across it.

The Standard Test Circuit

This is without doubt the most basic test circuit the world has ever known:

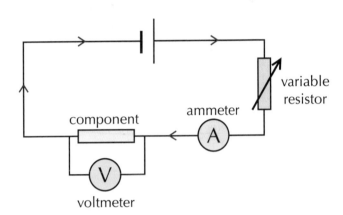

The Ammeter

1) Measures the current (in amps) flowing through the component.
2) Must be placed in series (see page 36) anywhere in the main circuit, but never in parallel like the voltmeter.

The Voltmeter

1) Measures the voltage (in volts) across the component.
2) Must be placed in parallel (see page 37) around the component under test — not around the variable resistor or the battery.

Five Important Points:

1) This circuit is used for testing components.
2) The component, the ammeter and the variable resistor are all in series, which means that they can be put in any order in the main circuit.
3) The voltmeter, on the other hand, can only be placed in parallel around the component under test, as shown.
4) As you alter the resistance of the variable resistor, the current flowing through the component changes.
5) You can take several pairs of readings from the ammeter and voltmeter to see how the voltage changes as the current changes. You can plot these values for current and voltage on an I-V graph (see next page).

Mains Supply is a.c., Battery Supply is d.c.

1) The UK mains electricity supply is approximately 230 volts.
2) It is an a.c. supply (alternating current), which means the current is constantly changing direction.
3) By contrast, cells and batteries supply direct current (d.c.). This just means that the current keeps flowing in the same direction.

The standard test circuit is used to measure current and voltage

If you build a standard test circuit (like the one above) and take readings from the ammeter and voltmeter, you can watch how the voltage across a component changes as you alter the current flowing through it.

Resistance and $V = I \times R$

The <u>voltage</u> across a component and the <u>current</u> flowing through it are linked by <u>resistance</u>.
If you plot them against each other, you can see how the resistance <u>changes</u>.

There's a **Formula** Linking **V** and **I**

You need to <u>know</u> this formula and be able to <u>use</u> and <u>rearrange</u> it:

> **Voltage = Current × Resistance**

> <u>Example:</u>   A <u>4 Ω</u> resistor in a circuit has a voltage of <u>6 V</u> across it.
>   What is the <u>current</u> through the resistor?
> <u>Answer:</u>   Use the formula <u>$V = I \times R$</u>.
>   You need to find I, so the version you need is $I = V/R$.
> $I = 6 \div 4 = 1.5$ A

I-V Graphs Show How Changing **Current** Affects **Voltage**

1)   If you have <u>pairs</u> of readings showing the <u>voltage</u> across a component at different <u>currents</u>,
     you can use them to plot a <u>graph</u> of current against voltage — also known as an <u>I-V graph</u>.

2)   Because <u>$R = V \div I$</u>, the <u>gradient</u> (slope) of an <u>I-V graph</u> is equal to the <u>resistance</u> of the component.
     The <u>steeper</u> the graph, the <u>lower</u> the resistance of the component at that point.

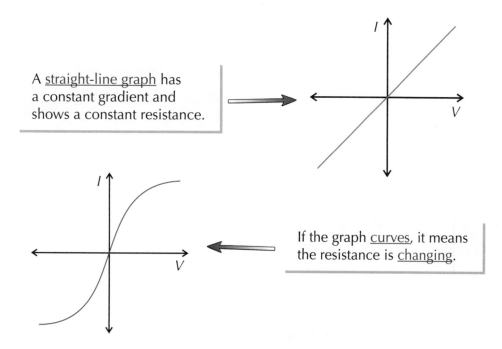

A <u>straight-line graph</u> has
a constant gradient and
shows a constant resistance.

If the graph <u>curves</u>, it means
the resistance is <u>changing</u>.

3)   You work out the resistance for any pair of values (V, I) from an <u>I-V graph</u>
     by sticking them in the <u>formula</u> $R = V \div I$.

You could be asked to interpret an *I-V* graph...

Make sure you take care when <u>reading values</u> off any <u>graph</u>. Pay close attention to the <u>axes</u>,
and make sure you've <u>converted</u> the values to the correct units <u>before</u> you do any calculations.

Resistance and $V = I \times R$

<u>Current-voltage graphs</u> look different for different circuit components.

Four Really Important Current-Voltage Graphs

<u>Current-voltage</u> (*I-V*) <u>graphs</u> show how the current varies as you change the voltage.
Learn these <u>four</u> examples well:

Metal Filament Lamp

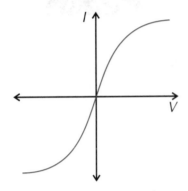

As the <u>temperature</u> of the metal filament <u>increases</u>, the <u>resistance increases</u>, hence the <u>curve</u>.

Wire

The current through a <u>wire</u> (at constant temperature) is <u>proportional to voltage</u>.

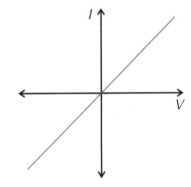

Different Resistors

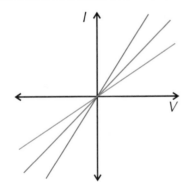

The current through a <u>resistor</u> (at constant temperature) is <u>proportional to voltage</u>. <u>Different resistors</u> have different <u>resistances</u>, hence the different <u>slopes</u>.

Diode

Current will only flow through a diode <u>in one direction</u>, as shown.

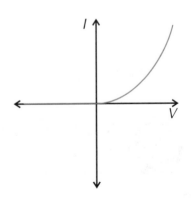

LEDs, LDRs and Thermistors

Here are some really useful <u>components</u> that can be used in <u>circuits</u> to make all sorts of things work...

Light-Emitting Diodes are Really Useful

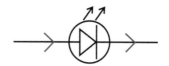

1) <u>Light-emitting diodes</u> (LEDs) emit light when a current flows through them in the forward direction.

2) LEDs have lots of <u>practical applications</u>. They are used for the numbers on <u>digital clocks</u>, in <u>traffic lights</u> and in <u>remote controls</u>.

3) Unlike a light bulb, they <u>don't have a filament that can burn out</u>.

LEDs, like lamps, <u>indicate</u> the presence of <u>current</u> in a circuit. They are often used in appliances to <u>show</u> that they are <u>switched on</u>.

Some Components Can Change Resistance

1) A <u>light-dependent resistor</u> (LDR) is a special type of resistor that changes its resistance depending on how much light falls on it.
2) In <u>bright light</u>, the resistance <u>falls</u> and in <u>darkness</u>, the resistance is <u>highest</u>.
3) This makes it a useful device for various <u>electronic circuits</u>, e.g. <u>burglar detectors</u>.

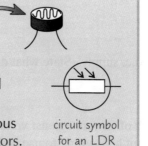

circuit symbol for an LDR

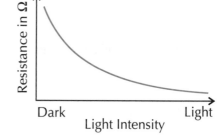

Resistance in Ω

Dark — Light
Light Intensity

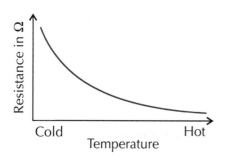

Resistance in Ω

Cold — Hot
Temperature

1) A <u>thermistor</u> is a temperature-dependent resistor.
2) In <u>hot</u> conditions, the resistance <u>drops</u> and in <u>cool</u> conditions, the resistance goes <u>up</u>.
3) Thermistors make useful <u>temperature detectors</u>, e.g. <u>car engine</u> temperature sensors, thermostats and fire alarms.

circuit symbol for a thermistor

Thermistors and LDRs have many applications...

...and they're not just limited to the examples on this page. For example, LDRs are used in digital cameras to control how long the shutter should stay open for. If the light level is low, changes in the resistance cause the shutter to stay open for longer than if the light level was higher. How interesting...

Warm-Up & Exam Questions

Phew — circuits aren't the easiest things in the world, are they? Make sure you've understood the last few pages by trying these questions. If you get stuck, just go back and re-read the relevant page.

Exam Questions

1   This question is about electricity supplies.

   (a)   Which describes the UK mains electricity supply?

       ☐   **A**   230 V a.c.

       ☐   **B**   320 V a.c.

       ☐   **C**   230 V d.c.

       ☐   **D**   320 V d.c.

[1 mark]

   (b)   Cells and batteries provide a d.c. supply. State what d.c. stands for and explain what it means.

[2 marks]

2   A student wants to produce a graph of current against voltage for component X.
An incomplete diagram of the circuit he is going to use is shown below.

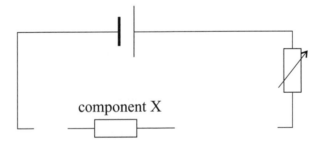

component X

   (a)   Copy the circuit diagram and complete it by adding an ammeter and a voltmeter.

[2 marks]

   (b)   The student increases the resistance of the variable resistor while keeping the voltage of the power supply the same. State what will happen to the current in the circuit.

[1 mark]

   (c)   Outline a method that the student could use to obtain a set of data to produce his graph from.

[3 marks]

Exam Questions

3 The diagram to the right shows a circuit that contains an LED, a light-dependent resistor and a cell. *Grade 4-6*

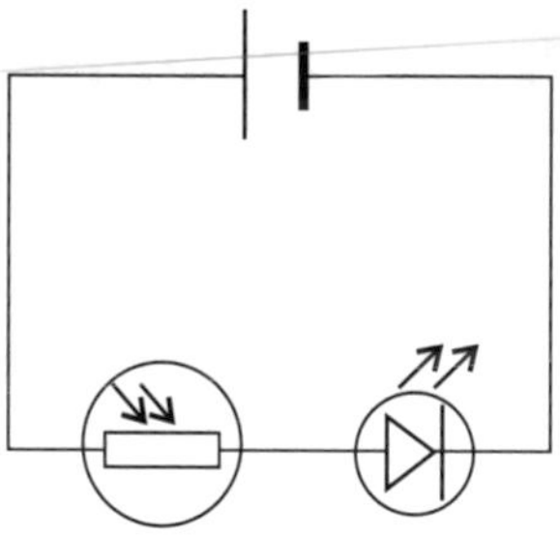

    (a) Describe how you could tell that a current is flowing in the circuit.

                                                [1 mark]

    (b) The circuit is placed in a well lit room.
        At the end of the day, the lights in the room are turned off.

        State and explain how the resistance of the circuit changes when the room lights are switched off.

                                                [2 marks]

4 The graph on the right shows current-voltage (*I-V*) graphs for four resistors at a constant temperature. *Grade 6-7*

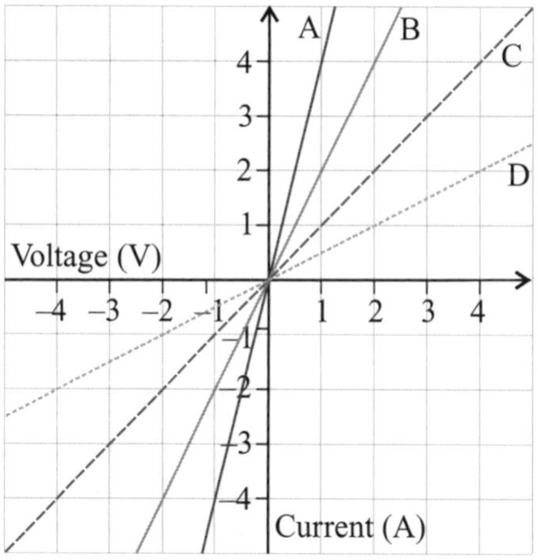

    (a) State which resistor has the highest resistance.

                                                [1 mark]

    (b) (i) State the equation linking voltage, current and resistance.

                                                [1 mark]

        (ii) Calculate the resistance of resistor B.
            Give your answer in ohms.

                                                  [3 marks]

        (iii) The resistance of resistor B is tested at different temperatures. At 30 °C, it has a resistance of 0.75 Ω when the voltage across it is 15 V. Calculate the current through the resistor at 30 °C. Give you answer in amps.

                                      [3 marks]

5 This question is about circuit components. *Grade 6-7*

    (a) (i) Which circuit symbol below represents a fuse?

        ☐ A   ☐ B   ☐ C   ☐ D

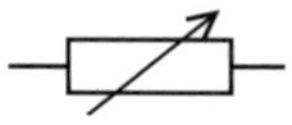

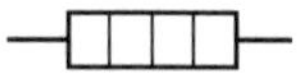

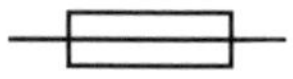

                                                  [1 mark]

        (ii) Which circuit symbol below does **not** represent a type of power source?

        ☐ A   ☐ B   ☐ C   ☐ D

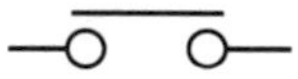

                                                  [1 mark]

    (b) (i) Draw a circuit diagram to represent a circuit in which the brightness of a lamp depends on temperature. The circuit should contain **three** components.

                                                [3 marks]

        (ii) Describe and explain how the current in the circuit changes as the room temperature increases.

                                                  [2 marks]

Series Circuits

You can connect circuits in two ways — in <u>series</u> or in <u>parallel</u> (see next page).
You need to make sure that you understand the <u>differences</u> between the two types of circuit.

Series Circuits — All or Nothing

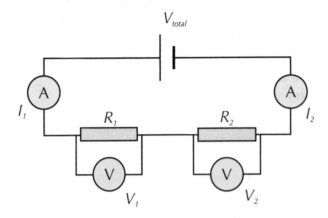

1) In <u>series circuits</u>, the different components are connected <u>in a line</u>, <u>end to end</u>, between the +ve and –ve of the power supply. (Except for <u>voltmeters</u>, which are <u>always</u> connected <u>in parallel</u>.)

2) If you remove or disconnect <u>one</u> component, the circuit is <u>broken</u> and they all <u>stop working</u>. This is generally <u>not very handy</u>, and in practice <u>only a few things</u> are connected in series, e.g. fairy lights.

3) For a <u>series</u> circuit:

- There's a bigger <u>supply p.d.</u> when more cells are in series (if they're all <u>connected</u> the <u>same way</u>). E.g. when two batteries with a p.d. of 1.5 V are <u>connected in series</u> they supply 3 V <u>between them</u>.

  Remember p.d. is potential difference or voltage.

- The <u>current</u> is the <u>same everywhere</u> in the circuit — $I_1 = I_2$ etc. The size of the current depends on the <u>total potential difference</u> and the <u>total resistance</u> of the circuit ($I = V_{total} \div R_{total}$).

- The total <u>potential difference</u> of the supply is <u>shared</u> between components. Different components can have <u>different voltages</u> across them — the p.d. of each component depends on its <u>resistance</u>.

- The <u>total resistance</u> of the circuit depends on the <u>number of components</u> and the <u>type</u> of components used. The <u>total resistance</u> is the <u>sum</u> of the resistance of <u>each component</u> in the circuit — $R_{total} = R_1 + R_2 + ...$

Series circuits — <u>s</u>ame <u>c</u>urrent everywhere...

...and that'll help you remember how <u>current</u> works in a <u>series circuit</u>. Unlike current, the different components in a series circuit have <u>different voltages</u> across them. But the voltages of all the individual components will always add up to the <u>total voltage</u> of the power supply. Handy.

Parallel Circuits

Parallel Circuits — Everything is Independent

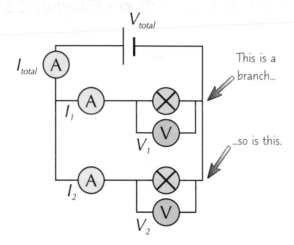

1) In <u>parallel circuits</u>, each component is <u>separately</u> connected to the +ve and –ve of the <u>supply</u>. (Except ammeters, which are <u>always</u> connected in <u>series</u>.)

2) If you remove or disconnect <u>one</u> component, it will <u>hardly affect</u> the others at all.

3) This is <u>obviously</u> how <u>most</u> things are connected, for example in <u>cars</u> and in <u>household electrics</u>. Each <u>light switch</u> in your house is part of a branch of a parallel circuit — it just turns <u>one</u> light (or one set of lights) on and off.

4) Everyday circuits often contain a <u>mixture</u> of series and parallel parts — when looking at components on the <u>same branch</u> the rules for <u>series</u> circuits apply.

5) For a <u>parallel</u> circuit:

- The <u>potential difference</u> is the <u>same</u> across all branches. $V_{total} = V_1 = V_2$ etc.

- <u>Current</u> is <u>shared</u> between <u>branches</u>. The <u>total current</u> flowing around the circuit is equal to the <u>total</u> of all the currents through the <u>separate components</u>. $I_{total} = I_1 + I_2$ etc.

- In a parallel circuit, there are <u>junctions</u> where the current <u>splits</u> or <u>rejoins</u>. The total current going <u>into</u> a junction equals the total current <u>leaving</u> it — charge <u>can't</u> disappear or appear.

- The <u>current</u> through a branch depends on the <u>resistance</u> of the branch — the higher the resistance, the harder it is for charge to flow, and so the lower the current in that branch. If two <u>identical components</u> are connected in parallel then the <u>same current</u> will flow through each component.

- The <u>total resistance</u> of the circuit <u>decreases</u> if you add a second resistor in parallel.

<u>Parallel</u> <u>c</u>ircuits — <u>p</u>art the <u>c</u>urrent...

...and that'll help you remember how <u>current</u> works in a <u>parallel circuit</u>. The current leaving the power supply <u>splits</u> between the branches, so each branch has a <u>different current</u> through it. But the <u>voltage</u> in each branch is the same — and is the same as the <u>total voltage</u> of the power supply.

Charge, Voltage and Energy Change

Charge can be <u>positive or negative</u> — and when <u>charge flows</u> it is called <u>current</u>.

Charge Through a Circuit Depends on Current and Time

1) Current is the <u>rate of flow of electrical charge</u> (in amperes, A) around a circuit (see page 29).

2) In <u>solid metal conductors</u> (e.g. copper wire) charge is carried by <u>negatively charged electrons</u>.

3) When <u>current</u> (*I*) flows past a point in a circuit for a length of <u>time</u> (*t*) then the <u>charge</u> (*Q*) that has passed is given by this formula:

Charge = Current × Time

4) <u>More charge</u> passes around a circuit when a <u>bigger current</u> flows.

> <u>Example:</u>   A battery charger passes a current of <u>2.5 A</u>
> through a cell over a period of <u>4 hours</u>.
> How much charge does the charger transfer to the cell altogether?
>
> <u>Answer:</u> $Q = I \times t = 2.5 \times (4 \times 60 \times 60) = 36\ 000$ C (36 kC)

The time needs to be in seconds.

Charge is measured in coulombs, C.

When a Charge Drops Through a Voltage it Transfers Energy

1) When an electrical <u>charge</u> (*Q*) goes through a <u>change</u> in voltage (*V*), then <u>energy</u> (*E*) is <u>transferred</u>.

2) Energy is <u>supplied</u> to the charge at the <u>power source</u> to 'raise' it through a voltage.

3) The charge <u>gives up</u> this energy when it '<u>falls</u>' through any <u>voltage drop</u> in <u>components</u> elsewhere in the circuit.

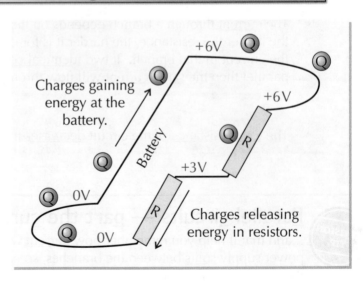

Charges gaining energy at the battery.

Charges releasing energy in resistors.

Charge, Voltage and Energy Change

You Can **Calculate** the **Amount of Energy Transferred**

1) The <u>bigger</u> the <u>change</u> in voltage, the <u>more energy</u> is transferred for a <u>given amount of charge</u> passing through the circuit.

2) That means that a battery with a <u>bigger voltage</u> will supply <u>more energy</u> to the circuit for every <u>coulomb</u> of charge which flows round it.

3) This is because the charge is raised up '<u>higher</u>' at the start — and as the diagram on the previous page shows, <u>more energy</u> will be <u>dissipated</u> in the circuit too.

<u>Voltage</u> is the <u>energy transferred</u> per <u>unit of charge passed</u>

4) The <u>unit</u> for voltage, the <u>volt</u>, is defined as:

<u>One volt</u> is <u>one joule</u> per <u>coulomb</u>

5) You can calculate the <u>energy transferred</u> (in <u>joules</u>, J) to or from an amount of <u>charge</u> as it passes through a <u>voltage</u> using the equation:

Energy transferred = Charge × Voltage

> Example: 1.5 kC of <u>charge</u> passes through a <u>kettle</u>
> when it boils water using a <u>230 V</u> supply.
> Calculate the amount of <u>energy transferred</u> as the kettle boils.
>
> Answer: $E = Q \times V$
> $= 1500 \times 230 = 345\ 000\ \text{J}\ (345\ \text{kJ})$

6) Combining this with $V = I \times R$ from page 31, you can also calculate the <u>energy transferred</u> by an amount of <u>charge</u> as it passes through a <u>resistance</u> using the equation:

Energy transferred = Charge × Current × Resistance

Make sure you always show your working...

...especially when you're substituting numbers into <u>formulas</u>, like the ones above. Writing out <u>each step</u> means that you're <u>less likely to make mistakes</u> when rearranging and substituting — and you'll usually still get some of the <u>marks</u> if you end up getting the final answer wrong.

Warm-Up & Exam Questions

Time to see what you can remember about parallel and series circuits, and energy change in circuits...

Warm-Up Questions

1) A series circuit contains a power supply, a lamp and a motor. The voltage across the lamp is 1.5 V. The voltage across the motor is 3.0 V. What is the voltage of the power supply?

2) True or false? The bigger the change in voltage, the more energy is transferred for a given charge.

Exam Questions

1 Two light bulbs are wired in series with a 12 V battery.

   (a) Give **one** advantage of wiring the lights in parallel instead.

[1 mark]

   (b) The current through one of the bulbs is 0.5 A.
Calculate the total resistance of the series circuit. Give your answer in ohms.

[3 marks]

   (c) Describe how the current in the circuit would change if there were three bulbs in series connected to the same battery.

[1 mark]

2 The diagram on the right shows a parallel circuit.

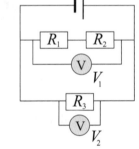

   (a) The battery supplies a voltage of 4.20 V.
Give the voltages V_1 and V_2.

[1 mark]

   (b) Each resistor has a resistance of 2.00 Ω.
Calculate the current through R_2. Give your answer in amps.

[4 marks]

3 A 3 V battery can supply a current of 5 A for 20 minutes before it needs recharging.

   (a) State what carries the charge in an electric current through a metal conductor.

[1 mark]

   (b) (i) State the equation that links charge, current and time.

[1 mark]

      (ii) Calculate how much charge will pass through the circuit before the battery needs recharging.

[3 marks]

   (c) State how much energy is transferred by the battery per coulomb of charge passed through the circuit. Explain your answer.

[2 marks]

   (d) A different battery is used to supply electricity to a circuit.
It transfers a charge of 12 C over 3.0 seconds.
Calculate the total resistance of the circuit in ohms if 36 J of energy is transferred in 3.0 s.

[4 marks]

Electrical Safety

Electricity can be <u>dangerous</u>, yet we use it every day — so it's important that we use it <u>safely</u>.

Appliances must be Earthed or Insulated

1) There are <u>three</u> wires in a plug — <u>live</u>, <u>neutral</u> and <u>earth</u>.

2) Only the <u>live</u> and <u>neutral wires</u> are usually needed, but if something goes wrong, the <u>earth wire</u> stops you getting hurt.

3) The <u>live wire</u> alternates between a <u>high positive and negative voltage</u> of about <u>230 V</u>.

4) The <u>neutral wire</u> is always at <u>0 V</u>.

5) Electricity normally flows in through the live wire and the neutral wire.

6) The <u>earth wire</u> and fuse (or circuit breaker) are just for <u>safety</u> and <u>work together</u> — see below.

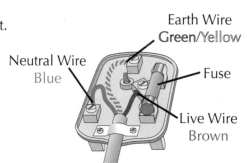

- All appliances with <u>metal cases</u> must be "<u>earthed</u>" to reduce the danger of <u>electric shock</u>. "Earthing" just means the case must be attached to an <u>earth wire</u>.

- An earthed conductor can <u>never become live</u>.

- If the appliance has a <u>plastic casing</u> and no metal parts <u>showing</u> then it's said to be <u>double insulated</u>.

- The plastic is an <u>insulator</u>, so it stops a current flowing — which means you can't get a shock.

- Anything with <u>double insulation doesn't need an earth wire</u> — just a live and neutral.

Earthing and Fuses Prevent Fires and Shocks

1) If a <u>fault</u> develops in which the <u>live wire</u> somehow touches the <u>metal case</u>, then because the case is <u>earthed</u>, a <u>big current</u> flows through the <u>live wire</u>, through the <u>case</u> and the <u>earth wire</u>.

2) This <u>surge</u> in current <u>'blows' (melts) the fuse</u> (or trips the circuit breaker — see next page), which <u>cuts off</u> the <u>live supply</u>.

3) This <u>isolates</u> the <u>whole appliance</u>, making it <u>impossible</u> to get an <u>electric shock</u> from the case. It also prevents the risk of <u>fire</u> caused by the heating effect of a large current.

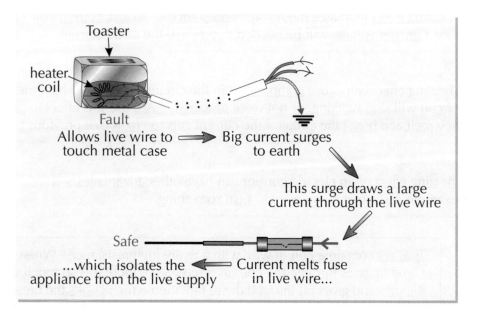

Electrical Safety and Resistors

Fuses are great, but circuit breakers are better. If you don't believe me, read on and decide for yourself. I think resistors aren't half bad either (but whether you agree or not, you have to learn about them).

Circuit Breakers Have Some Advantages Over Fuses

1) Circuit breakers are an electrical safety device used in some circuits.
   Like fuses, they protect the circuit from damage if too much current flows.

2) When circuit breakers detect a surge in current in a circuit, they break the circuit by opening a switch.

3) A circuit breaker (and the circuit it's in) can easily be reset by flicking a switch on the device.
   This makes them more convenient than fuses — which have to be replaced once they've melted.

4) One common type of circuit breaker is a Residual Current Circuit Breaker (RCCB):

   - Normally the same current flows through the live and neutral wires.
     If somebody touches the live wire, a current will flow through them to the earth.
     This means the neutral wire carries less current than the live wire. The RCCB
     detects this difference in current and cuts off the power by opening a switch.

   - They also operate much faster than fuses — they break the circuit
     as soon as there is a current surge — no time is wasted waiting for
     the current to melt a fuse. This makes them safer.

   - RCCBs even work for small current changes that might not be large enough to
     melt a fuse. Since even small currents could be fatal, this means RCCBs are
     more effective at protecting against electrocution.

Resistors Get Hot When an Electric Current Passes Through Them

1) When there is an electric current in a resistor there is an energy transfer which heats the resistor.

2) This happens because the electrons collide with the ions in the lattice that make up the resistor
   as they flow through it. This gives the ions energy, which causes them to vibrate and heat up.

3) This heating effect increases the resistor's resistance — so less current will
   flow, or a greater voltage will be needed to produce the same current.

4) This heating effect can cause components in the circuit to melt — which means
   the circuit will stop working, or not work properly. Fuses use this effect to protect circuits
   — they melt and break the circuit if the current gets too high (see previous page).

5) The heating effect of an electric current can have other advantages.
   For example, it's useful if you want to heat something.

   Toasters contain a coil of wire with a really high resistance. When a
   current passes through the coil, its temperature increases so much that
   it glows and gives off infrared (heat) radiation which cooks the bread.

Energy and Power in Circuits

Most electrical appliances come with a <u>power rating</u> and a <u>voltage rating</u>.
You can use these to work out which fuse is most <u>appropriate</u> for the device.

Electrical Power and Fuse Ratings

1) <u>Electrical power</u> is the <u>rate</u> at which an appliance transfers <u>energy</u>.

2) An appliance with a <u>high power rating</u> transfers a <u>lot</u> of <u>energy</u> in a <u>short time</u>.

3) This energy comes from the <u>current</u> flowing through it. This means that an appliance with a <u>high power rating</u> will draw a <u>large current</u> from the supply.

4) Power is measured in <u>watts</u> (W). The formula for <u>electrical power</u> is:

$$\text{Electrical Power} = \text{Current} \times \text{Voltage}$$

5) Most electrical goods show their <u>power rating</u> and <u>voltage rating</u>.

6) <u>Fuses</u> have <u>current ratings</u> and should be <u>rated</u> as near as possible but <u>just higher</u> than the <u>normal operating current</u>.

The most common fuse ratings in the UK are 3 A, 5 A and 13 A.

7) To work out the <u>fuse</u> needed, you need to work out the <u>current</u> that the item will normally use.

> <u>Example:</u>   A hair dryer is rated at <u>230 V</u> and <u>1 kW</u>. Find the <u>fuse</u> that it needs.
> <u>Answer:</u>   1 kW = 1000 W
> $I = P \div V = 1000 \div 230 = 4.34... \text{ A}$
> Normally, the fuse should be rated just a little higher than
> the normal current, so a 5 amp fuse is ideal for this one.

Electrical Appliances Transfer Energy Electrically

1) The <u>energy transferred</u> by an appliance depends on the <u>power of the appliance</u> and <u>how long</u> it is on for (measured in seconds, s): <u>Energy Transferred = Electrical Power × Time</u>.

2) Join that with the formula for electrical power above, and you get this formula for <u>energy transferred</u>:

$$\text{Energy transferred} = \text{Current} \times \text{voltage} \times \text{time}$$

> <u>Example:</u>   The <u>motor</u> in an electric toothbrush is attached to a <u>3 V</u> battery.
> If a current of <u>0.8 A</u> flows through the motor for <u>3 minutes</u>,
> calculate the <u>energy transferred</u> by the motor.
> <u>Answer:</u>   Use $E = I \times V \times t = 0.8 \times 3 \times (3 \times 60) = 432 \text{ J}$

Time needs to be in seconds.

Choose the right fuse for the job

You need to make sure a fuse is rated <u>as close as possible</u> to the <u>normal operating current</u> of the appliance.
If it's too low, the fuse will keep blowing all the time. If it's too high, the fuse won't blow when it needs to.

Warm-Up & Exam Questions

Now for some more questions — this time they're about safety, energy and power in circuits.

Warm-Up Questions

1) Name the three wires in a standard three-pin plug.
2) What happens to a resistor when an electric current passes through it?
   How is this useful in toasters?

Exam Questions

1 The picture below shows an old-fashioned household fuse box.
Grade 4-6

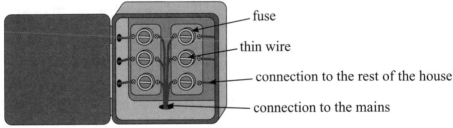

— fuse

— thin wire

—— connection to the rest of the house

—— connection to the mains

(a) Explain why houses have fuse boxes.

[1 mark]

(b) In old-fashioned fuse boxes like this, home-owners sometimes replaced old fuses
with pennies. Explain why replacing fuses with pennies like this was dangerous.

[1 mark]

2 The heating element in a kettle usually contains a coil of wire made of Nichrome.
When the kettle is turned on, current flows through the coil of wire.
Grade 6-7

(a) Explain why the coil of wire in the heating element is designed to have a high resistance.

[2 marks]

(b) The table below shows the power and voltage ratings for two kettles.

	Power (kW)	Voltage (V)
Kettle A	2.8	230
Kettle B	3.0	230

(i) State the equation linking electrical power, voltage and current.

[1 mark]

(ii) Calculate the current drawn from the mains supply by kettle A.
Give your answer in amps.

[3 marks]

(iii) A student is deciding whether to buy kettle A or kettle B.
She wants to buy the kettle that boils water faster. Both kettles are 90% efficient.
Suggest which kettle she should choose. Give a reason for your answer.

[2 marks]

Static Electricity

Static electricity is all about charges which are not free to move. Read on for more...

Like Charges Repel, Opposite Charges Attract

1) Two things with opposite electric charges are attracted to each other.

2) Two things with the same electric charge will repel each other.

3) These forces get weaker the further apart the two things are.

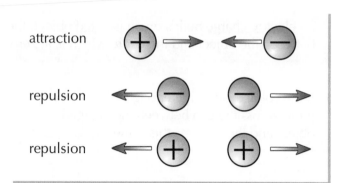

attraction

repulsion

repulsion

Conductors Conduct Charge — Insulators Don't

1) Materials that are electrical conductors conduct charge easily — a current can flow through them. They're usually metals, e.g. copper and silver.

2) Electrical insulators don't conduct charge very well — so a current can't flow. Examples include plastic and rubber.

A Static Charge Cannot Move

1) A static charge is a charge which builds up in one place and is not free to move. These are more common on insulators, where current cannot flow, rather than on conductors.

2) A common cause of static electricity is friction. When two insulating materials are rubbed together, electrons will be scraped off one and dumped on the other.

3) This'll leave a positive electrostatic charge on one and a negative electrostatic charge on the other.

4) Which way the electrons are transferred depends on the two materials involved.

5) Both positive and negative electrostatic charges are only ever produced by the movement of electrons. The positive charges definitely do not move. A positive static charge is always caused by electrons moving away elsewhere.

6) Static charges can occur on conductors too — cars often get a static charge on the outside because they've gained or lost electrons from the air rushing past them as they travel at high speeds.

7) A charged conductor can be discharged safely by connecting it to earth with a metal strap. The electrons flow down the strap to the ground if the charge is negative and flow up the strap from the ground if the charge is positive.

electron flow

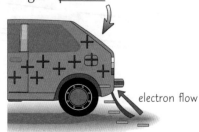

electron flow

Investigating Static Electricity

When lots of static charge builds up, it often ends with a spark or a shock when it does finally move.

As Charge Builds Up, So Does the Voltage

1) As electric charge builds on an isolated object, the voltage between the object and the earth (which is at zero volts) increases.

2) If the voltage gets large enough, electrons can jump across the gap between the charged object and the earth — this is the spark.

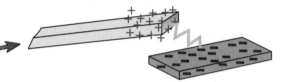

3) They can also jump to any earthed conductor that is nearby — which is why you can get static shocks from clothes, or getting out of a car.

4) This usually happens when the gap is fairly small. (But not always — lightning is just a really big spark, see page 48.)

Experiments Can Show the Effects of Static Electricity

1) As you saw on the previous page, static charges can be caused by friction.

2) The classic examples of this are polythene and acetate rods being rubbed with a cloth duster, as shown in the diagrams below. You can test these out for yourself in the lab.

3) When the polythene rod is rubbed with the duster, electrons move from the duster to the rod. The rod becomes negatively charged and the duster is left with an equal positive charge.

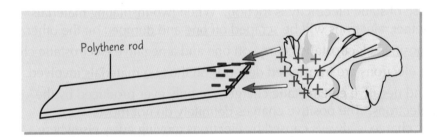

Polythene rod

4) When the acetate rod is rubbed, electrons move from the rod to the duster. The duster becomes negatively charged and the rod is left with an equal positive charge.

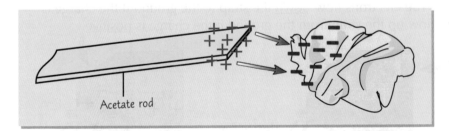

Acetate rod

5) You can confirm that these rods have become charged using the methods outlined on the next page.

Paper 2

Paper 2

Investigating Static Electricity

How to **Check** if a Material is **Charged**:

1) **Gold-Leaf Electroscope**  PRACTICAL

1) You can see whether a material is <u>charged</u> by using a <u>gold-leaf electroscope</u>.

2) A gold-leaf electroscope has a <u>metal disc</u> connected to a <u>metal rod</u>, at the bottom of which are attached two thin pieces of gold <u>leaf</u>.

3) When a rod with a <u>charge</u> is brought near to the disc of the electroscope, <u>electrons</u> will either be <u>attracted</u> to, or <u>repelled</u> from, the metal disc — depending on the charge of the rod.

4) This induces a charge in the <u>metal disc</u>, which in turn induces a charge in the <u>gold leaves</u>. Both gold leaves will have the <u>same charge</u>, so they will <u>repel</u> each other, causing them to <u>rise</u>.

5) When the rod is taken away, the gold leaves will <u>discharge</u> and <u>fall</u> again.

6) If the foil <u>does not rise</u> when the rod is brought near the disc, the rod is <u>not charged</u>.

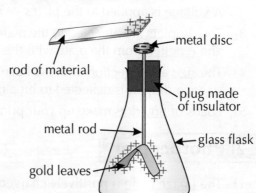

metal disc

rod of material

plug made of insulator

metal rod

glass flask

gold leaves

2) **Suspending** a **Charged Rod**  PRACTICAL

1) Another way of testing whether a rod of material is charged is to <u>suspend</u> a rod with a <u>known charge</u> on a thread and see if there is <u>repulsion</u> or <u>attraction</u> when the rod you're testing is brought close to it.

2) If there is an <u>attraction</u>, then the <u>test rod</u> has the <u>opposite</u> charge to the suspended rod.

3) If there is a <u>repulsion</u>, then the test rod has the <u>same</u> charge as the suspended rod.

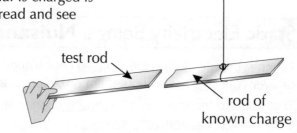

test rod

rod of known charge

Van de Graaff Generators Make Your **Hair** Stand on End

1) A <u>Van de Graaff generator</u> is used to demonstrate electrostatic charges.

2) It's made up of a <u>rubber belt</u> moving round <u>plastic rollers</u> underneath a <u>metal dome</u>.

3) An electrostatic <u>charge</u> is built up on the metal dome as the belt goes round.

4) If you stand on an <u>insulated</u> chair and place your hands on the dome, electrons will move between your body and the dome, giving your body a charge.

5) The human body <u>conducts charge</u>, and <u>like</u> charges <u>repel</u>, so the charges will <u>spread out</u> as much as possible throughout your body.

6) The charge is strong enough to make your hairs <u>repel</u> each other and stand on end.

 PRACTICAL TIP

Always take a moment to think about safety...

When you do any experiment, you should always <u>assess</u> the <u>risks</u> and try to <u>reduce</u> them as much as possible. Be <u>careful</u> not to <u>shock</u> yourself or others when working with static electricity.

Static Electricity — More Examples

They like asking you to give <u>quite detailed examples</u> in exams. Make sure you <u>learn all these details</u>.

Static Electricity Being **Helpful**:

1) **Inkjet Printer**

1) Tiny droplets of ink are forced out of a <u>fine nozzle</u>, making them <u>electrically charged</u>.
2) The droplets are <u>deflected</u> as they pass between two metal plates.
   A <u>voltage</u> is applied to the plates — one is <u>negative</u> and the other is <u>positive</u>.
3) The droplets are <u>attracted</u> to the plate of the <u>opposite</u> charge and <u>repelled</u> from the plate with the <u>same</u> charge.
4) The <u>size</u> and <u>direction</u> of the voltage across each plate changes so each droplet is deflected to hit a <u>different place</u> on the paper.
5) Loads of <u>tiny dots</u> make up your printout. Clever.

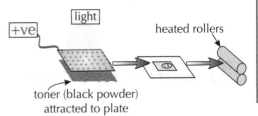

jet of ink

charged plates

printout

2) **Photocopier**

1) The <u>image plate</u> is positively charged. An image of what you're copying is projected onto it.
2) Whiter bits of what you're copying make <u>light</u> fall on the plate and the charge <u>leaks away</u> in those places.
3) The charged bits attract negatively charged <u>black powder</u>, which is transferred onto positively charged paper.
4) The paper is <u>heated</u> so the powder sticks.
5) Voilà, a <u>photocopy</u> of your piece of paper.

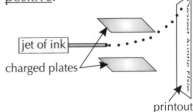

+ve

light

heated rollers

toner (black powder)
attracted to plate

Static Electricity Being a **Nuisance**: Clothing Crackles

When <u>synthetic clothes</u> are <u>dragged</u> over something else (like <u>other clothes</u> in a <u>tumble dryer</u>, or over your <u>head</u> as you put them on), electrons get scraped off, leaving <u>static charges</u> on both parts.
That leads to the inevitable — <u>attraction</u> (they stick together) and little <u>sparks</u> and <u>shocks</u> as the charges <u>rearrange themselves</u>.

Static Electricity Being a **Serious Problem**:

1) **Lightning**

Raindrops and ice <u>bump together</u> inside storm clouds, knocking off electrons and leaving the top of the cloud positively charged and the bottom of the cloud <u>negative</u>. This creates a <u>huge voltage</u> and a <u>big spark</u>.

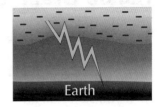

Earth

2) The **Fuel-Filling Nightmare**

1) As <u>fuel</u> flows out of a <u>filler pipe</u>, <u>static can build up</u>.
2) This can easily lead to a <u>spark</u> and in <u>dusty</u> or <u>fumy</u> places — BOOM!
3) <u>The solution</u>: make the nozzles out of <u>metal</u> so that the charge is <u>conducted away</u>, instead of building up.
4) It's also good to have <u>earthing straps</u> between the <u>fuel tank</u> and the <u>fuel pipe</u>.

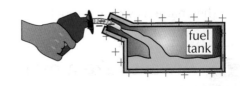

fuel tank

Warm-Up & Exam Questions

You might not be ecstatic about static electricity, but luckily you're nearly at the end of this section. There's only a few questions between you and a well deserved break...

Warm-Up Questions

1) What is an electrical conductor? Give an example.
2) What is an electrical insulator? Give an example.

Exam Questions

PAPER 2 | **PRACTICAL**

1   A student rubs a polythene rod with a dusting cloth. The rod becomes negatively charged and the dusting cloth becomes positively charged.

   (a)   Describe what happens to the electrons as the polythene rod is rubbed.

   [2 marks]

   (b)   The polythene rod is now suspended from a string tied around its centre. The student has another charged object, with an unknown charge on it. Explain how the student can use the negatively charged polythene rod to determine the type of charge (positive or negative) on the object.

   [3 marks]

PAPER 2

2   A student prints a document from a computer using an inkjet printer.

   (a)   An inkjet printer works by firing charged droplets of ink towards a piece of paper. Explain how the printer can control and alter the direction of the droplets of ink.

   [3 marks]

   (b)   The student then photocopies the document. The diagram below shows the main steps that a photocopier uses to make a paper copy of a document.

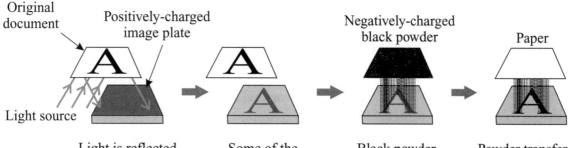

   (i)   Before the process starts, the image plate is positively charged. Describe what causes some parts of the image plate to lose their charge.

   [1 mark]

   (ii) Describe how the original image is transferred to the paper after the light source has been reflected off it.

   [5 marks]

Revision Questions for Section 2

That's it for Section 2 — time to power through these questions while you still have the energy.
- Try these questions and tick off each one when you get it right.
- When you've done all the questions under a heading and are completely happy with it, tick it off.

Circuit Properties and Components (p.29-33) ☑

1) Explain what current, voltage and resistance are in an electric circuit. ☑
2) In a standard test circuit, describe where the ammeter and the voltmeter should be placed. ☑
3) What is the difference between a.c. and d.c.? ☑
4) *Calculate the resistance of a wire if the voltage across it is 12 V and the current through it is 2.5 A. ☑
5) Sketch typical current-voltage graphs for:
   a) a wire (at constant temperature),   b) a resistor (at constant temperature),
   c) a filament lamp,   d) a diode.
   Explain the shape of each graph. ☑
6) Describe how the resistance of an LDR varies with light intensity. Give an application of an LDR. ☑

Series and Parallel Circuits (p.36-37) ☑

7) True or False? The current is the same everywhere in a series circuit. ☑
8) Why are parallel circuits often more useful than series ones? ☑

Charge, Voltage and Energy Change (p.38-39)

9) *If 80 C of charge is carried past a certain point in a wire in 2 s, how much current is flowing? ☑
10) Give the definition of a volt. ☑

Electrical Safety and Energy in Circuits (p.41-43) ☐

11) Sketch a properly wired three-pin plug. ☑
12) Explain how a fuse and earth wire work together in a plug. ☑
13) Explain how a Residual Current Circuit Breaker (RCCB) works. ☑
14) Give two advantages of using an RCCB instead of a fuse and an earth wire. ☑
15) Why does the wire in a fuse melt when the current gets too high? ☑
16) *Find the appropriate fuse (3 A, 5 A or 13 A) for these appliances:
   a) a toaster rated at 230 V, 1100 W   b) an electric heater rated at 230 V, 2000 W ☑

Static Electricity (p.45-48) ☑

17) What causes the build-up of static electricity? Which particles move when static builds up? ☑
18) Describe how an acetate rod becomes electrically charged when it is rubbed with a duster. ☑
19) Give two examples of how static electricity can be dangerous. ☑

*Answers on page 207.

Waves — The Basics

We're constantly bombarded by <u>waves</u> (<u>light</u>, <u>sound</u>, <u>heat</u>)... and they've all got stuff in common.

All Waves Have **Wavelength, Frequency, Amplitude** and **Speed**

1) <u>Wavelength</u> (λ) is the <u>distance</u> from one peak to the next.

2) <u>Frequency</u> (f) is how many <u>complete waves</u> there are <u>per second</u> (passing a certain point). It's measured in <u>hertz</u> (Hz). 1 Hz is 1 wave per second.

3) <u>Amplitude</u> is the <u>height</u> of the wave (from <u>rest</u> to <u>crest</u>).

4) The <u>Speed</u> (v, for <u>velocity</u>) is, well, how fast the wave goes.

$$f = \frac{1}{T}$$

5) The <u>Period</u> (T) is the <u>time</u> it takes (in <u>s</u>) for <u>one complete wave</u> to pass a point. E.g. a wave with period <u>0.002 s</u> has a frequency of 1 ÷ 0.002 = <u>500 Hz</u>.

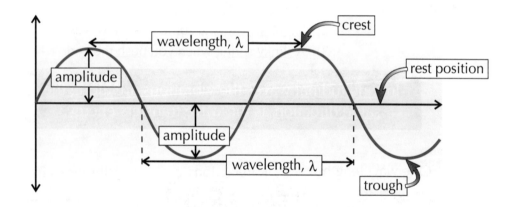

Wave Speed = Frequency × Wavelength

1) You need to learn this equation — and <u>practise</u> using it.

Speed = Frequency × Wavelength
(m/s)   (Hz)   (m)

OR

$$v = f \times \lambda$$

2) You won't <u>always</u> be asked for the speed though, so you might need this <u>formula triangle</u> too...

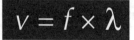

> <u>Example:</u>   Find the frequency of a light wave with wavelength 1×10^{-7} m.
>   (Speed of light = 3×10^8 m/s.)
>
> <u>Answer:</u>   Frequency = speed ÷ wavelength = $(3 \times 10^8) ÷ (1 \times 10^{-7}) = 3 \times 10^{15}$ Hz.

3) Waves often have <u>high frequencies</u> which are given in awkward units like <u>kHz</u> or <u>MHz</u>:
1 kHz (kilohertz) = 1000 Hz, and 1 MHz (megahertz) = 1 000 000 Hz.
For example, 900 MHz = <u>900 000 000 Hz</u>.

Waves — The Basics

Waves Can Be **Transverse**...

Most waves are transverse:
  1) Light and all other EM waves (see p.55).
  2) A slinky spring wiggled up and down.
  3) Waves on strings.
  4) Ripples on water.

> In transverse waves the vibrations are at 90° to the
> direction energy is transferred by the wave.

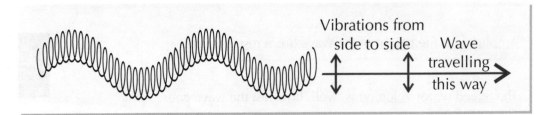

...or **Longitudinal**

Some longitudinal waves are:
  1) Sound and ultrasound.
  2) Shock waves, e.g. some seismic waves.
  3) A slinky spring when you push the end.

> In longitudinal waves the vibrations are along the
> same direction as the wave transfers energy.

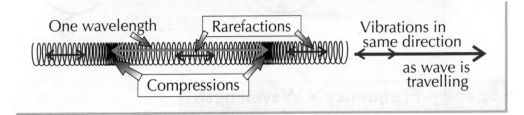

Waves Transfer **Energy** and **Information** Without Transferring **Matter**

1) All waves carry and transfer energy in the direction they're travelling. E.g. microwaves in an oven make things warm up — their energy is transferred to the food you're cooking. Sound waves can make things vibrate or move, e.g. loud bangs can start avalanches.

2) Waves can also be used as signals to transfer information from one place to another — e.g. light in optical fibres, or radio waves travelling through the air. There's more on this on pages 55-56.

Waves only transfer energy and information — not matter...

It's really important that you understand this stuff, or the rest of this section is likely to be a bit of a blur. Make sure you understand the diagrams of the two types of wave above and can distinguish between them.

Wave Behaviour

If you've ever wondered why the sound of a fast car speeding past you <u>changes</u> as it <u>comes towards</u> you and then as it <u>moves away</u> from you, I reckon you're going to enjoy this page.

Two or More Waves Moving Together Have Wavefronts

1) Often when we talk about waves approaching an obstacle or boundary, there are <u>multiple</u> waves moving together in the same direction.

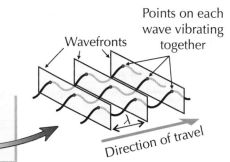

2) In this case it's useful to talk about <u>wavefronts</u>. Wavefronts are imaginary <u>planes</u> that cut across all the waves, connecting the points on adjacent waves which are <u>vibrating together</u>.

3) The distance between each wavefront is equal to <u>one wavelength</u>, i.e. each wavefront is at the <u>same point</u> in the <u>cycle</u>.

The Motion of a Source Affects Frequency and Wavelength

1) If a <u>wave source</u> is moving <u>towards</u> an observer, the <u>frequency</u> of the wave they observe will be <u>higher</u> and the <u>wavelength</u> will be <u>shorter</u> than the original wave emitted by the source.

2) If a <u>wave source</u> is moving <u>away</u> from an observer, the <u>frequency</u> of the wave they observe will be <u>lower</u> and the <u>wavelength</u> will be <u>longer</u> than the original wave emitted by the source.

3) This is because the wave's <u>speed</u> is <u>constant</u> — if the source is moving, it 'catches up' to the waves in front of it. This causes the wavefronts to <u>bunch up</u> in front of the moving source and <u>spread out</u> behind it.

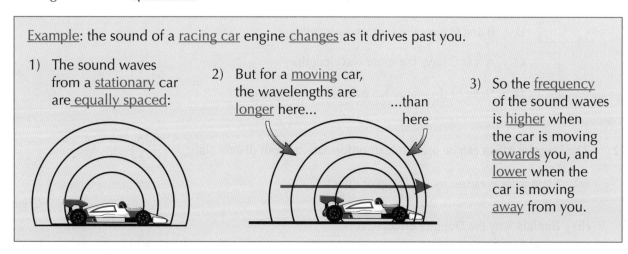

<u>Example</u>: the sound of a <u>racing car</u> engine <u>changes</u> as it drives past you.

1) The sound waves from a <u>stationary</u> car are <u>equally spaced</u>:

2) But for a <u>moving</u> car, the wavelengths are <u>longer</u> here... ...than here

3) So the <u>frequency</u> of the sound waves is <u>higher</u> when the car is moving <u>towards</u> you, and <u>lower</u> when the car is moving <u>away</u> from you.

4) This is called the <u>Doppler effect</u>.

Moving the source of a wave will affect what you observe

The <u>Doppler effect</u> is tricky to get your head round, so don't panic if it takes a while to sink in. You'll have <u>heard</u> it in everyday life with <u>sound waves</u>, e.g. how the sound of an ambulance siren changes as it passes you. But remember, it applies to <u>all waves</u> — there's a bit about how it works in <u>light waves</u> on page 150.

Warm-Up & Exam Questions

Now to check what information's actually been transferred to your brain over the last three pages...

Warm-Up Questions

1) Define the following: a) wavelength b) period (of a wave).
2) Find the wavelength of a wave with a frequency of 6×10^6 Hz that is travelling at 3×10^8 m/s.
3) Describe how transverse and longitudinal waves are different in terms of the direction of their vibrations.
4) True or false? Waves transfer energy, information and matter.
5) Explain what is meant by a wavefront.

Exam Questions

1   The diagram shows the graphs of three waves A, B and C. Each graph has the same scale.

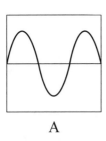   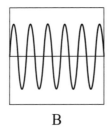   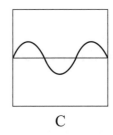

   A   B   C

(a)   What is meant by the amplitude of a wave?

[1 mark]

(b)   Which of the following is correct?

   ☐   **A**   A and B have the same wavelength.

   ☐   **B**   B and C have the same wavelength.

   ☐   **C**   A and C have the same wavelength.

   ☐   **D**   None of the waves have the same wavelength.

[1 mark]

2   The Doppler effect can be used to learn information about distant stars.

(a)   State what is meant by the Doppler effect.

[2 marks]

(b)   Explain why the Doppler effect occurs.

[3 marks]

(c)   An astronomer measures the frequencies of the electromagnetic waves emitted by a distant star. She finds that they are slightly lower than those of a similar star that is known not to be moving either towards or away from the Earth.

   Suggest whether this indicates that the distant star is moving towards or away from the Earth. Explain your reasoning.

[2 marks]

Uses of Electromagnetic Waves

EM waves are great — there's so much you can do with them. Here's a good look at the uses of EM waves.

There are Seven Types of Electromagnetic (EM) Waves

1) Electromagnetic (EM) waves with different wavelengths have different properties. They're grouped into seven types by their wavelength (but the types actually merge to form a continuous spectrum).

RADIO WAVES	MICRO-WAVES	INFRA-RED	VISIBLE LIGHT	ULTRA-VIOLET	X-RAYS	GAMMA RAYS	Wavelength
$1\,m - 10^4\,m$	$10^{-2}\,m$ (1 cm)	$10^{-5}\,m$ (0.01 mm)	$10^{-7}\,m$	$10^{-8}\,m$	$10^{-10}\,m$	$10^{-12}\,m$	

Increasing Frequency and Decreasing Wavelength

2) All types of EM radiation are transverse waves and travel at the same speed through free space (a vacuum).

3) The different colours of visible light depend on the wavelength — red has the longest wavelength (and lowest frequency) and violet has the shortest wavelength (and highest frequency).

Radio Waves are Used Mainly for Communications

1) Radio waves are EM radiation with wavelengths longer than about 10 cm.

2) Long-wave radio (wavelengths of 1 – 10 km) can be transmitted a long way, because long wavelengths are bent around the curved surface of the Earth.

3) Short-wave radio signals (wavelengths of about 10 m – 100 m) can also be received at long distances from the transmitter. That's because they are reflected from the ionosphere (a layer of the Earth's atmosphere).

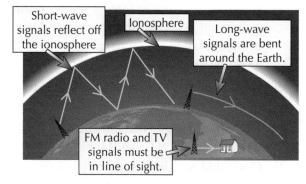

Short-wave signals reflect off the ionosphere

Ionosphere

Long-wave signals are bent around the Earth.

FM radio and TV signals must be in line of sight.

4) The radio waves used for TV and FM radio broadcasting have very short wavelengths (10 cm – 10 m). To get reception, you must be in direct sight of the transmitter — the signal doesn't bend around hills.

Microwaves are Used for Satellite Communication and Cooking

1) Microwaves have a wavelength of around 1 – 10 cm, and can also be used for communication.

2) Satellite communication (including satellite TV signals and satellite phones) uses microwaves.

3) For satellite TV, the signal from a transmitter is transmitted into space, where it's picked up by the satellite receiver dish orbiting thousands of kilometres above the Earth. The satellite transmits the signal back to Earth where it's received by a satellite dish on the ground.

4) Mobile phone calls also travel as microwaves from your phone to the nearest transmitter.

5) Microwaves are also used for cooking. These microwaves are absorbed by the water molecules in the food. They penetrate a few centimetres into the food before being absorbed. The energy is then conducted or convected to other parts (see pages 82-83) of the food.

REVISION TIP

You need to remember the seven types of EM waves...

...and you need to remember them in order. A mnemonic can make this easier. My favourite is: Raging Martians Invaded Venus Using X-ray Guns. But you can make up your own if you prefer.

Uses of Electromagnetic Waves

Infrared radiation and visible light are both ridiculously useful EM waves that we use all the time.

Infrared Radiation is Used for Heating and to Monitor Temperature

1) Infrared radiation (or IR) is also known as heat radiation. Electrical heaters radiate IR to keep us warm, and things like grills use IR to cook food.

2) IR is given out by all objects — the hotter the object, the more IR radiation it gives out.

3) The infrared radiation given out by objects can be detected in the dark of night by night-vision equipment. The equipment turns it into an electrical signal, which is displayed on a screen as a picture, allowing things which would otherwise be hidden in the dark (e.g. criminals on the run) to be seen.

Light Signals Can Travel Through Optical Fibres

1) As well as using it to look at things around us, visible light can be used for communication using optical fibres — which carry data over long distances as pulses of light.

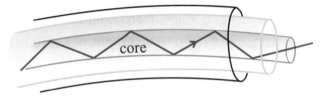

This is known as total internal reflection — see p.65.

2) Optical fibres work by bouncing waves off the sides of a very narrow core.

3) The pulse of light enters the fibre at a certain angle at one end and is reflected again and again until it emerges at the other end.

4) Optical fibres are increasingly being used for telephone and broadband internet cables. They're also used for medical purposes to 'see inside' the body without having to operate.

Visible Light is Also Useful for Photography

It sounds pretty obvious, but photography would be tricky without visible light.

1) Cameras use a lens to focus visible light onto a light-sensitive film or sensor.

2) The lens aperture controls how much light enters the camera.

3) The shutter speed determines how long the film or sensor is exposed to the light.

4) By varying the aperture and shutter speed (and also the sensitivity of the film or the sensor), a photographer can capture as much or as little light as they want in their photograph.

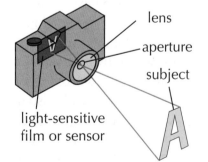

Optical fibres are amazingly useful...

Optical fibres are used to send information over long distances. The EM waves travel fast. And the signal is less prone to interference than in a copper wire, so there's more chance of it reaching the other end clearly.

Uses of Electromagnetic Waves

That's right — yet another page on the uses of EM waves. Ultraviolet, X-rays and gamma rays are the shortest waves in the spectrum, and we use them for all sorts of fancy stuff...

Ultraviolet is Used in Fluorescent Lamps

The Sun also emits a lot of UV radiation — it can cause damage to skin cells (see p.58).

1) Fluorescence is a property of certain chemicals, where ultraviolet radiation (UV) is absorbed and then visible light is emitted. That's why fluorescent colours look so bright — they actually emit light.

2) Fluorescent lights (like the ones you might have in your classroom) use UV radiation to emit visible light. They're safe to use as nearly all the UV radiation is absorbed by a phosphor coating on the inside of the glass which emits visible light instead.

3) Fluorescent lights are more energy-efficient (see page 76) than filament light bulbs.

X-Rays Let Us See Inside Things

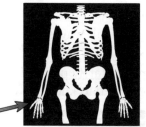

1) X-rays are used to view the internal structure of objects and materials, including our bodies — which is why they're so useful in medicine.

2) To make an X-ray image, X-rays are directed through the object or body onto a detector plate. The brighter bits are where fewer X-rays get through. This is a negative image.

3) Radiographers in hospitals take X-ray photographs to help doctors diagnose broken bones — X-rays pass easily through flesh but not through denser material like bones or metal.

4) Exposure to X-rays can cause mutations that lead to cancer. Radiographers and patients are protected as much as possible by lead aprons and shields and exposure to the radiation is kept to a minimum.

Gamma Radiation Can be Very Useful For...

...Sterilising Medical Equipment

1) Gamma rays are used to sterilise medical instruments by killing all the microbes.

2) This is better than trying to boil plastic instruments, which might be damaged by high temperatures.

...Sterilising Food

1) Food can be sterilised in the same way as medical instruments — again killing all the microbes.

2) This keeps the food fresh for longer, without having to freeze it, cook it or preserve it some other way.

3) The food is not radioactive afterwards, so it's perfectly safe to eat.

Each type of EM wave has multiple uses

You're probably getting the idea by now that we use electromagnetic radiation an awful lot. There are even more uses than the examples on these pages, but these are the ones you need to make sure you know.

58

Dangers of Electromagnetic Waves

Okay, so you know how <u>useful</u> electromagnetic radiation can be — well, it can also be pretty <u>dangerous</u>.

Some EM Radiation Can be Harmful to People

When EM radiation enters <u>living tissue</u> — like <u>you</u> — it's often harmless, but sometimes it creates havoc.

1) Some EM radiation mostly <u>passes through soft tissue</u> without being absorbed — e.g. radio waves.
2) Other types of radiation are absorbed and cause <u>heating</u> of the cells — e.g. microwaves.
3) Some radiations can cause <u>cancerous changes</u> in living cells — e.g. gamma rays can cause cancer.

Higher Frequency EM Radiation is Usually More Dangerous

1) The <u>effects</u> of <u>EM radiation</u> depend on its <u>frequency</u>. The higher the <u>frequency</u> of EM radiation, the more <u>energy</u> it has and generally the more <u>harmful</u> it can be.
2) In general, waves with <u>lower frequencies</u> (like <u>radio waves</u> — which are <u>harmless</u> as far as we know) are <u>less harmful</u> than <u>high frequency</u> waves like X-rays and gamma rays.
3) From a <u>safety</u> point of view, it's how radiation affects <u>human tissue</u> that's most vital. You need to know how the <u>body</u> can be affected if exposed to too much of the following radiation:

Microwaves

1) <u>Microwaves</u> have a <u>similar frequency</u> to the <u>vibrations</u> of many <u>molecules</u>, and so they can increase these vibrations. The result is <u>internal heating</u> — the heating of molecules inside things (as in <u>microwave ovens</u>). Microwaves <u>heat human body tissue</u> internally in this way.
2) <u>Microwave ovens</u> need to have <u>shielding</u> to prevent microwaves from reaching the user.

Infrared

1) The <u>infrared</u> (IR) range of frequencies can make the <u>surface molecules</u> of any substance <u>vibrate</u> — and like microwaves, this has a <u>heating effect</u>. But infrared has a <u>higher frequency</u>, so it carries <u>more energy</u> than microwave radiation. If the <u>human body</u> is exposed to <u>too much</u> <u>infrared</u> radiation, it can cause some nasty <u>skin burns</u>.
2) You can protect yourself using <u>insulating materials</u> to reduce the amount of IR reaching your skin.

Ultraviolet

1) UV radiation can <u>damage surface cells</u> and cause <u>blindness</u>. Some frequencies of UV radiation are 'ionising' — they carry <u>enough energy</u> to knock electrons off atoms. This can cause <u>cell mutation or destruction</u>, and cancer.
2) You should wear sunscreen with <u>UV filters</u> whenever you're out in the sun, and stay out of <u>strong sunlight</u> to protect your skin from UV radiation.

Gamma

1) <u>Very high-frequency</u> waves, such as <u>gamma rays</u>, are also <u>ionising</u>, and carry <u>much more energy</u> than UV rays. This means they can be <u>much more damaging</u> and they can <u>penetrate further</u> into the body. Like all ionising radiation, they can cause <u>cell mutation</u> or <u>destruction</u>, leading to <u>tissue damage</u> or <u>cancer</u>.
2) Radioactive sources of gamma rays should be kept in <u>lead-lined boxes</u> when not in use. When people need to be exposed to them, e.g. in medical treatment, the exposure time should be as <u>short</u> as possible.

Increasing Frequency

Warm-Up & Exam Questions

There are quite a few different sorts of electromagnetic waves — and you never know which ones might come up in the exams... So use these questions to check which ones you're still a bit hazy on.

Warm-Up Questions

1) Of the seven types that electromagnetic waves are usually grouped into, which has the longest wavelength?

2) True or false? Radio waves travel more slowly than visible light through free space.

3) What type of EM radiation is used in grills and electric heaters?

4) Explain how gamma rays can be dangerous for the human body and describe one way of reducing the risk when using them.

Exam Questions

1 The diagram shows electromagnetic radiation being used to sterilise a surgical instrument. *(Grade 3-4)*

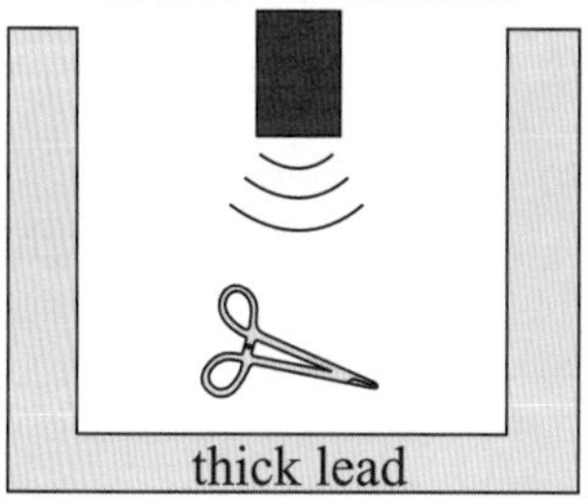

   source of radiation

   (a) State what type of electromagnetic radiation is being used.

   [1 mark]

   (b) A similar process can be used to treat fruit before it is exported to other countries. Suggest why this process is used.

   [2 marks]

   thick lead

2 Optical fibres have many practical uses. *(Grade 4-6)*

   (a) Which type of electromagnetic wave is typically transmitted in optical fibres?

   ☐ **A** radio waves   ☐ **B** visible light

   ☐ **C** microwaves   ☐ **D** X-rays

   [1 mark]

   (b) Explain how data is transmitted through optical fibres.

   [2 marks]

   (c) Give **one** application of optical fibres.

   [1 marks]

3 Mobile phones use microwaves to transmit signals. *(Grade 6-7)*

   (a) Suggest why people might be worried that excessive mobile phone use could be harmful.

   [1 mark]

   (b) Explain why it would be more dangerous to use infrared radiation instead of microwaves for mobile phone signals.

   [2 marks]

Exam Questions

4 The radio transmitter shown transmits long-wave and short-wave radio signals.
The house receiving the signal is a long way from the transmitter.

radio transmitter

    (a) Describe how the long-wave and short-wave radio signals from
the transmitter are each able to reach the house.

[2 marks]

    (b) The owner of the house decides to get satellite TV installed.

        (i) State what type of electromagnetic radiation is used to send signals to satellites.

[1 mark]

        (ii) Describe how satellite TV signals are transmitted from a transmitter
on the ground to the house.

[2 marks]

5 A naturalist uses a night-vision camera to capture an image of a fox, as shown below.

    Explain how the night-vision camera allowed this image to be taken.

[2 marks]

6 X-rays are used by truck scanners at country border control points.

    (a) X-rays are passed through a truck. Explain how an image of the objects in the truck is formed.

[4 marks]

    (b) During a scan, the driver and any passengers are asked to step outside the vehicle
for their own safety. Suggest why this happens.

[2 marks]

7 Ultraviolet radiation can damage skin cells and cause cancer in humans.

    (a) Fluorescent lamps make use of ultraviolet radiation.
State whether or not fluorescent lamps are harmful to humans. Explain your answer.

[2 marks]

    (b) Photographers sometimes use ultraviolet filters to prevent ultraviolet radiation from
reaching the camera's sensor or film. Describe how a camera creates a photograph using
visible light, and how the photographer can control the amount of visible light entering it.

[3 marks]

Reflection of Waves

All waves can be <u>reflected</u>. Reflection happens when light <u>bounces</u> off a surface.

Reflection of Light Lets Us See Things

1) <u>Visible light</u> is a <u>transverse</u> wave (see page 52), like all EM waves.

2) <u>Reflection of visible light</u> is what allows us to see most objects. Light bounces off them into our eyes.

You can draw ray diagrams, like the ones below, to show the path that light waves travel along.

3) When light reflects from an <u>uneven surface</u> such as a piece of paper, the light reflects off at all different angles and you get a <u>diffuse reflection</u>.

4) When light reflects from an <u>even surface</u> (smooth and shiny like a mirror) then it's all reflected at the <u>same angle</u> and you get a <u>clear reflection</u>.

Rays are always drawn as straight lines.

5) The <u>law of reflection</u> applies to every reflected ray:

> ## Angle of incidence = Angle of reflection

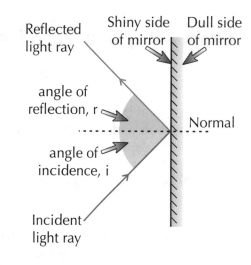

6) The <u>normal</u> is an imaginary line that's <u>perpendicular</u> (at right angles) to the surface at the <u>point of incidence</u> (the point where the wave hits the boundary). The normal is usually shown as a <u>dotted line</u>.

7) The <u>angle of incidence</u> is the angle between the <u>incoming wave</u> and the <u>normal</u>. The <u>angle of reflection</u> is the angle between the <u>reflected wave</u> and the <u>normal</u>.

- You'll probably have gathered from years of looking in mirrors that they form <u>images</u> of whatever's in front of them.
- <u>Virtual images</u> are formed when the light rays bouncing off an object onto a mirror are <u>diverging</u>, so the light from the object appears to be coming from a completely different place. This ray diagram shows how an <u>image</u> is formed in a <u>plane mirror</u>.

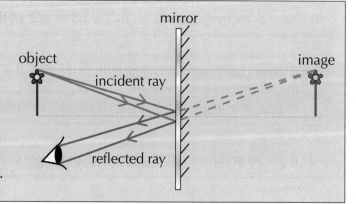

The law of reflection applies to all reflected rays...

...if you know the <u>angle of incidence</u> then you know the <u>angle of reflection</u> — it's as simple as that.

Refraction of Waves

Refraction occurs when a wave slows down or speeds up at a <u>boundary between two materials</u>.

Waves Can be **Refracted**

1) Waves travel at <u>different speeds</u> in substances which have <u>different densities</u>. EM waves travel more <u>slowly</u> in <u>denser</u> media (usually). Sound waves travel faster in <u>denser</u> substances.

2) So when a wave crosses a boundary between two substances, from glass to air, say, it <u>changes speed</u>.

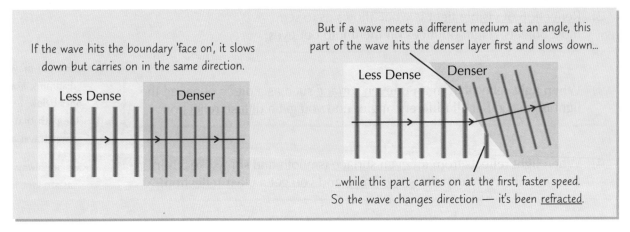

If the wave hits the boundary 'face on', it slows down but carries on in the same direction.

Less Dense   Denser

But if a wave meets a different medium at an angle, this part of the wave hits the denser layer first and slows down...

Less Dense   Denser

...while this part carries on at the first, faster speed. So the wave changes direction — it's been <u>refracted</u>.

Draw a **Ray Diagram** for a **Refracted Wave**

There are more ray diagrams on pages 63 and 64.

A <u>ray diagram</u> shows the <u>path</u> that a <u>wave</u> travels. You can draw one for a <u>refracted light ray</u>:

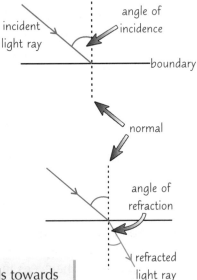

1) First, start by drawing the <u>boundary</u> between your two materials and the <u>normal</u> (a line that is at 90° to the boundary).

2) Draw an <u>incident ray</u> that <u>meets</u> the <u>normal</u> at the <u>boundary</u>.

3) The angle <u>between</u> the <u>ray</u> and the <u>normal</u> is the <u>angle of incidence</u>. (If you're <u>given</u> this angle, make sure to draw it <u>carefully</u> using a <u>protractor</u>.)

4) Now draw the <u>refracted ray</u> on the other side of the boundary.

5) If the second material is <u>denser</u> than the first, the refracted ray <u>bends towards</u> the normal (like on the right). The <u>angle</u> between the <u>refracted</u> ray and the <u>normal</u> (the angle of <u>refraction</u>) is <u>smaller</u> than the <u>angle of incidence</u>.

6) If the second material is <u>less dense</u>, the angle of refraction is <u>larger</u> than the angle of incidence.

Hitting a boundary at an angle can lead to refraction

If you're asked to draw a ray diagram in an exam, make sure it's clear and a sensible size. You should always use a ruler, a protractor and a nice sharp pencil to draw ray diagrams too.

Refraction of Waves

Didn't get your fill of <u>refraction</u> from the last page? Don't worry, we've got you covered...

Rays Passing Through a **Glass Block** are Refracted **Twice**

1) You can <u>experiment</u> with refraction using a light source and a <u>rectangular block</u> of a particular material (e.g. glass) resting on top of a piece of paper...

2) Shine a light ray at an angle into the block, as shown. Some of the light is reflected, but a lot of it passes through the glass and gets <u>refracted</u> as it does so.

3) <u>Trace</u> the <u>incident</u> and <u>emergent</u> rays on to the paper and remove the block. You can <u>draw in</u> the <u>refracted ray</u> through the block by joining the ends of the other two rays with a straight line.

4) You should see that as the light passes from the air into the block (a <u>denser</u> medium), it bends <u>towards</u> the normal. This is because it <u>slows down</u>.

5) When the light reaches the boundary on the other side of the block, it's passing into a <u>less dense</u> medium. So it <u>speeds up</u> and bends <u>away</u> from the normal. (Some of the light is also <u>reflected</u> at this boundary.)

6) The light ray that emerges on the other side of the block is now travelling in the <u>same direction</u> it was to begin with — it's been <u>refracted</u> towards the normal and then back again by the <u>same amount</u>.

Triangular Prisms **Disperse** White Light

1) You'll get an interesting effect if you shine white light into a <u>triangular prism</u>.

2) <u>Different wavelengths</u> of light refract by <u>different amounts</u>, so <u>white light</u> (which is a mixture of all visible frequencies) disperses into <u>different colours</u> as it <u>enters the prism</u> and the different wavelengths are refracted by different amounts.

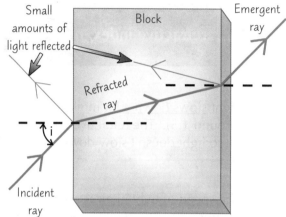

Red is bent the least and violet is bent the most.

3) A similar effect happens as the light leaves the prism, which means you get a nice <u>rainbow effect</u>.

Use appropriate equipment to get better results...

Try to use a <u>thin, bright beam of light</u> because it will be <u>much easier to trace</u>. Not only will you be able to see the light <u>more clearly</u>, but your measurements will be <u>more accurate</u> too.

Refractive Index and Snell's Law

Make sure you're <u>happy</u> with the last two pages before going on, because there's more <u>refraction</u> coming...

Every Transparent Material Has a **Refractive Index**

1) The <u>refractive index</u> of a <u>transparent material</u> tells you <u>how fast</u> light travels in that material. The <u>refractive index</u> of a material is defined as:

$$\text{refractive index, n} = \frac{\text{speed of light in a vacuum, } c}{\text{speed of light in that material, } v} \qquad n = \frac{c}{v}$$

2) Light <u>slows down a lot</u> in <u>glass</u>, so the <u>refractive index</u> of glass is <u>high</u> (around 1.5). The refractive index of <u>water</u> is a bit <u>lower</u> (around 1.33) — so light doesn't slow down as much in water as in glass.

3) The <u>speed of light in air</u> is about the <u>same</u> as in a <u>vacuum</u>, so the <u>refractive index</u> of <u>air</u> is 1.00 (to 2 d.p.).

4) According to <u>Snell's law</u>, the <u>angle of incidence</u>, <u>angle of refraction</u> and <u>refractive index</u> are all <u>linked</u>...

Snell's Law Says...

...when an <u>incident ray</u> passes into a material:

$$n = \frac{\sin i}{\sin r}$$

So if you know <u>any two</u> of <u>n</u>, <u>i</u> or <u>r</u>, you can work out the <u>missing one</u>.

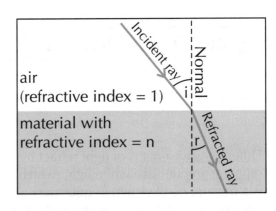

Remember, if a wave is travelling along (or parallel to) the normal when it crosses a boundary between materials, it doesn't refract.

<u>Example:</u> A beam of light travels from air into water. The angle of incidence is <u>23°</u>. The refractive index of water is <u>1.33</u>. Calculate the <u>angle of refraction</u> to the nearest degree.

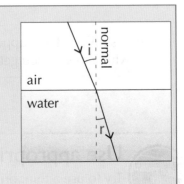

<u>Answer:</u> Rearrange the equation: $\sin r = \dfrac{\sin i}{n}$

Then substitute the values in: $\sin r = \dfrac{\sin 23^{o}}{1.33} = 0.29....$

Use the inverse function of sine to find r:

$r = \sin^{-1}(0.29...) = 17.08.... = 17°$

Refractive Index and Snell's Law  PRACTICAL

Believe it or not, there are another couple of <u>practicals</u> that you can do with <u>glass blocks</u> coming right up.

Find the **Refractive Index** of **Glass** Using a **Glass Block**

You need to be able to describe an <u>experiment</u> to find the <u>refractive index of a glass block</u>
— it's pretty much the same as the rectangular block experiment on the page 63.

1) Draw around a <u>rectangular glass block</u> on a piece of paper and
   direct a <u>ray of light</u> through it at an <u>angle</u>. Trace the <u>incident</u>
   and <u>emergent</u> rays, remove the block, then draw in the
   <u>refracted ray</u> between them.

2) You then need to <u>draw in the normal</u> at <u>90°</u> to the edge of the
   block, at the point where the ray <u>enters</u> the block.

3) Use a <u>protractor</u> to measure the <u>angle of incidence</u> (i) and the
   <u>angle of refraction</u> (r), as shown. Remember — these are the
   angles made with the <u>normal</u>.

4) Calculate the <u>refractive index</u> (n) using <u>Snell's law</u>: $n = \dfrac{\sin i}{\sin r}$.

5) Et voilà — you should have found the
   <u>refractive index</u> of the block.

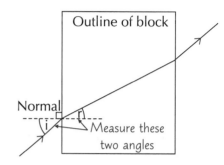

The refractive index of glass should be
around 1.5, so if you get a ridiculous answer
then you've gone wrong somewhere.

Use **Semicircular Blocks** to Show **Total Internal Reflection**

1) As you've seen, light going from a material with a <u>higher</u> refractive index to a material with a <u>lower</u>
   refractive index <u>speeds up</u> and bends <u>away from the normal</u> (e.g. when travelling from <u>glass into air</u>).

2) If you keep <u>increasing</u> the <u>angle of incidence</u> (i), the <u>angle of refraction</u> (r) gets closer and closer to <u>90°</u>.

3) Eventually i reaches a <u>critical angle</u> (C) for which <u>r = 90°</u>.
   The light is refracted right along the <u>boundary</u>.

4) Above this critical angle, you get <u>total internal reflection</u> — no light leaves the medium.

5) An <u>experiment</u> to demonstrate this uses a <u>semicircular block</u> instead of a rectangular one.
   The incident light ray is aimed at the <u>curved edge</u> of the block so that it always <u>enters at right angles</u> to
   the edge. This means it <u>doesn't bend</u> as it <u>enters</u> the block, only when it <u>leaves</u> from the <u>straight edge</u>.

6) To investigate the critical angle, C, mark the positions of the <u>rays</u> and the <u>block</u> on paper and use a
   <u>protractor</u> to measure i and r for <u>different angles of incidence</u>. <u>Record</u> your results in a <u>table</u>.

<u>If the angle of incidence (i) is...</u>

Remember — the angle of incidence and the angle of
reflection are equal, and always measured from the normal.

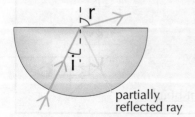

partially
reflected ray

Critical angle C

stronger
reflected ray

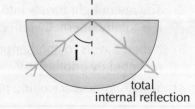

total
internal reflection

<u>...less than the critical angle:</u>
Most of the light <u>passes</u>
<u>out</u> but a <u>little</u> bit of it is
<u>internally reflected</u>.

<u>...equal to the critical angle:</u>
The emerging ray comes out
<u>along the surface</u>. There's quite
a bit of <u>internal reflection</u>.

<u>...greater than the critical angle:</u>
<u>No light comes out</u>.
It's <u>all</u> internally reflected,
i.e. <u>total internal reflection</u>.

Snell's Law and Critical Angles

You'll be pleased to know that this page covers the final bits and bobs you need to know about <u>Snell's law</u>.

You Can Use **Snell's Law** to find **Critical Angles**

You can find the <u>critical angle</u>, *C*, of a material using this equation:

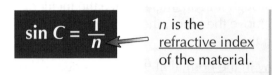

This equation comes from Snell's law that you saw on page 64 — you don't need to know how, but you do need to learn both equations.

$$\sin C = \frac{1}{n}$$

n is the <u>refractive index</u> of the material.

The <u>higher the refractive index</u>, the <u>lower the critical angle</u>. For water, *C* is 49°.

Optical Fibres and **Prisms** Use **Total Internal Reflection**

Optical Fibres

1) <u>Optical fibres</u> (see page 56) that are made of <u>plastic</u> or <u>glass</u> consist of a <u>central core</u> surrounded by <u>cladding</u> with a <u>lower</u> refractive index.
2) The core of the <u>fibre</u> is so <u>narrow</u> that <u>light</u> signals passing through it <u>always</u> hit the core-cladding boundary at angles <u>higher than C</u> — so the light is <u>always totally internally reflected</u>.
3) It only <u>stops working</u> if the fibre is bent <u>too sharply</u>.

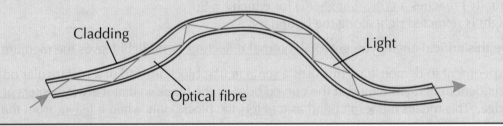

Cladding

Light

Optical fibre

Prisms

1) Total internal reflection also allows us to use <u>prisms</u> to see objects that aren't in our direct line of sight. This is how a <u>periscope</u> works.
2) The ray of light travels into one prism where it is totally internally reflected by 90°.
3) It then travels to <u>another prism</u> lower down and is totally internally reflected by another 90°.
4) The ray is now travelling <u>parallel</u> to its initial path but at a <u>different height</u>.

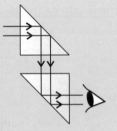

The critical angle is always measured from the normal...

Remember that total internal reflection <u>only works</u> when light tries to pass into something <u>less dense</u> (i.e. with a <u>lower refractive index</u>), for example, when light passes from a glass block into the air.

Warm-Up & Exam Questions

There you go — a little reflection, a lot of refraction. Here are a few questions to check it all went in.

Warm-Up Questions

1) Is visible light a transverse or longitudinal wave?
2) A ray of light passes into a rectangular glass block, through it, and out again. How many times will the light ray have been refracted?
3) State Snell's law.
4) Describe an experiment you could do to find the refractive index of a glass block.

Exam Questions

1   A student shines a beam of light into a mirror.

(a)   State the law of reflection.

[1 mark]

(b)   A ray of light with an angle of incidence of 35° is reflected from a mirror. Copy the diagram of the mirror and the normal shown below and sketch a ray diagram to show both the incident and reflected rays.

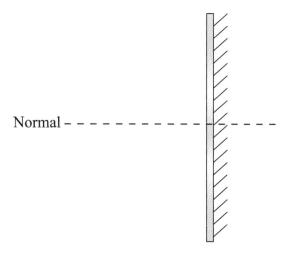

Normal – – – – – – – – – – – – – – –

[2 marks]

(c)   The student swaps the mirror for a glass block, and shines the beam of light into it at an angle to the normal. Explain why the beam of light changes direction when it travels from the air into the block and state the name of this effect.

[3 marks]

2   Endoscopes use optical fibres to look inside a patient's body. When light meets the boundary between the optical fibre core and the outer cladding, there is total internal reflection.

(a)   An optical fibre core has a refractive index of 1.54. Calculate the critical angle of the core material.

[3 marks]

Exam Questions

(b) Suggest why bending the endoscope too sharply may result in reduced image quality.

[2 marks]

3 A semicircular acrylic block is placed in water. Light passes through the block into the water. The critical angle (*C*) of the acrylic-water boundary for the light is 63.2°.

(a) State what is meant by the **critical angle** for a boundary.

[1 mark]

(b) A ray of light meets the acrylic-water boundary at an angle of incidence of 75°. Describe what will happen to the ray of light at the boundary.

[1 mark]

(c) The diagram shows a ray of light hitting the boundary between the same acrylic block and the air. Calculate the refractive index of the acrylic.

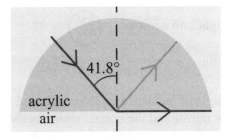

[3 marks]

4 The diagram shows white light refracting at an air-glass boundary and separating into colours.

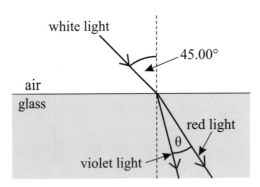

(a) The refractive index of glass for red light is 1.514. Calculate the angle of refraction for red light.

[4 marks]

(b) Explain why the ray of white light would not separate into colours if it crossed the boundary along the normal.

[2 marks]

(c) The refractive index of glass for violet light is 1.528. Calculate the angle θ shown in the diagram.

[4 marks]

Sound Waves

You hear <u>sounds</u> when <u>vibrations</u> reach your eardrums. Read on to find out how <u>sound waves</u> work...

Sound Travels as a Wave

1) <u>Sound waves</u> are <u>longitudinal waves</u> caused by <u>vibrating objects</u>. The vibrations are passed through the surrounding medium as a series of compressions.

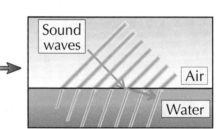

compressions

Vibrations of particles

Direction of sound wave — same direction as vibrations

rarefactions

2) The sound may eventually reach someone's <u>eardrum</u>, at which point the person might <u>hear it</u> — the <u>human ear</u> is capable of hearing sounds with frequencies between <u>20 Hz</u> and <u>20 000 Hz</u>.

Although in practice some people can't hear some of the higher frequency sounds.

3) Because sound waves are caused by <u>vibrating particles</u>, in general the <u>denser</u> the medium, the <u>faster</u> sound travels through it. This also means it <u>can't</u> travel through a <u>vacuum</u>, where there <u>aren't any particles</u>.

4) Sound generally travels <u>faster in solids</u> than in liquids, and faster in liquids than in gases.

5) Sound waves will be <u>reflected</u> by <u>hard flat surfaces</u>. Things like <u>carpets</u> and <u>curtains</u> act as <u>absorbing surfaces</u>, which will <u>absorb</u> sounds rather than reflect them.

6) <u>Sound waves</u> will also <u>refract</u> (change direction) as they enter <u>different media</u>. As they enter <u>denser</u> material, they <u>speed up</u>.

   However, since sound waves are always spreading out so much, the change in direction is hard to spot under normal circumstances.

Sound waves

Air

Water

An Oscilloscope Can Display Sound Waves

1) A <u>sound wave receiver</u>, such as a <u>microphone</u>, can pick up sound waves travelling through the air.

2) To <u>display</u> these sound waves, and <u>measure their properties</u>, you can plug the microphone into an <u>oscilloscope</u>. The microphone <u>converts</u> the sound waves to electrical signals.

3) An <u>oscilloscope</u> is a device which can display the microphone signal as a <u>trace</u> on a screen.

4) The <u>appearance</u> of the wave on the screen tells you whether the sound is <u>loud</u> or <u>quiet</u>, and <u>high-</u> or <u>low-pitched</u>. You can even take <u>detailed measurements</u> to calculate the <u>frequency</u> of the sound (see next page) by <u>adjusting the settings</u> of the display.

Loudness Increases with Amplitude

The <u>greater the amplitude</u> of a wave, the <u>more energy</u> it carries. In <u>sound</u> this means it'll be <u>louder</u>. <u>Louder</u> sound waves will also have a trace with a larger <u>amplitude</u> on an oscilloscope.

Louder

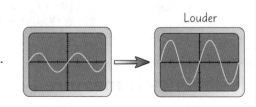

Paper 2

Sound Waves

All sounds have <u>pitch</u>. You can <u>measure</u> the pitch of sounds using an <u>oscilloscope</u>. Here's how...

The **Higher** the **Frequency**, the Higher the **Pitch**

1) <u>Frequency</u> is the number of <u>complete vibrations</u> each second, and it's measured in hertz (Hz) — 1 Hz is equal to 1 vibration per second. Other common <u>units</u> are <u>kHz</u> (1000 Hz) and <u>MHz</u> (1 000 000 Hz).

2) You can <u>compare</u> the <u>frequency</u> of waves on an <u>oscilloscope</u> — the <u>more complete cycles</u> displayed on the screen, the <u>higher the frequency</u> (if the waves are being compared on the <u>same scale</u> — see below).

3) If the source of sound vibrates with a <u>high frequency</u> the sound is <u>high-pitched</u>, e.g. a <u>squeaking mouse</u>. If the source of sound vibrates with a <u>low frequency</u> the sound is <u>low-pitched</u>, e.g. a <u>mooing cow</u>.

4) The <u>traces</u> below are <u>very important</u>, so make sure you know them.

Original Sound   Higher pitched   Lower pitched   Higher pitched and louder

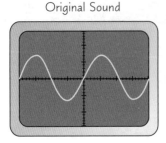
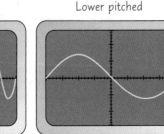

Use an **Oscilloscope** to Find the **Frequency** of a **Wave**   PRACTICAL

1) The <u>horizontal axis</u> on the oscilloscope display is <u>time</u>.
2) The time between <u>each division</u> on the scale can be <u>adjusted</u> to get a clear, readable trace. Here, each division has been set to show <u>0.00001 s</u>.
3) Adjust the <u>time division setting</u> until the display shows <u>at least 1 complete cycle</u>, like this.
4) Read off the <u>period</u> — the <u>time</u> taken for <u>one complete cycle</u>.

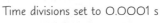
Time divisions set to 0.0001 s

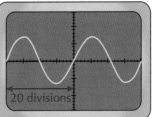
20 divisions

Here 1 cycle crosses <u>20 divisions</u>, so
<u>period</u> = 20 × 0.00001 s = <u>0.0002 s</u>.
<u>Frequency</u> = 1 ÷ period (see page 51)
     = 1 ÷ 0.0002 s = 5000 Hz = <u>5 kHz</u>.

Frequency is measured in hertz (Hz)

Remember: if the waves on the oscilloscope get <u>closer together</u>, the <u>frequency</u> has <u>increased</u> and the sound will be <u>higher pitched</u>. If they get taller, the <u>amplitude</u> has <u>increased</u> and the sound will be <u>louder</u>.

Sound Waves

This page is all about how to measure the <u>speed</u> of sound. Exciting stuff.

You Can Use an **Oscilloscope** to Measure the **Speed** of Sound

1) By attaching a <u>signal generator</u> to a speaker you can generate sounds with a <u>specific frequency</u>. You can use <u>two microphones</u> and an <u>oscilloscope</u> to find the <u>wavelength</u> of the sound waves generated:

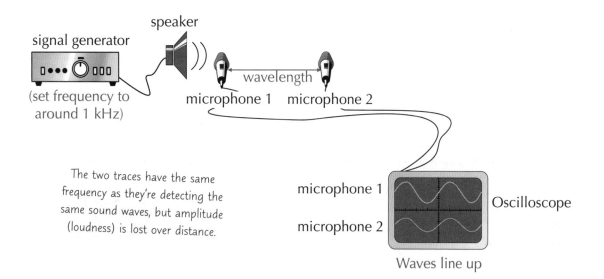

The two traces have the same frequency as they're detecting the same sound waves, but amplitude (loudness) is lost over distance.

2) The <u>detected waves</u> at each microphone can be seen as <u>a separate wave</u> on the oscilloscope.

3) Start with <u>both microphones</u> next to the speaker, then slowly <u>move one away</u> until the <u>two waves</u> are <u>aligned</u> on the display, but exactly <u>one wavelength apart</u>.

4) <u>Measure the distance</u> between the microphones to find the <u>wavelength</u> (λ).

5) You can then use the formula <u>$v = f \times \lambda$</u> (see page 51) to find the <u>speed</u> (v) of the <u>sound waves</u> passing through the <u>air</u> — the <u>frequency</u> (f) is whatever you set the <u>signal generator</u> to in the first place.

6) The speed of sound in air is around <u>340 m/s</u>, so check your results <u>roughly agree</u> with this.

You can measure the speed of sound in other ways...

For example, you can ask a friend to stand a long distance away (e.g. 100 m) and bang a drum (or do something else that makes a loud bang). You can use a stopwatch to measure the time taken between you seeing the person make the noise, and when you hear it. Then use "speed = distance ÷ time" (see page 1) to work out the speed of the sound waves.

Warm-Up & Exam Questions

Now for some more questions — work through them all to see if you've got your sound wave facts sorted.

Warm-Up Questions

1) Is sound a transverse or longitudinal wave?
2) What is the frequency range for human hearing?
3) What is the relationship between the loudness of a sound and its amplitude?

Exam Question

PAPER 2 **PRACTICAL**

1   The diagram below shows how an oscilloscope can be used to display sound waves by connecting microphones to it. Trace 1 on the oscilloscope shows the sound waves detected by microphone 1 and trace 2 shows the sound waves detected by microphone 2.

signal generator   speaker

microphone 1   microphone 2

oscilloscope

(a) (i) A student used this equipment to find the speed of sound. The steps below show the method he used. Put the steps into the correct order by copying the table and numbering the boxes. The first one has been done for you.

Statements	Order
Measure the distance between the microphones. This is the wavelength.	
Stop moving microphone 2 when the traces line up.	
Use the measured distance and the frequency of the signal generator to find the wave speed.	
Begin with both microphones at an equal distance from the speaker.	1
Keeping microphone 1 fixed, slowly move microphone 2 away from the speaker (keeping it in line with microphone 1), causing trace 2 to move.	

[3 marks]

(ii) With the signal generator set to 50 Hz, the distance between the microphones was measured to be 6.8 m. Calculate the speed of sound in air in m/s.

[2 marks]

(b) One microphone is removed and the signal generator is adjusted. The diagram shows the trace produced on the oscilloscope.

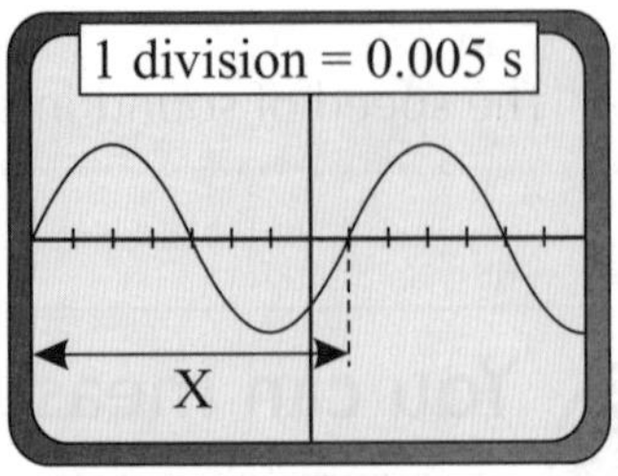

(i) Which quantity is represented by X on the trace?

☐ **A** wavelength   ☐ **B** amplitude

☐ **C** frequency   ☐ **D** time period

[1 mark]

1 division = 0.005 s

X

(ii) Calculate the frequency of the wave in hertz.

[2 marks]

Revision Questions for Section 3

That wraps up <u>Section 3</u> — time to put yourself to the test and find out <u>how much you really know</u>.
- Try these questions and <u>tick off each one</u> when you <u>get it right</u>.
- When you've done <u>all the questions</u> under a heading and are <u>completely happy</u> with it, tick it off.

Wave Basics (p.51-53) ☑

1) Draw a diagram to illustrate frequency, wavelength and amplitude. ☑
2) What is the formula used to calculate the frequency of a wave from the period? ☑
3) *Find the frequency in hertz of a wave with a wavelength of 0.3 m and a speed of 150 m/s. ☑
4) What is the main difference between a transverse wave and a longitudinal wave? ☑

Electromagnetic Waves (p.55-58) ☑

5) Write down all seven types of EM radiation in order of increasing frequency
   and decreasing wavelength. ☑
6) Write down all the colours of visible light in order of increasing frequency and
   decreasing wavelength. ☑
7) Describe one common use of each of the seven types of EM waves. ☑
8) Which is generally more hazardous — low frequency or high frequency EM radiation? ☑
9) Describe the harmful effects on the human body that can be caused by UV rays. ☑

Reflection and Refraction (p.61-66) ☑

10) *A ray of light hits the surface of a mirror at an incident angle of 10° to the normal.
    What is the angle of reflection for the ray of light? ☑
11) Draw a diagram to show the path of a ray of light that travels from air, enters a rectangular block of
    glass, then exits the block back into air on the other side (use an angle of incidence larger than 0°). ☑
12) *A beam of light travelling through air enters a material with $i = 30°$.
    It refracts so that $r = 20°$. What is the refractive index of the material? ☑
13) *For each of the diagrams A to D below, state whether the ray of light would be
    totally internally reflected or not. (The critical angle for glass is approximately 42°.) ☑

14) Give one practical use of total internal reflection. ☑

Sound Waves (p.69-71) ☑

15) True or false? Sound waves are reflected by hard surfaces. ☑
16) This is a diagram of a sound wave displayed on an oscilloscope. ⟶
    a) What is happening to the loudness of the sound? ☑
    b) What is happening to the pitch of the sound? ☑
17) Explain how you would find the frequency of a wave from an oscilloscope display. ☑

*Answers on page 209.

Conservation of Energy

I hope you're feeling lively, because this module is all about <u>energy</u>. The main thing to remember about energy is that you can never make it or destroy it — you just <u>transfer it</u> from one energy store to another.

Energy is Transferred Between Energy Stores

<u>Energy</u> can be held in different <u>stores</u>. Here are the stores you need to learn, plus examples of <u>objects</u> with energy in each of <u>these stores</u>:

1) <u>Kinetic</u> .... anything <u>moving</u> has energy in its <u>kinetic energy store</u>.
2) <u>Thermal</u> .... <u>any object</u> — the <u>hotter</u> it is, the <u>more</u> energy it has in this <u>store</u>.
3) <u>Chemical</u>. .... anything that can release energy in a <u>chemical reaction</u>, e.g. <u>food</u>, <u>fuel</u>.
4) <u>Gravitational Potential</u> ..... anything in a <u>gravitational field</u> (i.e. anything which can <u>fall</u>).
5) <u>Elastic Potential</u> .... anything stretched, like <u>springs</u> and <u>rubber bands</u>.
6) <u>Electrostatic</u> .... e.g. two <u>charges</u> that attract or repel each other.
7) <u>Magnetic</u> .... e.g. two <u>magnets</u> that attract or repel each other.
8) <u>Nuclear</u> .... <u>atomic nuclei</u> release energy from this store in <u>nuclear reactions</u>.

Energy can be <u>transferred between stores</u> in <u>four</u> main ways:

<u>Mechanically</u> — an object moving due to a <u>force</u> acting on it,
e.g. pushing, pulling, stretching or squashing.

<u>Electrically</u> — a charge moving through a <u>potential difference</u>, e.g. charges moving round a circuit.

<u>By heating</u> — energy transferred from a <u>hotter</u> object to a <u>colder</u> object,
e.g. heating a pan of water on a hob.

<u>By radiation</u> — energy transferred by <u>electromagnetic waves</u> (like <u>light</u> or <u>sound</u> — see page 55),
e.g. energy from the Sun reaching Earth as light.

There is a Principle of Conservation of Energy

There are plenty of different <u>stores</u> of energy, but <u>energy always obeys the principle below</u>:

> <u>Energy</u> can be <u>stored</u>, <u>transferred</u> between <u>stores</u>, or
> <u>dissipated</u> — but it can never be <u>created or destroyed</u>.
> The <u>total energy</u> of a <u>closed system</u> has <u>no net change</u>.

Dissipated is a fancy way of saying that the energy is spread out and lost.

A <u>closed system</u> is just a system (a collection of objects) that can be treated completely on its own, <u>without any matter</u> being exchanged with the <u>surroundings</u>.

No matter what store it's in, it's all energy...

In the exam, make sure you refer to <u>energy</u> in terms of the <u>store</u> it's in. For example, if you're describing energy in a <u>hot object</u>, say it 'has energy in its thermal energy store'.

Wasted Energy

So energy is <u>transferred</u> between different <u>stores</u>. But not all of the energy is transferred to <u>useful</u> stores.

Most **Energy Transfers** Involve Some **Losses**, Often by **Heating**

1) Another <u>important principle</u> you need to know is:

> Energy is <u>only useful</u> when it is <u>transferred</u> from one store to a <u>useful store</u>.

2) <u>Useful devices</u> can <u>transfer energy</u> from <u>one store</u> to a <u>useful store</u>.

3) However, some of the <u>input energy</u> is always <u>lost or wasted</u>, often to <u>thermal energy stores</u> by <u>heating</u>.

> For example, a <u>motor</u> will transfer energy to its <u>kinetic energy store</u> (<u>useful</u>), but will also transfer energy to the <u>thermal energy stores</u> of the motor and the surroundings (<u>wasted</u>).

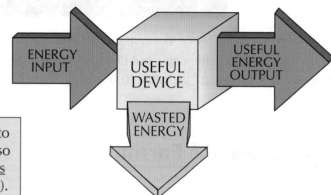

4) The law of conservation of energy means that:
<u>total energy input = useful energy output + wasted energy</u>.

5) The <u>less energy</u> that's <u>wasted</u>, the <u>more efficient</u> the device is said to be.

The amount of energy wasted can often be reduced — see page 84.

We Generally **Can't Do Anything Useful** with **Wasted Energy**

1) <u>The wasted energy</u> that's <u>output</u> by a device is transferred to less useful stores — normally by <u>heating</u>, or by <u>light</u> or <u>sound</u>. As the energy is <u>transferred</u> away from the device to its surroundings, the <u>energy</u> often spreads out and becomes <u>less concentrated</u> — we say it <u>dissipates</u>.

> For example, a <u>pan of water</u> on a <u>hob</u> — the hob will transfer energy to the water, but <u>some energy</u> will be <u>dissipated</u> to the surrounding air by heating.

2) According to the <u>principle of conservation of energy</u> (see previous page), the <u>total</u> amount of <u>energy</u> stays the <u>same</u>. So the energy is still there, but it <u>can't be easily used</u> or <u>collected back in</u> again.

Before you know what's waste, you've got to know what's useful...

If you're trying to work out <u>how</u> a device is <u>wasting energy</u>, the first thing you should do is figure out which store is <u>useful</u>. For example, for a <u>phone charger</u>, only energy that's transferred to the <u>chemical energy store</u> of the phone's battery is <u>useful</u>. Then you know any energy that ends up <u>anywhere else</u> is <u>wasted</u>.

Energy Efficiency

Devices have <u>energy transferred</u> to them, but only transfer <u>some</u> of it to <u>useful energy stores</u>. Wouldn't it be great if we could tell <u>how much</u> the device <u>usefully transfers</u>? That's where <u>efficiency</u> comes in.

You can **Calculate** the **Efficiency** of an **Energy Transfer**

The <u>efficiency</u> of any device is defined as:

$$\text{efficiency} = \frac{\text{useful energy output}}{\text{total energy output}} \times 100\%$$

The total energy <u>output</u> will be the same as the total energy <u>input</u>, because of the principle of conservation of energy (see p.74).

You should give efficiency as a <u>percentage</u>, e.g. <u>75%</u>.

All devices have an efficiency, but because some energy is <u>always wasted</u>, the efficiency <u>can never be</u> equal to or higher than <u>100%</u>.

How to **Use** the **Formula**:

1) You find how much energy is <u>supplied</u> to a machine — the <u>total</u> energy <u>input</u>. This equals the <u>total</u> energy <u>output</u>.

2) You find how much <u>useful energy</u> the machine <u>delivers</u> — the <u>useful</u> energy <u>output</u>. An exam question either tells you this directly or tells you how much is <u>wasted</u>.

3) Either way, you get those <u>two important numbers</u> and then just <u>divide</u> the <u>smaller one</u> by the <u>bigger one</u>, then multiply by 100, to get a value for <u>efficiency</u> somewhere between <u>0 and 100%</u>. Easy.

> <u>Example:</u> A toaster transfers <u>216 000 J</u> of energy electrically from the mains. <u>84 000 J</u> of energy is transferred to the bread's thermal energy store. Calculate the efficiency of the toaster.
>
> <u>Answer:</u> $\text{efficiency} = \dfrac{\text{useful energy output}}{\text{total energy output}} \times 100\%$
>
> $= \dfrac{84\,000}{216\,000} \times 100 = 38.888... = 39\%$ (to 2 s.f.)

4) The other way they might ask it is to tell you the <u>efficiency</u> and the <u>total energy output</u> and ask for the <u>useful energy output</u>, or they could tell you the <u>efficiency</u> and <u>useful energy output</u> and ask for the <u>total energy output</u>. You need to be able to swap the formula round.

You can compare devices more easily if you calculate their efficiencies...

As long as you remember to <u>multiply by 100</u> to get a <u>percentage</u>, the efficiency equation's not too bad to use. Where it can get tricky is working out what is <u>useful energy</u> — some devices may transfer energy to <u>more than one</u> useful store, so make sure that you've factored them <u>all</u> into your calculation.

Energy Transfers

More! More! Tell me more about <u>energy transfers</u> please! OK, since you insist:

You Need to be Able to **Describe Energy Transfers**

In the exam, they can ask you about <u>any device</u> or <u>energy transfer system</u> they feel like. So it's no good just learning the examples — you need to <u>understand the patterns</u>, and analyse how energy moves between stores in different situations.

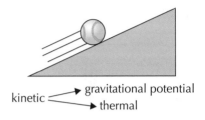

kinetic ⟶ gravitational potential
⟶ thermal

A BALL ROLLING UP A SLOPE:
Energy is transferred <u>mechanically</u> from the <u>kinetic</u> energy store of the ball to its <u>gravitational potential</u> energy store. Some energy is transferred <u>mechanically</u> to the <u>thermal</u> energy stores of the ball and the <u>slope</u> (due to <u>friction</u>), and then <u>by heating</u> to the <u>thermal</u> energy stores of the <u>surroundings</u> — this energy is <u>wasted</u>.

A BAT HITTING A BALL:
Some energy is <u>usefully transferred mechanically</u> from the <u>kinetic energy store</u> of the bat to the <u>kinetic energy store</u> of the ball. The rest of the energy is <u>wasted</u>. Some energy in the kinetic energy store of the bat is transferred <u>mechanically</u> to the <u>thermal energy stores</u> of the bat, the ball and their surroundings. The remaining energy is carried away by <u>sound</u>.

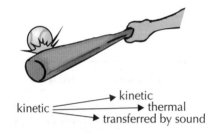

kinetic ⟶ kinetic
⟶ thermal
⟶ transferred by sound

thermal ⟶ thermal

AN ELECTRIC KETTLE BOILING WATER:
Energy is transferred <u>electrically</u> from the mains to the <u>thermal energy store</u> of the kettle's <u>heating element</u>. It is then transferred <u>by heating</u> to the <u>thermal energy store</u> of the water. Some energy is <u>wasted</u>, and transferred <u>by heating</u> from the thermal energy stores of the heating element and the water to the thermal energy stores of the <u>surroundings</u>.

A BATTERY-POWERED TOY CAR:
Energy is usefully transferred <u>electrically</u> from the <u>chemical energy store</u> of the battery to the <u>kinetic energy store</u> of the car and carried away by <u>light</u> from the headlights. <u>Wasteful</u> energy transfers also occur, to <u>thermal energy stores</u> of the car and surroundings, and wastefully carried away by <u>sound</u>.

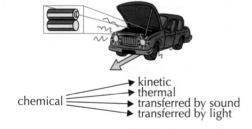

chemical ⟶ kinetic
⟶ thermal
⟶ transferred by sound
⟶ transferred by light

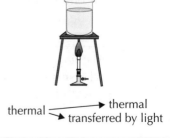

thermal ⟶ thermal
⟶ transferred by light

A BUNSEN BURNER AND BEAKER:
Energy is usefully transferred <u>by heating</u> from the <u>chemical energy store</u> of the gas to the <u>thermal energy stores</u> of the beaker and the water. Energy is also <u>wastefully</u> transferred by heating to the <u>thermal energy stores</u> of the stand and the surroundings. Some energy is also carried away by <u>light</u>.

Energy is transferred between the different stores of objects...

REVISION TIP

Energy stores pop up <u>everywhere</u> in physics. You need to be able to describe <u>how energy is transferred</u>, and <u>which stores</u> it gets transferred between, for <u>any scenario</u>. So make sure you know all the <u>energy stores</u> and <u>transfer methods</u> like the back of your hand.

Sankey Diagrams

This is another bit of physics where you'll have to tackle some maths-based questions. Fantastic.
So best prepare yourself — here's what <u>Sankey diagrams</u> are all about...

The **Thickness** of the **Arrow** Represents the **Amount** of **Energy**

The idea of <u>Sankey (energy transformation) diagrams</u> is to make it <u>easy to see</u> at a glance how much
of the <u>input energy</u> is being <u>usefully employed</u> compared with how much is being <u>wasted</u>.

The <u>thicker the arrow</u>, the <u>more energy</u> it represents
— so you see a big <u>thick arrow going in</u>, then
several <u>smaller arrows going off</u> it to show the
different energy transformations taking place.

You can have either a little <u>sketch</u> or a properly
<u>detailed diagram</u> where the width of each arrow is
proportional to the number of joules it represents.

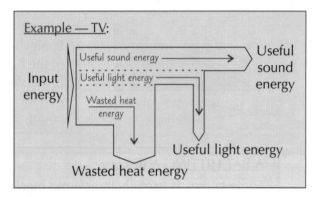

Example — Sankey Diagram for a **Simple Motor**:

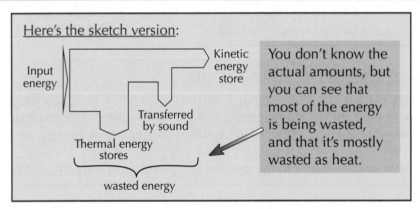

You don't know the actual amounts, but you can see that most of the energy is being wasted, and that it's mostly wasted as heat.

<u>Exam Questions:</u>
With sketches, you might be asked to <u>compare</u> two different devices and say which is <u>more efficient</u>. You generally want to be looking for the one with the <u>thickest</u> useful energy arrow(s).

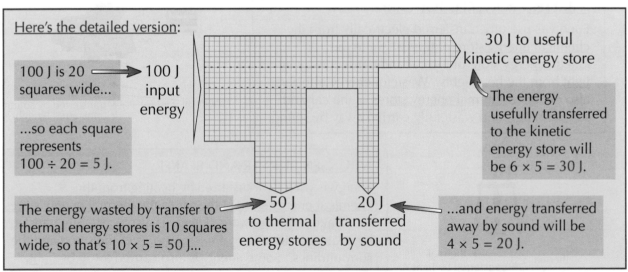

<u>Exam Questions:</u>
In an exam, the <u>most likely question</u> you'll get about detailed Sankey diagrams
is <u>filling in</u> one of the numbers or <u>calculating the efficiency</u>. The efficiency is
straightforward enough if you can work out the numbers (see page 76).

Warm-Up & Exam Questions

You must be getting used to the routine by now — the warm-up questions get you, well, warmed up, and the exam questions give you some idea of what you'll have to cope with on the day.

Warm-Up Questions

1) What type of useful energy store is food?
2) State the principle of the conservation of energy.
3) Describe the energy transfers that take place when a ball is hit with a bat.

Exam Questions

1   This question is about energy transfers.

Copy and complete the table below.
For each scenario, state the energy store that energy is transferred away from.

Scenario	Energy Transferred From...
A skydiver falling from an aeroplane.	
A substance undergoing a nuclear reaction.	
A stretched spring returning to its original shape.	
A piece of burning coal.	

[3 marks]

2   Fan A transfers 20 J of energy per second away from its battery's chemical energy store. 8 J is transferred to the fan's kinetic energy stores, 11.5 J is transferred to the thermal energy stores of the fan's moving parts and the surroundings and 0.5 J is carried away by sound.

(a)   Name the store that energy is usefully transferred to by fan A.

[1 mark]

(b)   (i)   State the equation linking percentage efficiency, useful energy output and total energy input.

[1 mark]

(ii) Calculate the percentage efficiency of fan A.

[2 marks]

(c)   Fan B has an efficiency of 55% and usefully transfers 10 J of energy to its kinetic energy store each second. Calculate how much energy is supplied to fan B per second.

[3 marks]

(d)   Each fan is powered by an identical battery. A student claims that the battery in fan B will go 'flat' quicker than in fan A because it transfers more energy to its kinetic store. Do you agree or disagree? Explain your answer.

[1 mark]

Exam Questions

3   The manufacturer of a toy crane creates a Sankey diagram to show the energy transfers involved when the crane is in operation.

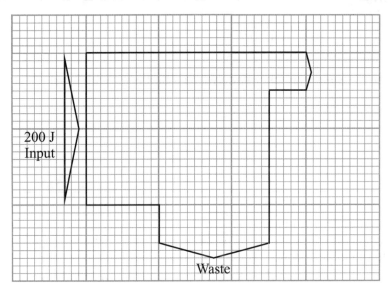

(a)   Calculate the value represented by each small square.

[1 mark]

(b)   Calculate how much energy, in J, is transferred usefully by the toy crane for every 200 J of energy supplied.

[1 mark]

4   A winch uses a cable and a hook to lift a weight by winding the cable around a drum.

On the right is a Sankey diagram for the winch lifting a weight.

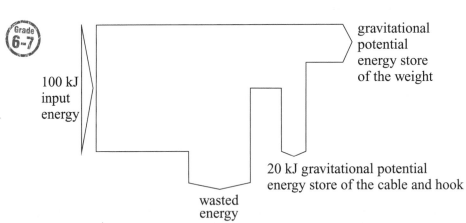

(a)   Suggest **one** type of energy store that energy is transferred to when energy is wasted by the winch.

[1 mark]

(b)   The winch wastes a total of 50 kJ. Calculate the energy, in kJ, transferred to the gravitational potential energy store of the weight by the winch.

[1 mark]

(c)   The weight is released and falls to the ground. 1.5 kJ of energy is wastefully transferred to thermal energy stores and carried away by sound, due to air resistance acting on the weight during the fall.

Sketch and label a Sankey diagram to show the energy transfers that take place during the weight's fall.

[3 marks]

Conduction, Convection and Radiation

Energy tends to be transferred <u>away</u> from a hotter object to its <u>cooler surroundings</u>.

Energy Transfer by Heating can Happen in Three Different Ways

1) <u>Energy</u> can be transferred by heating through <u>radiation</u>, <u>conduction</u> or <u>convection</u>.

2) <u>Thermal radiation</u> is the transfer of energy by heating by <u>infrared electromagnetic waves</u> (see below).

3) <u>Conduction</u> and <u>convection</u> are energy transfers that involve the transfer of energy by <u>particles</u>.

4) <u>Conduction</u> is the main form of energy transfer by heating in <u>solids</u> (see next page).

5) <u>Convection</u> is the main form of energy transfer by heating in <u>liquids and gases</u> (see the next page).

6) Emission of <u>thermal radiation</u> occurs in <u>solids, liquids and gases</u>. Any object can both absorb and emit thermal radiation, whether or not conduction or convection are also taking place.

7) The <u>bigger the temperature difference</u>, the <u>faster energy is transferred</u> between the thermal energy stores of a body and its surroundings.

Thermal Radiation Involves Emission of Electromagnetic Waves

<u>Thermal radiation</u> can also be called <u>infrared (IR) radiation</u>, and it consists purely of electromagnetic waves of a certain range of frequencies. It's next to visible light in the <u>electromagnetic spectrum</u> (see page 55).

1) <u>All objects</u> are <u>continually</u> emitting and absorbing <u>infrared radiation</u>.
2) An object that's <u>hotter</u> than its surroundings <u>emits more radiation</u> than it <u>absorbs</u> (as it <u>cools</u> down). And an object that's <u>cooler</u> than its surroundings <u>absorbs more radiation</u> than it <u>emits</u> (as it <u>warms</u> up).
3) You can <u>feel</u> this <u>radiation</u> if you stand near something <u>hot</u> like a fire.
4) Some colours and surfaces <u>absorb</u> and <u>emit</u> radiation better than others — see pages 84-85 for more on this.

Energy transfer by radiation happens constantly...

Conduction, convection and radiation are <u>separate processes</u>. But more than one of them can happen at once. So if you're asked to think about how thermal energy is being <u>transferred</u> away from an object, make sure you think about <u>everything</u> that might be going on, both in the <u>object</u> and in its <u>surroundings</u>.

Conduction, Convection and Radiation

There's more about <u>heat transfer</u> coming up on this page. It's all about <u>conduction</u> (which happens mainly in solids) and <u>convection</u> (which only happens in liquids and gases).

Conduction — Occurs **Mainly in Solids**

In a solid, the particles are held <u>tightly</u> together. So when one particle <u>vibrates</u>, it <u>collides</u> with other particles nearby and the vibrations quickly pass from particle to particle.

<u>Thermal conduction</u> is the process where vibrating particles transfer energy from their kinetic energy store to the kinetic energy stores of neighbouring particles.

This process continues <u>throughout the solid</u> and gradually some of the energy is passed all the way through, causing a <u>rise in temperature</u> at the other side of the solid. It's then usually transferred to the thermal energy stores of the surroundings (or anything else touching the object).

You Can do an **Experiment** to **Demonstrate** Conduction

1) Attach <u>beads</u> at regular intervals (e.g. <u>every 5 cm</u>) to one half of a <u>long</u> (at least 30 cm) <u>metal bar</u> using <u>wax</u>.

2) Hold the metal bar in a clamp stand. Using a Bunsen burner, <u>heat</u> the side of the bar with <u>no beads</u> attached from the <u>very end</u>.

3) As time goes on, <u>energy</u> is transferred along the bar by <u>conduction</u> and the <u>temperature increases</u> along the rod.

4) The wax holding the beads in place will gradually <u>melt</u> and the beads will <u>fall</u> as the temperature increases, <u>starting</u> with the bead <u>closest</u> to the point of heating. This illustrates <u>conduction</u>.

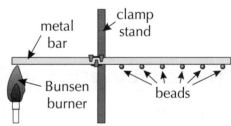

Convection of Heat — **Liquids** and **Gases** Only

1) <u>Gases and liquids</u> are usually free to <u>move about</u> — and that allows them to transfer energy by <u>convection</u>, which is a <u>much more effective process</u> than conduction.

<u>Convection</u> occurs when the more energetic particles <u>move</u> from a <u>hotter region</u> to a <u>cooler region</u> — <u>and transfer energy as they do</u>.

2) This is how <u>immersion heaters</u> in <u>kettles</u>, <u>hot water tanks</u> and <u>convector heaters</u> work.

3) Convection simply <u>can't happen in solids</u> because the particles <u>can't move</u> (apart from vibrating — see page 103).

Conduction, Convection and Radiation

Take a deep breath — here are some examples of <u>convection</u> in action...

The **Immersion Heater** Example

In a bit more detail:

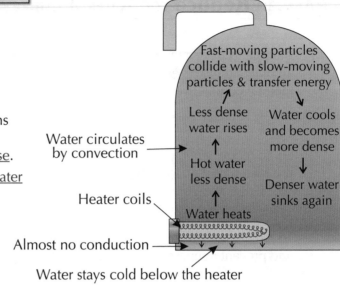

1) <u>Energy</u> is <u>transferred</u> from the heater coils to the thermal energy store of the water by <u>conduction</u> (particle collisions).

2) The <u>particles</u> near the coils get <u>more energy</u>, so they start <u>moving</u> around <u>faster</u>. This means there's more distance between them, i.e. the water <u>expands</u> and becomes <u>less dense</u>.

3) This reduction in density means that <u>hotter water</u> tends to <u>rise above</u> the <u>denser</u>, <u>cooler water</u>.

4) As the <u>hot water</u> rises, the <u>colder</u> water <u>sinks</u> towards the heater coils.

5) This cold water is then <u>heated by the coils</u> and rises — and so it goes on. You end up with <u>convection currents</u> going up, round and down, <u>circulating</u> the energy through the water.

6) Because the <u>hot water rises</u> (because of the <u>lower density</u>), you only get convection currents in the water <u>above the heater</u>. The water below it <u>stays cold</u> because there's almost no conduction.

Image labels: Fast-moving particles collide with slow-moving particles & transfer energy; Less dense water rises; Water cools and becomes more dense; Water circulates by convection; Hot water less dense; Denser water sinks again; Heater coils; Water heats; Almost no conduction; Water stays cold below the heater

> <u>Convection</u> is <u>most efficient</u> in <u>round-ish or square-ish containers</u>, because they allow the <u>convection currents</u> to <u>work best</u>. Shallow, wide containers or tall, thin ones just don't work quite so well.

<u>CONVECTION CURRENTS</u> are all about <u>CHANGES IN DENSITY</u>.

You Can See **Convection Currents** Using **Coloured Crystals**

1) Place some <u>purple</u> potassium permanganate crystals in a beaker of <u>cold water</u>. Aim to put the crystals to <u>one side</u> of the beaker.

2) Using a Bunsen burner, <u>gently heat</u> the side of the beaker with the crystals at the bottom.

3) As the <u>temperature</u> of the water around the potassium permanganate crystals <u>increases</u>, they begin to <u>dissolve</u>, forming a <u>bright purple solution</u>.

4) This purple solution is <u>carried</u> through the water by <u>convection</u>, and so <u>traces out</u> the path of the <u>convection currents</u> in the beaker.

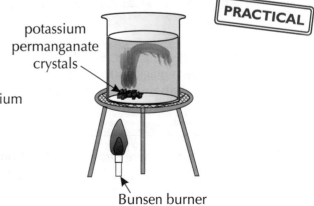

PRACTICAL

potassium permanganate crystals

Bunsen burner

In convection, particles move from hotter areas to cooler areas...

...so the particles <u>move</u>, taking their energy with them. Don't get this confused with <u>conduction</u>, where the particles can't move from their fixed positions, but <u>vibrate</u> to transfer energy to neighbouring particles. Have a flick back to the previous page if you need to remind yourself about conduction.

Energy Transfers by Heating

Energy transfer can be a problem if you're trying to keep the energy you've got. But never fear — there are things you can do to reduce the energy transferred away by radiation, convection and conduction.

You Can **Reduce** the Rate of Energy Transfer

1) All objects have a thermal conductivity — it describes how well an object transfers energy by conduction. Materials with a high thermal conductivity transfer energy between their particles quickly.

2) So, to reduce energy transfers away from a system by conduction, use materials with low thermal conductivity.

3) To reduce convection, you need to stop the fluid moving, and prevent convection currents from forming.

4) Insulation uses both of these techniques to reduce energy transfers.

5) Insulation such as clothes, blankets and foam cavity wall insulation all work by trapping pockets of air. The air can't move, so the energy has to conduct very slowly through the pockets of air, as well as the material in between, both of which have a low thermal conductivity.

For example, this building has cavity wall insulation — the foam layer traps air between the inner and outer walls.

6) Some colours and surfaces will absorb and emit IR radiation better than others. For example, a black surface is better at absorbing and emitting radiation than a white one, and a matt (dull) surface is better at absorbing and emitting radiation than a shiny one.

7) So to reduce the energy transfers away from an object by thermal radiation, the object should be designed with a surface that is a poor emitter (e.g. shiny and white).

Some substances are better thermal conductors than others...

Denser materials (see page 101) are usually better conductors than less dense materials. It's easy to see why — particles that are right next to each other can pass energy between their kinetic energy stores far more effectively than particles that are far apart. For example, water is a much better thermal conductor than air.

Energy Transfers by Heating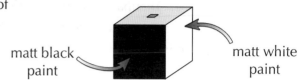

Here comes another <u>practical</u> that you can do to investigate <u>energy transfer</u> by <u>heating</u> — this one focuses on <u>radiation</u>, and involves a fun piece of kit called a <u>Leslie cube</u>.

You Can Investigate **Emission of IR Radiation** with a **Leslie Cube**

A <u>Leslie cube</u> is a <u>hollow</u>, <u>watertight</u>, metal cube made of e.g. aluminium, whose four <u>vertical faces</u> have <u>different surfaces</u> (for example, matt black paint, matt white paint, shiny metal and dull metal). You can use them to <u>investigate infrared (IR) emission</u> by different surfaces:

matt black paint   matt white paint

1) Place an <u>empty Leslie cube</u> on a <u>heat-proof</u> mat.

2) <u>Boil</u> water in a kettle and <u>fill</u> the <u>Leslie cube</u> with boiling water.

3) Wait a while for the cube to <u>warm up</u>, then hold a <u>thermometer</u> against each of the four vertical faces of the cube. You should find that all four faces are the <u>same temperature</u>.

4) Hold an <u>infrared detector</u> a <u>set distance</u> (e.g. 10 cm) away from one of the cube's vertical faces, and record the <u>amount of IR radiation</u> it detects.

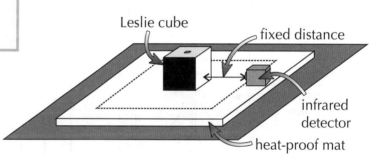

Leslie cube   fixed distance

infrared detector

heat-proof mat

5) <u>Repeat</u> this measurement for <u>each</u> of the cube's <u>vertical faces</u>. Make sure you position the detector at the <u>same distance</u> from the cube each time.

6) You should find that you detect <u>more infrared radiation</u> from the <u>black</u> surface than the <u>white</u> one, and more from the <u>matt</u> surfaces than the <u>shiny</u> ones.

7) As always, you should do the experiment <u>more than once</u>, to make sure your results are <u>reliable</u> (see page 156).

8) It's important to be <u>careful</u> when you're doing this experiment. <u>Don't</u> try to <u>move the cube</u> when it's full of <u>boiling water</u> — you might burn your hands. And be careful if you're carrying a <u>full kettle</u> too.

You can also investigate how the <u>absorption</u> of IR radiation depends on the surface absorbing it. One way is to stick ball bearings to pieces of two different materials using wax. Then place the backs of the materials at an equal distance from a heat source and see which ball bearing falls off first.

Carry out your practicals carefully...

...and that means <u>both</u> being careful when <u>collecting data</u>, and when dealing with any potential <u>hazards</u>. Watch out when you're pouring or carrying <u>boiling water</u>, and make sure any water or equipment has <u>cooled down</u> enough before you start handling it after your experiment is done.

Warm-Up & Exam Questions

Hopefully the last few pages have stuck, but there's only one way to check — and that's with some questions. Warm-up questions to get you started, and then exam questions to really get your teeth into.

Warm-Up Questions

1) True or false? Thermal radiation can also be called ultraviolet radiation.
2) Explain how energy is transferred through a solid by conduction.
3) Why does convection only take place in liquids and gases?
4) Explain how an immersion heater works.

Exam Questions

1   Three flasks, each containing 100 ml of water, are placed in closed boxes filled with a clear gel at an initial temperature of 50 °C.
    The water in each flask is at a different temperature, as shown.

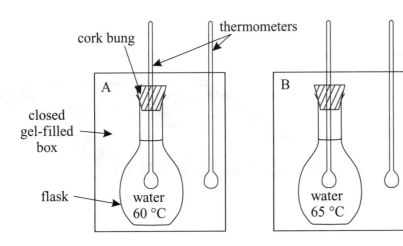

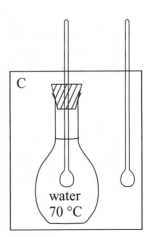

a)   Name **two** ways in which the flasks will transfer heat to the gel surrounding them.

[2 marks]

b)   State which flask will transfer heat to the gel the fastest. Explain your answer.

[2 marks]

2   A homeowner is worried that her house is losing a lot of heat energy through its walls and windows. The outer walls of the house are made up of two layers of bricks separated by an air cavity.

(a)   Which type of energy transfer does having an air gap in the wall help to reduce?

[1 mark]

(b)   The homeowner is considering having cavity wall insulation installed.
      Explain how this will help to reduce energy transfer by convection.

[1 mark]

Exam Questions

3 Energy can be transferred by convection. Grade 6-7

  (a) Give the state of matter in which convection cannot take place. Give a reason for your answer.

      [2 marks]

  (b) A student is carrying out an experiment in class to demonstrate convection.
She fills a rectangular glass tube with water and heats one of the bottom corners, as shown.

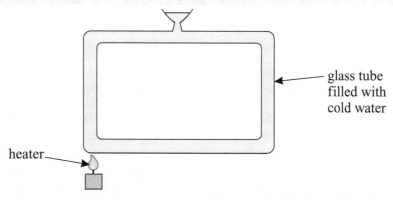

glass tube filled with cold water

heater

    (i) Copy the diagram above and draw **two** arrows to show the movement of the water in the tube.

      [1 mark]

    (ii) Explain why the water in the tube moves in the way that you have shown in part (i).

      [3 marks]

  (c) Which of the following is **not** an example of convection?

    ☐ **A** the heating of a large room by a radiator

    ☐ **B** the heating of water in a kettle

    ☐ **C** the transfer of energy by heating through a copper pan

    ☐ **D** hot air rising up a chimney

      [1 mark]

PRACTICAL

4 A student uses a Leslie cube, shown in the diagram to the right, to investigate how different surfaces radiate energy. A Leslie cube is a hollow cube with faces that have differently textured and coloured surfaces. Grade 6-7

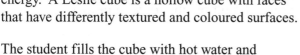

Leslie cube

The student fills the cube with hot water and places his hand near to each surface.
He records how warm his hand feels in front of each surface.
The four sides of the cube are matt black, shiny black, matt white and shiny white.

  (a) Predict which side the student's hand would feel warmest in front of.

      [1 mark]

  (b) Predict which side the student's hand would feel coolest in front of.

      [1 mark]

  (c) Suggest **one** way that the student could improve his method.

      [1 mark]

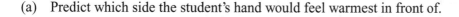

Work

Work (like a lot of things) means something slightly different in Physics to what it means in everyday life...

'Work Done' is Just 'Energy Transferred'

> When a force moves an object through a distance,
> WORK IS DONE on the object and ENERGY IS TRANSFERRED.

1) To make something move, some sort of force needs to act on it.
   The thing applying the force needs a source of energy (like fuel or food).

2) The force does 'work' to move the object and energy is
   transferred mechanically from one store to another (see page 74).

3) Whether energy is transferred usefully (e.g. lifting a load) or is wasted (see page 75), you can
   still say that work is done, because work done and energy transferred are the same thing.

> For example, when you push something along a rough surface (like a carpet) you are
> doing work against frictional forces. Energy is being transferred to the kinetic energy store
> of the object because it starts moving, but some is also being transferred to thermal energy
> stores of the object and the surface due to the friction. This causes the temperature of the
> object and the surface to increase. (Like rubbing your hands together to warm them up.)

There's a **Formula** to Learn for **Work Done**:

> **Work done = Force × Distance moved**

$$\frac{W}{F \times d}$$

This formula only works if the
force is in exactly the same
direction as the movement.

FORCE

Distance

Whether the force is friction or weight or tension in a rope, it's the same equation.
To find how much work has been done (in joules), you just multiply the force in newtons
by the distance moved in metres.

> Example: Some people drag an old tractor tyre 5 m over flat ground.
>   They pull with a total force of 340 N. Find the work done.
>
> Answer: $W = F \times d$
> $= 340 \times 5 = 1700$ J

Doing work involves a force acting over a distance...

MATHS TIP Whenever you use a formula in Physics, always make sure that the values you're putting in are in
the right units. For example, when you're using the formula above, make sure that your force is in
newtons and your distance is in metres — or the answer you get for work done won't be in joules.

Power

The <u>more powerful</u> a device is, the <u>more energy</u> it will transfer in a certain amount of <u>time</u>.

Power is the '**Rate of Doing Work**' — i.e. How Much **per Second**

1) <u>Power</u> is a measure of <u>how quickly work</u> is being <u>done</u>.
As <u>work done</u> = <u>energy transferred</u>, you can <u>define</u> power like this:

> <u>Power</u> is the <u>rate</u> at which <u>energy is transferred</u>.

2) So, the power of a <u>machine</u> is the <u>rate</u> at which it <u>transfers energy</u>.

> For example, if an <u>electric drill</u> has a power of <u>700 W</u>, this means it can transfer <u>700 J</u> of energy <u>every second</u>.

3) This is the <u>formula</u> for power:

$$\text{Power} = \frac{\text{Work done}}{\text{Time taken}}$$

4) The proper unit of power is the <u>watt (W)</u>.
<u>1 W = 1 J of energy transferred per second</u> (J/s).

> <u>Example:</u>   A motor transfers <u>4.8 kJ</u> of useful energy in <u>2 minutes</u>.
> Find its power output.
>
> <u>Answer:</u>   energy = 4.8 kJ = 4800 J
>   time = 2 minutes = 120 s
> $P = W \div t$
>   = 4800 ÷ 120 = 40 W (or 40 J/s)

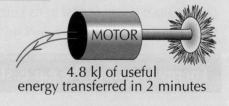

4.8 kJ of useful
energy transferred in 2 minutes

A large power doesn't always mean a large force...

The power that a <u>car</u> has is often measured in a funny unit called <u>horsepower</u>. 1 horsepower is the rate at which energy is transferred when a horse raises a mass of 550 lb through a height of 1 ft in 1 second...
I think I'd stick to <u>watts</u> if I were you. Anyway, make sure that you've learnt the <u>formula for power</u>.

Kinetic and Potential Energy Stores

Now you've got your head around <u>energy stores</u>, it's time to see how you can calculate the amount of energy in <u>two</u> of the most common ones — <u>kinetic</u> and <u>gravitational potential</u> energy stores.

Movement Means Energy in an Object's Kinetic Energy Store

1) Anything that is <u>moving</u> has energy in its <u>kinetic energy store</u>. Energy is transferred <u>to</u> this store when an object <u>speeds up</u> and is transferred <u>away</u> from this store when an object <u>slows down</u>.

2) The energy in the <u>kinetic energy store</u> depends on the object's <u>mass</u> and <u>speed</u>. The <u>greater its mass</u> and the <u>faster</u> it's going, the <u>more energy</u> there will be in its kinetic energy store.

3) There's a <u>slightly tricky</u> formula for it:

$$\text{Energy in kinetic energy store} = \tfrac{1}{2} \times \text{mass} \times (\text{speed})^2$$

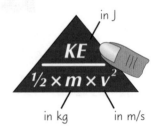

> Example: A car of mass <u>2450 kg</u> is travelling at <u>38 m/s</u>. Calculate its kinetic energy.
>
> Answer: $KE = \tfrac{1}{2}mv^2 = \tfrac{1}{2} \times 2450 \times 38^2 = 1\,768\,900$ J

Raised Objects Store Energy in G.P.E. Stores

g.p.e. = gravitational potential energy

1) <u>Lifting</u> an object in a <u>gravitational field</u> requires <u>work</u>. This causes a <u>transfer of energy</u> to the <u>gravitational potential</u> energy (g.p.e.) store of the raised object. The <u>higher</u> the object is lifted, the <u>more</u> energy is transferred to this store.

2) The amount of energy in a g.p.e. store depends on the object's <u>mass</u>, its <u>height</u> and the <u>strength</u> of the gravitational field the object is in (see page 5).

$$\text{Energy in gravitational potential energy store} = \text{mass} \times \text{gravitational field strength} \times \text{height}$$

On Earth,
$g = 10 \text{ m/s}^2$
(This is the same as 10 N/kg, since $1 \text{ m/s}^2 = 1$ N/kg.)

3) You can use this equation to find the <u>change in energy</u> in an object's gravitational potential energy store for a <u>change in height</u>, <u>h</u>.

Falling Objects Also Transfer Energy

1) When something <u>falls</u>, energy from its <u>gravitational potential energy store</u> is transferred to its <u>kinetic energy store</u>.

2) For a falling object when there's <u>no air resistance</u>:

Energy lost from the g.p.e. store = Energy gained in the kinetic energy store

3) It's all to do with the Principle of the Conservation of Energy — see page 74.

4) In real life, <u>air resistance</u> acts against all falling objects (see page 16)— it causes some energy to be transferred to <u>other energy stores</u>, e.g. the <u>thermal</u> energy stores of the <u>object</u> and <u>surroundings</u>.

Greater height means more energy in G.P.E. stores...

If you're struggling to remember any of these <u>formulas</u> that you need to know, you could make up a handy <u>mnemonic</u> to help you. Like "<u>k</u>itten <u>e</u>ats <u>half</u> <u>m</u>y <u>v</u>illage <u>s</u>quare" for $KE = \tfrac{1}{2}mv^2$.

Warm-Up & Exam Questions

There were lots of definitions and equations to get to grips with on the last few pages.
Try these questions to see what you can remember.

Warm-Up Questions

1) What is meant by the work done by a force?
2) What's the formula linking power and work done?
3) State the equation linking kinetic energy, mass and speed.

Exam Questions

1 Which of these is the definition of power? (Grade 4-6)

☐ **A** Power is the total work done by an object.

☐ **B** Power is the rate at which energy is transferred.

☐ **C** Power is the total energy transferred to an object.

☐ **D** Power is the minimum work done to an object to cause it to move.

[1 mark]

2 A woman pushes a 20 kg wheelbarrow 15 m along a flat path using a horizontal force of 50 N. (Grade 6-7)

(a) (i) State the equation that links work done, force applied and
distance moved in the direction of the force.

[1 mark]

(ii) Calculate the work done by the woman, in J.

[2 marks]

(b) Work has to be done against the frictional forces acting on the wheel of the wheelbarrow.
Explain the effect this has on the temperature of the wheel.

[2 marks]

3 A roller coaster cart with a mass of 105 kg is
rolling along a horizontal track at 2.39 m/s. (Grade 7-9)

2.39 m/s

(a) Calculate the energy in the kinetic energy store of the cart, in J.

[3 marks]

(b) The cart reaches a downhill slope in the track with a vertical height of 20.2 m.
It rolls down the slope with no driving force other than gravity.

(i) Calculate the energy lost from the gravitational potential energy
store of the cart as it rolls down the slope, in J.

[3 marks]

(ii) Assuming no friction acts against the cart, explain what happens to the
energy that is lost from the gravitational potential energy store.

[1 mark]

Non-Renewable Energy and Power Stations

There are different types of <u>energy resource</u>, but they fit into <u>two types</u>: <u>renewable</u> and <u>non-renewable</u>.

Non-Renewable Energy Resources Will Run Out One Day

The <u>non-renewables</u> are the <u>three fossil fuels</u> and <u>nuclear</u>:

1) <u>Coal</u>
2) <u>Oil</u>
3) <u>Natural gas</u>
4) <u>Nuclear fuels</u> (e.g. <u>uranium</u> and <u>plutonium</u>)

a) They will <u>all 'run out'</u> one day.
b) They all do <u>damage</u> to the environment.
c) But they provide <u>most of our energy</u>.

Most Power Stations Use Steam to Drive a Turbine

<u>Most</u> electricity we use is <u>generated</u> from the four <u>non-renewable</u> sources of energy (<u>coal</u>, <u>oil</u>, <u>natural gas</u> and <u>nuclear</u>) in <u>big power stations</u>, which are all <u>pretty much the same</u> (apart from the <u>boiler</u>, which is a bit different in nuclear power stations — see page 93):

1) As the fossil fuel <u>burns</u> (in oxygen) the energy in its <u>chemical energy store</u> is transferred to the <u>thermal energy store</u> of the water <u>by heating</u>.

2) The water <u>boils</u> to form <u>steam</u>, which <u>turns</u> a <u>turbine</u>, transferring energy <u>mechanically</u> to the <u>kinetic energy store</u> of the turbine.

3) As the turbine revolves, so does the <u>generator</u>, which produces an electric current (see p.121). The generator transfers the energy <u>electrically</u> away from the power station, via the <u>national grid</u>.

Boiler | steam | Turbine | Generator | Grid
Fuel
chemical energy store → thermal energy store → water → kinetic energy store → kinetic energy store → transferred away electrically

Fossil Fuels are Linked to Environmental Problems

Burning <u>fossil fuels</u> (<u>oil</u>, <u>natural gas</u> and <u>coal</u>) causes a lot of problems, mainly <u>environmental</u>. But at the moment we still rely on them the <u>most</u> to provide the energy needed to generate electricity.

Advantages

1) <u>Burning fossil fuels</u> releases a <u>lot of energy</u>, relatively <u>cheaply</u>.
2) Energy from fossil fuels <u>doesn't</u> rely on the <u>weather</u>, like a lot of renewable energy (see pages 93-97), so it's a <u>reliable</u> energy source.
3) We have lots of fossil fuel power stations already, so we <u>don't</u> need to spend money on <u>new technology</u> to use them.

Disadvantages

1) All three fossil fuels release <u>carbon dioxide</u> (CO_2) into the <u>atmosphere</u> when burned in power stations. All this CO_2 contributes to <u>global warming</u> and <u>climate change</u>.
2) Burning <u>coal</u> and <u>oil</u> also releases <u>sulfur dioxide</u> (SO_2), which causes <u>acid rain</u>. Acid rain can <u>harm trees</u> and <u>soils</u> and can have a huge impact on <u>wildlife</u>.
3) And a massive disadvantage of using fossil fuels is that <u>they're eventually going to run out</u>.

Paper 2

Nuclear and Geothermal Energy

Well, who'd have thought... there's <u>energy</u> lurking about inside <u>atoms</u> and <u>deep underground</u>.

Nuclear Reactors are Just Fancy Boilers

1) A <u>nuclear power station</u> is mostly the same as the one on page 92. The difference is that <u>nuclear fission</u> (see page 139), e.g. of <u>uranium</u>, produces the <u>heat</u> to make <u>steam</u> to drive <u>turbines</u> etc., rather than burning. So the <u>boiler</u> is a bit different:

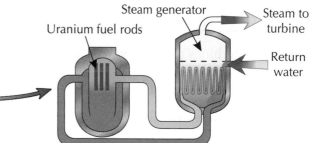

Steam generator

Uranium fuel rods

Steam to turbine

Return water

2) During the process, energy is transferred from <u>nuclear</u> energy stores to <u>thermal</u> energy stores by heating, then mechanically to <u>kinetic</u> energy stores, and finally transferred electrically through the national grid.

3) Nuclear reactors are expensive to <u>build</u> and <u>maintain</u>, and take <u>longer</u> to <u>start up</u> than fossil fuel ones.

4) <u>Processing</u> the <u>uranium</u> before you use it causes pollution, and there's always a risk of <u>leaks</u> of radioactive material, or even a <u>major catastrophe</u> like at <u>Chernobyl</u>.

5) A big problem with nuclear power is the <u>radioactive waste</u> that you always get.

6) When they're too old and inefficient, nuclear power stations have to be <u>decommissioned</u> (shut down and made safe) — that's expensive too.

7) But there are many <u>advantages</u> to nuclear power. It <u>doesn't</u> produce any of the <u>greenhouse gases</u> which contribute to <u>global warming</u>. Also, there's still plenty of <u>uranium</u> left in the ground (although it can take a lot of money and energy to make it suitable for use in a reactor).

Paper 2

Paper 2

Geothermal Power — Heat from Underground

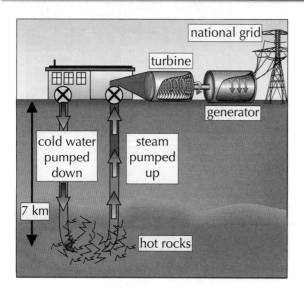

national grid

turbine

generator

cold water pumped down

steam pumped up

7 km

hot rocks

1) This is <u>only possible</u> in <u>certain places</u> where <u>hot rocks</u> lie quite near to the <u>surface</u>. The source of much of the energy is the <u>slow decay</u> of various <u>radioactive elements</u> (including <u>uranium</u>) deep inside the Earth.

2) <u>Water is pumped</u> in pipes down to the <u>hot rocks</u> and forced back up due to <u>pressure</u> to turn a turbine which drives a <u>generator</u>. So the energy is transferred from <u>thermal energy stores</u> to <u>kinetic energy stores</u> and used to generate electricity.

3) In some places, geothermal <u>energy</u> is used to <u>heat buildings directly</u>.

4) This is <u>free</u>, <u>renewable energy</u> with no real <u>environmental problems</u>.

5) The <u>main drawback</u> is the <u>cost of drilling</u> down <u>several km</u>.

6) The <u>cost</u> of building a power plant is often <u>high</u> compared to the <u>amount</u> of energy we can get out of it.

7) So there are <u>very few places</u> where this seems to be an <u>economic option</u> (for now).

Wind and Wave Energy

A nice, cool <u>breeze</u> and <u>waves</u> lapping against the shore... two more ways of <u>generating electricity</u>.

Wind Farms — Lots of Wind Turbines

1) Wind power involves putting lots of wind turbines up in <u>exposed places</u> — like on <u>moors</u>, around the <u>coast</u>, or <u>out at sea</u>.

2) Wind turbines use energy from the <u>kinetic energy</u> store of moving air to <u>generate electricity</u>. <u>Wind</u> turns the <u>blades</u>, which turn a <u>generator</u> inside it.

3) Wind turbines are quite cheap to run — they're very <u>tough</u> and reliable, and the wind is <u>free</u>.

4) Wind power doesn't produce any <u>polluting waste</u> and it's <u>renewable</u> — the wind's never going to run out.

5) But there are <u>disadvantages</u>. Some people think they <u>spoil the view</u>. You need about <u>1500 wind turbines</u> to replace <u>one coal-fired power station</u> and 1500 of them cover <u>a lot</u> of ground — which would have a big effect on the scenery. And they can be <u>noisy</u>, which can be annoying for people living nearby.

6) Another problem is that sometimes the wind isn't <u>strong enough</u> to generate any power. It's also impossible to increase supply when there's extra demand.

7) And although the wind is free, it's <u>expensive</u> to <u>set up</u> a wind farm, especially <u>out at sea</u>.

Wave Power — Lots of Little Wave Converters

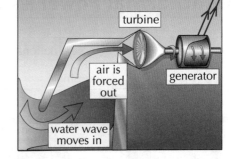

1) One way of harvesting wave power is with lots of small <u>wave converters</u> located <u>around the coast</u>. As waves come in to the shore they provide an <u>up and down motion</u> which can be used to drive a <u>generator</u>.

2) The energy is transferred from the <u>kinetic energy store</u> of the waves to the <u>kinetic energy store</u> of the turbine, and used to generate electricity.

3) There's <u>no pollution</u> and it's <u>renewable</u>.

4) The main problems are <u>spoiling the view</u> and being a <u>hazard to boats</u>.

5) It's <u>fairly unreliable</u>, since waves tend to die out when the <u>wind drops</u>.

6) <u>Initial costs are high</u> but there are <u>no fuel costs</u> and <u>minimal running costs</u>.

7) Wave power is unlikely to provide energy on a <u>large scale</u> but it can be <u>very useful</u> on <u>small islands</u>.

More renewable energy resources to learn

For the exam, you'll need to be able to describe the <u>energy transfers</u> involved in all these methods of generating electricity, as well as the ones described over the next few pages. You'll also need to be able to write about the advantages and disadvantages of each method.

Solar Energy

Energy from <u>the Sun</u> can be used to generate <u>electricity</u> too, or harnessed directly for <u>heating</u>.

You Can **Capture** the Sun's Energy Using **Solar Cells**

1) <u>Solar cells</u> (<u>photocells</u>) use <u>energy</u> from the Sun to directly generate electricity. They generate <u>direct current</u> (d.c.) — the same as a <u>battery</u> (not like the <u>mains electricity</u> in your home, which is a.c. (alternating current) — see page 30).

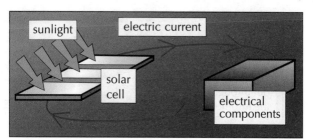

2) The Sun provides a <u>renewable</u> energy resource — it won't run out (not for 5 billion years anyway).

3) Solar cells are very <u>expensive initially</u>, but after that the energy is <u>free</u> and <u>running costs</u> are almost <u>nil</u>. And there's <u>no pollution</u> produced while using them (although some is produced during their manufacture).

4) They're usually used to generate electricity on a <u>relatively small scale</u>, e.g. powering <u>individual homes</u>.

5) It's often <u>too expensive</u> or <u>not practical</u> to connect them to the <u>national grid</u> — the cost of connecting them can be enormous compared with the value of the electricity generated.

6) Solar cells can only <u>generate</u> enough <u>electricity</u> to be useful if they have <u>enough sunlight</u> — which can be a problem at <u>night</u> (and in <u>winter</u> in some places). But the cells can be linked to <u>rechargeable batteries</u> to create a system that can <u>store energy</u> during the day for use at <u>night</u>.

7) Solar cells are often the best way to power <u>calculators</u> or <u>watches</u> that don't use much energy. They're also used in <u>remote places</u> where there's not much choice (e.g. deserts) and in satellites.

Solar Heating Systems — No Complex Mechanical Stuff

Solar Water Heating Panels

Solar water heating panels are more simple than solar cells — they're basically just <u>black water pipes</u> inside a <u>glass</u> box. The <u>glass</u> lets <u>energy</u> from the Sun in, which is then <u>absorbed</u> by the black pipes and heats up the water.

Like solar cells, they cost money to <u>set up</u>, but are <u>renewable</u> and <u>free</u> after that. They're only used for <u>small-scale</u> energy production.

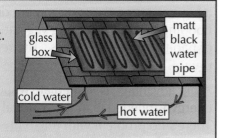

Cooking with Solar Power

If you get a <u>curved mirror</u>, then you can <u>focus</u> the Sun's light. This is what happens in a solar oven. They provide a <u>renewable</u> energy resource for outdoor cooking. But they're <u>slow</u>, <u>bulky</u> and <u>unreliable</u> — they need strong sunlight to work.

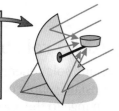

All the radiation that lands on the curved mirror is focused right on your pan.

Paper 2

Paper 2

Generating Electricity Using Water

Water, water, everywhere. Perfect for generating electricity.

Tidal Barrages Generate Energy When the Tide Goes In and Out

1) Tidal barrages are big dams built across river estuaries, with turbines in them. As the tide comes in it fills up the estuary to a height of several metres. This water can then be allowed out through turbines at a controlled speed. It also drives the turbines on the way in.

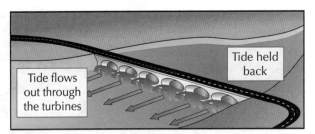

Tide held back

Tide flows out through the turbines

2) The energy is transferred from the kinetic energy stores of the water to the kinetic energy store of the turbine, and used to generate electricity.

3) There's no pollution and it's renewable. The main problems are preventing free access by boats, spoiling the view and altering the habitat of the wildlife.

4) Tides are pretty reliable, but the height of the tide is variable, so lower tides will provide less energy than higher ones.

5) Initial costs are moderately high, but there's no fuel costs and minimal running costs.

Hydroelectricity — Catching Rainwater

1) Hydroelectric power often requires the flooding of a valley by building a big dam. Rainwater is caught and allowed out through turbines, transferring energy from the gravitational potential energy store of the water to kinetic energy stores as it falls. This is used to generate electricity.

dam

national grid

water stored

turbines

generator

2) It's a renewable energy resource.

3) There is no pollution (as such), but there's a big impact on the environment due to flooding the valley (rotting vegetation releases methane and CO_2) and possible loss of habitat for some species. The reservoirs can also look very unsightly when they dry up. Location in remote valleys can avoid some of these problems.

4) A big advantage is immediate response to increased demand. If more energy is needed than the national grid can supply, the water's released. There's no problem with reliability except in times of drought.

5) Initial costs are high, but there's no fuel and low running costs.

Renewable AND reliable, but a big impact on the local environment...

Unlike wind, wave and solar energy, tidal barrages and hydroelectric power installations are able to generate a fairly constant supply of electricity (or even vary their output to match demand). However, they can cause lasting change to the appearance of the surrounding area and to the wildlife that lives there.

Generating Electricity Using Water

Nearly at the end of all this <u>energy resources</u> stuff now. Just one more page...

Pumped Storage Gives Extra Supply Just When it's Needed

Most large power stations have <u>huge boilers</u> which have to be kept running <u>all night</u> even though demand is <u>very low</u>. This means there's a <u>surplus</u> of electricity at night — and it's surprisingly <u>difficult</u> to find a way of <u>keeping</u> this spare energy for <u>later use</u>. Pumped storage is one of the <u>best solutions</u>.

Here's How it Works...

1) In pumped storage, 'spare' <u>night-time electricity</u> is used to pump water up to a <u>higher reservoir</u>.

2) This can then be <u>released quickly</u> during periods of <u>peak demand</u>, such as at <u>teatime</u> each evening, to supplement the <u>steady delivery</u> from the big power stations.

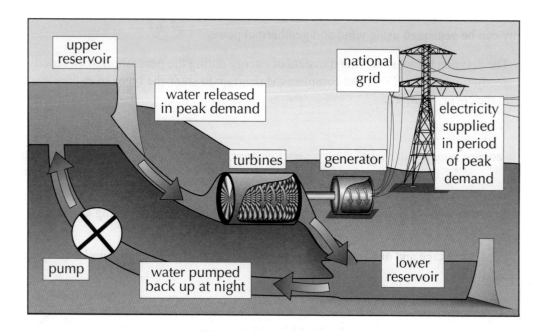

It's a really clever idea — the 'spare' electricity is used to <u>transfer energy</u> back to the water's <u>gravitational potential energy stores</u>, so that it can generate more electricity when it is needed by flowing through the dam.

Paper 2

Paper 2

Pumped storage doesn't generate power — it stores it

There tend to be surges in demand for electricity at certain times — for example, there's often a surge in demand when it gets to half-time in a big football match, as everyone switches their kettles on. Clever people at the National Grid have to try to predict what electricity we'll need and when. They can then employ pumped storage facilities, like the one at Dinorwig in Wales, to try to meet demand.

Warm-Up & Exam Questions

It's very nearly the end of this section. But don't shed a tear — try these questions instead.

Warm-Up Questions

1) How does burning coal contribute to acid rain? Give one problem caused by acid rain.
2) Give two advantages of using solar energy to generate electricity instead of fossil fuels.
3) What does it mean if an energy resource is 'renewable'?

Exam Questions

PAPER 2

Grade 3-4

1   Which of the following energy sources is a renewable energy source?

☐ **A**   coal   ☐ **B**   nuclear   ☐ **C**   wind   ☐ **D**   oil

[1 mark]

PAPER 2

Grade 4-6

2   Electricity can be generated using wind and geothermal power.

(a) (i)   The diagram below shows the transfers of energy during the generation of electricity using geothermal power. Copy and complete the diagram to show the types of energy store involved in the energy transfers.

.... → .... → ....

energy store of hot rocks   energy store of water   energy stores of turbine
and generator

[3 marks]

(ii) Give **one** advantage and **one** disadvantage of generating electricity using geothermal resources.

[2 marks]

(b)   Give **one** advantage and **one** disadvantage of generating electricity using wind.

[2 marks]

PAPER 2

Grade 4-6

3   In some coastal regions, electricity is generated from waves using wave converters.

(a)   Which of the following statements about wave converters is true?

☐ **A**   They generate electricity all the time.

☐ **B**   The initial costs of wave converters are low.

☐ **C**   They produce pollution when generating electricity.

☐ **D**   They can be hazardous to boats.

[1 mark]

(b)   Describe the energy transfer that occurs in a wave converter when it is used to generate electricity.

[1 mark]

Exam Questions

PAPER 2

4   In a nuclear power station, water is heated to produce steam.
Grade 6-7

(a)   Describe the energy transfer(s) that occur in a nuclear power station to produce the steam.

[1 mark]

(b)   (i)   One argument for building more nuclear power stations is that generating electricity from nuclear fuel does not directly contribute to global warming. Explain why this is the case.

[1 mark]

(ii)   Give **two** ways in which generating nuclear power can harm the environment.

[2 marks]

PAPER 2

5   Energy from the Sun is used in different ways. Grade 6-7

(a)   Name **one** type of device that uses energy from the Sun to directly generate electricity.

[1 mark]

(b)   Electricity generated from the Sun's energy can be used to heat water in a home.
Name and describe **one** other way the Sun's energy can be used to heat water in a home.

[2 marks]

(c)   Give **two** reasons why electricity generated from the Sun is rarely supplied to the national grid.

[2 marks]

PAPER 2

6   Water can be used in many ways to generate electricity. In some countries, electricity is generated using hydroelectric dams. Water is held back behind the dam before being allowed to flow out through turbines to produce electricity.
Grade 6-7

(a)   Describe the energy transfers involved when water flowing through the turbines is used to produce electricity.

[3 marks]

(b)   Hydroelectric power stations don't produce any carbon dioxide when generating electricity.
Give **two** ways that using hydroelectric power stations to generate electricity damages the environment.

[2 marks]

(c)   In some hydroelectric power stations, energy is used to pump water back into the reservoir during times of low electricity demand. Give the name of this type of system.

[1 mark]

(d)   Sea tides can also be used to generate electricity using tidal barrages.
Give **two** advantages of generating electricity using tidal barrages.

[2 marks]

Revision Questions for Section 4

Phew, that was a fairly hefty section. Time to check you've taken it all in — I hope you're feeling energised...
- Try these questions and <u>tick off each one</u> when you <u>get it right</u>.
- When you've done <u>all the questions</u> for a topic and are <u>completely happy</u> with it, tick off the topic.

Energy Transfers and Efficiency (p.74-78) ☑

1) Name eight types of energy store. ☑

2) *What is the percentage efficiency of a motor that has an input energy transfer of 120 J and transfers 90 J usefully to the motor's kinetic energy store? ☑

3) Describe the energy transfers that occur in a battery-powered toy car. ☑

4) *The Sankey diagram below shows how energy is transferred in a catapult.

100 J input energy transfer → kinetic energy store → thermal energy stores

    a) How much energy is transferred to the kinetic energy store?

    b) How much energy is wasted?

    c) What is the percentage efficiency of the catapult? ☑

Energy Transfers by Heating (p.81-85) ☑

5) Describe the three ways that energy can be transferred by heating. ☑

6) Describe how the energy is transferred from a heating element throughout the water in a kettle. What is this process called? ☑

7) Describe how insulation reduces energy transfers. ☑

Calculating Energy and Power (p.88-90) ☑

8) *A dog dragged a big branch 12 m over the next-door neighbour's front lawn, pulling with a force of 535 N. How much work was done? ☑

9) *An electric motor uses 540 kJ of electrical energy in 4.5 minutes. What is its power consumption? ☑

10) *Find the energy in the kinetic energy store of a 78 kg sheep moving at 2.3 m/s. ☑

11) What happens to the amount of energy in an object's gravitational potential energy store when it is lifted above the ground? ☑

12) Write down the formula used to find the energy in an object's gravitational potential energy store. ☑

Energy Resources (p.92-97) ☑

13) List four different types of renewable energy resource. ☑

14) Describe the energy transfers that take place when burning fossil fuels to generate electricity in a typical power station. ☑

15) State two advantages and two disadvantages of using fossil fuels to generate electricity. ☑

16) Describe the energy transfers that take place when a tidal barrage is used to generate electricity. ☑

*Answers on page 211.

Density

Density tells you how much <u>mass</u> is packed into a given <u>volume</u> of space. You need to be able to work it out, as well as carry out <u>practicals</u> to work out the densities of liquids and solids. Lucky you.

Density is **Mass** per Unit **Volume**

Density is a measure of the '<u>compactness</u>' (for want of a better word) of a substance.
It relates the <u>mass</u> of a substance to how much <u>space</u> it <u>takes up</u>.

$$\text{Density } (\rho) = \frac{\text{mass } (m)}{\text{volume } (V)}$$

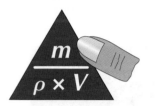

The symbol for density is a Greek letter rho (ρ) — it looks like a p, but it isn't.

1) The units of density are g/cm^3 or kg/m^3. $1\ g/cm^3 = 1000\ kg/m^3$

2) The density of an object depends on what it's made of. Density <u>doesn't vary</u> with <u>size</u> or <u>shape</u>.

3) The average <u>density</u> of an object determines whether it <u>floats</u> or <u>sinks</u> —
a solid object will <u>float</u> on a fluid if it has a <u>lower density</u> than the fluid.

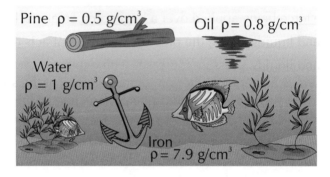

Pine $\rho = 0.5\ g/cm^3$
Oil $\rho = 0.8\ g/cm^3$
Water $\rho = 1\ g/cm^3$
Iron $\rho = 7.9\ g/cm^3$

You Can Find the **Density** of an Object from its **Mass** and **Volume**

PRACTICAL

1) To <u>measure</u> the <u>density</u> of a substance, use a balance to measure its <u>mass</u>.

2) If it's a box shape, start by measuring its <u>length</u>, <u>width</u> and <u>height</u> with an <u>appropriate</u> piece of equipment (e.g. a <u>ruler</u>). Then calculate its <u>volume</u> by <u>multiplying</u> the length, width and height together.

3) For an irregular solid, you can find its volume by <u>submerging</u> it in a <u>eureka can</u> filled with water. The water <u>displaced</u> by the object will be <u>transferred</u> to the <u>measuring cylinder</u>.

4) Record the <u>volume</u> of water in the measuring cylinder. This is also the <u>volume</u> of the <u>object</u>.

5) Plug the object's <u>mass</u> and <u>volume</u> into the <u>formula</u> above to find its <u>density</u>.

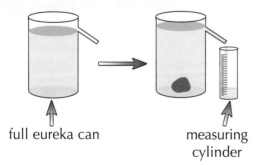

full eureka can

measuring cylinder

A dense material has a lot of mass in a small volume

Dense materials tend to feel really heavy for their size. If you look at the formula for finding the density of an object, you'll see that a dense material must have a big mass in comparison to its volume.

Pressure

You probably hear about <u>pressure</u> a fair bit in everyday life, but (as always) there are some lovely <u>equations</u> to describe it in Physics. Better get your calculator out...

Pressure is **Force** per Unit **Area**

1) <u>Pressure</u> is a measure of the <u>force</u> being applied to the surface of something.

2) It relates how much force is being applied to an object (in N) to the <u>area</u> that it is applied over (in m²).

$$\text{Pressure} = \frac{\text{force}}{\text{area}}$$

The symbol for pressure is a p — don't confuse it with density (ρ).

3) Pressure is usually measured in <u>pascals</u>, Pa (or <u>kilopascals</u>, kPa).   1 kPa = 1000 Pa
   1 pascal is defined as 1 N/m².

- The <u>same force</u> being applied over a <u>larger area</u> creates a <u>lower pressure</u>.
- In <u>gases</u> and <u>liquids</u> at rest, the pressure at any point acts <u>equally in all directions</u>.
- In <u>gases</u> and <u>liquids</u>, pressure increases with <u>depth</u>.
  The pressure is higher at the bottom of the sea than at the surface, and it is lower high up in the atmosphere than close to the Earth.

Pressure **Difference** in Liquids and Gases Depends on **Density**

1) <u>Pressure difference</u> is the difference in pressure between two points in a liquid or gas.

2) It depends on the <u>height difference</u> (in m), and the <u>density</u> (in kg/m³) of the substance.

3) <u>Gravity</u> has an effect too — g is the <u>gravitational field strength</u>, which is around 10 m/s².

Pressure difference = height × density × gravitational field strength

Formula triangles can make using equations easier

<u>Formula triangles</u> can be a handy way of helping you <u>rearrange equations</u>. Just <u>cover up</u> the variable you're interested in, and then the positions of the other variables will show you how you need to write the equation. As long as you can <u>remember</u> the triangle, it makes life easier.

Changes of State

Solid ⇌ melts ⟶ Liquid ⇌ boils ⟶ Gas ⇌ condenses ⟶ Liquid ⇌ solidifies ⟶ Solid. Easy peasy.

Kinetic Theory Can Explain the Three States of Matter

1) The three states of matter are solid (e.g. ice), liquid (e.g. water) and gas (e.g. water vapour). The particles of a substance in each state are the same — only the arrangement and energy of the particles are different.

Solids

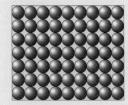

Strong forces of attraction hold the particles close together in a fixed, regular arrangement. The particles don't have much energy so they can only vibrate about their fixed positions.

Liquids

There are weaker forces of attraction between the particles. The particles are close together, but can move past each other, and form irregular arrangements. They have more energy than the particles in a solid — they move in random directions at low speeds.

Gases

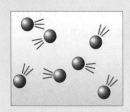

There are almost no forces of attraction between the particles. The particles have more energy than those in liquids and solids — they are free to move, and travel in random directions and at high speeds.

2) The energy in a substance's thermal energy store is held by its particles in their kinetic energy stores — this is what the thermal energy store actually is.

3) When you heat a liquid, the extra energy is transferred into the particles' kinetic energy stores, making them move faster. When enough of the particles have enough energy to overcome their attraction to each other, big bubbles of gas form in the liquid — this is boiling.

The boiling point of a substance is the temperature at which a liquid becomes a gas.

4) It's similar when you heat a solid. The extra energy makes the particles vibrate faster until eventually the forces between them are partly overcome and the particles start to move around — this is melting.

The melting point of a substance is the temperature at which it turns from a solid to a liquid.

5) When a substance is melting or boiling, you're still putting in energy, but the energy's used for breaking bonds between particles rather than raising the temperature. So the substance stays at a constant temperature.

6) When a substance is condensing or freezing, bonds are forming between particles, which releases energy. This means the temperature doesn't go down until all of the substance has changed state.

Evaporation

There are two processes by which a liquid can turn into a gas — boiling and evaporation. You've come across boiling already, so here's how evaporation works:

Evaporation is a Special Example of Changing States

1) Evaporation is when particles escape from a liquid and become gas particles.

2) Particles can evaporate from a liquid at temperatures that are much lower than the liquid's boiling point.

3) Particles near the surface of a liquid can escape and become gas particles if:

- The particles are travelling in the right direction to escape the liquid.
- The particles are travelling fast enough (they have enough energy in their kinetic energy stores) to overcome the attractive forces of the other particles in the liquid.

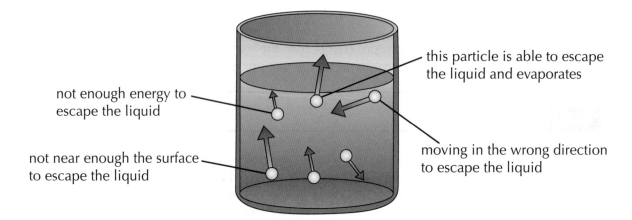

not enough energy to escape the liquid

not near enough the surface to escape the liquid

this particle is able to escape the liquid and evaporates

moving in the wrong direction to escape the liquid

4) The fastest particles (with the most energy) are most likely to evaporate from the liquid — so when they do, the average speed and energy in the kinetic energy stores of the remaining particles decreases.

5) This decrease in average particle energy means the temperature of the remaining liquid falls — the liquid cools.

6) This cooling effect can be really useful. For example, you sweat when you exercise or get hot. As the water from the sweat on your skin evaporates, it cools you down.

Evaporation depends on kinetic energy

Particles in a liquid need to have a high kinetic energy to evaporate. When a particle evaporates, it takes its kinetic energy with it — so the average energy in the kinetic stores of the particles in the liquid decreases.

Warm-Up & Exam Questions

It's time again to test what you've learnt from the last few pages. Have a go at these...

Warm-Up Questions

1) Describe how you would measure the volume of an irregularly shaped object.
2) What basic unit is pressure measured in?
3) How is the energy in a substance's thermal energy store held?
4) State the conditions necessary for particles near the surface of a liquid to escape by evaporation.

Exam Questions

1   A company that manufactures a water-resistant digital watch tests the watch under high pressure in salt water. They only recommend it is used underwater if the pressure difference from the surface is 245 kPa or less.

(a)   State the equation linking pressure difference, height, density and gravitational field strength (g).

[1 mark]

(b)   (i)   The mass of a 0.5000 m³ volume of salt water is 514.0 kg. Calculate the density of the salt water in kg/m³.

[2 marks]

(ii)   Calculate the maximum depth in m from the surface of the salt water that the watch can be used at. Gravitational field strength, $g = 10$ m/s².

[3 marks]

PAPER 2

2   Substances can exist in different states of matter.

(a)   (i)   Describe the arrangement and movement of the particles in a solid.

[2 marks]

(ii)   Give the name of the state of matter that possesses the **highest** average energy per particle.

[1 mark]

(b)   If a substance is heated to a certain temperature it can change from a solid to a liquid.
(i) Give the name of this process.

[1 mark]

(ii) Explain why the temperature of the substance does not increase during this process.

[2 marks]

(c)   If a liquid is heated to a certain temperature it starts to boil and become a gas.
(i)   Name the other process by which a liquid starts to become a gas.
Explain how it is different to boiling.

[3 marks]

(ii) Explain why the remaining liquid cools down when a liquid starts to turn into a gas by the process named in part (i).

[3 marks]

PRACTICAL Temperature and Particle Theory

Here's another _experiment_ that you might do _in class_, or be asked about in your _exams_.
Make sure you know the _method_, and can remember the _shape_ of the _graph_ you'd expect to obtain.

You Can Obtain a **Temperature-Time Graph** for **Water**

You can do a simple _experiment_ to show that temperature remains
constant during changes of state:

1) Fill a _beaker_ with _crushed ice_. Place a _thermometer_
   into the beaker and record the _temperature_ of the ice.

2) Using the Bunsen burner, _gradually heat_
   the beaker full of ice.

3) Every twenty seconds, record the _temperature_ and the
   current state of the ice (e.g. partially melted, completely
   melted). Continue this until the water begins to _boil_.

4) Plot a graph of _temperature against time_
   for your experiment.

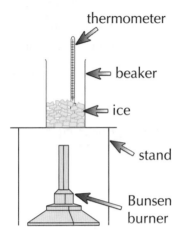

Your graph should look like this:

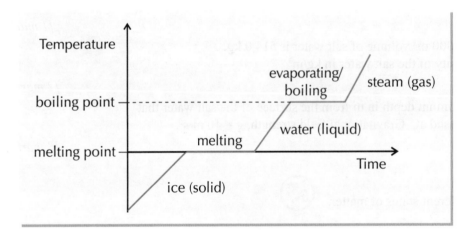

You get a similar one for _condensing_ and _freezing_:

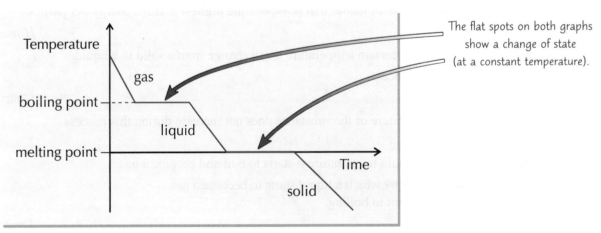

The flat spots on both graphs
show a change of state
(at a constant temperature).

The temperature of a substance is constant as it changes state...

Remember: energy isn't being transferred to the particles' kinetic energy stores during a _change of state_,
so the _temperature_ of the substance stays the _same_ and you get _flat spots_ on a temperature-time graph.

Temperature and Particle Theory

You've probably heard of Celsius and Fahrenheit, but did you know there's yet another temperature scale? This one's often used by scientists as well, so read on to find out more...

Absolute Zero is as Cold as Stuff Can Get — 0 Kelvins

1) If you increase the temperature of something, you give its particles more energy
— they move about more quickly or vibrate more. Similarly, if you cool
a substance down, you reduce the energy of the particles.

2) The coldest that anything can ever get is –273 °C — this temperature is known as absolute zero.
At absolute zero, the particles have as little energy in their kinetic stores as it's possible to get.

3) Absolute zero is the start of the Kelvin scale of temperature.

4) A temperature change of 1 °C is also a change of 1 kelvin. The two
scales are similar — the only difference is where the zero occurs.

5) To convert from degrees Celsius to kelvins, just add 273.
And to convert from kelvins to degrees Celsius,
all you need to do is subtract 273.

	Absolute zero	Freezing point of water	Boiling point of water
Celsius scale	–273 °C	0 °C	100 °C
Kelvin scale	0 K	273 K	373 K

For some reason, there's no
degree symbol ° when you
write a temperature in kelvins
— you just write K (not °K).

Energy in Particles' Kinetic Stores is Proportional to Temperature

1) Particle theory says that gases consist of very small particles which
are constantly moving in completely random directions. The particles
hardly take up any space — most of the gas is empty space.

2) The particles constantly collide with and bounce off of each other and the container walls.

3) If you increase the temperature of a gas, you give its particles more
energy. If you double the temperature (measured in kelvins), you double
the average energy in the kinetic energy stores of the particles.

> The temperature of a gas (in kelvins) is proportional to
> the average energy in the kinetic energy stores of its particles.

4) As you heat up a gas, the average speed of its particles increases. Anything that's moving has
energy in its kinetic energy store. This energy is equal to $\frac{1}{2}mv^2$, as you saw on page 90.

273 is the magic number...

Doubling the temperature of a substance in Celsius doesn't double the energy in its particles' kinetic energy
stores — that's only true for the Kelvin scale. So always check the scale that's being used for temperature.

Particle Theory and Pressure in Gases

Particle theory helps explain how temperature, pressure, volume and the energy in kinetic stores are related.

Particle Theory Says Colliding Gas Particles Create Pressure

1) As gas particles move about, they randomly bang into each other and whatever else gets in the way.

2) Gas particles are very light, but they definitely aren't massless. When they collide with something, they exert a force on it and their momentum and direction change. In a sealed container, gas particles smash against the container's walls — creating an outward pressure.

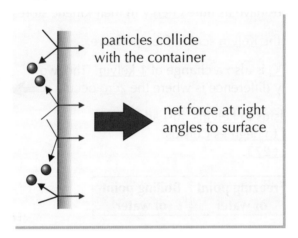

particles collide with the container

net force at right angles to surface

3) This pressure depends on how fast the particles are going and how often they hit the walls.

Increasing the Temperature Increases the Pressure

1) If you heat a gas, the particles move faster and have more energy in their kinetic stores.

2) This increase in energy means the particles hit the container walls harder and more frequently, resulting in a larger force, creating more pressure.

3) In fact, temperature (in K) and pressure are proportional — double the temperature of a fixed amount of gas, and you double the pressure.

Increasing the Volume Decreases the Pressure

1) If you put the same fixed amount of gas in a bigger container, the pressure will decrease, because there'll be fewer collisions between the gas particles and the container's walls.

2) When the volume's reduced, the particles get more squashed up and so they hit the walls more frequently, producing a larger force over a smaller surface area, which increases the pressure.

The pressure equation is simple to apply to gas pressure

Gas pressure is the amount of force exerted by the gas particles per unit area of the container wall that they're colliding with. It's 'force divided by area', just like it would be for any other type of pressure.

Particle Theory and Pressure in Gases

These equations are basically the maths-y way of describing what you learnt on the previous page...

At Constant Temperature "pV = Constant"

This all applies to so-called ideal gases. Ideal gases are ones that are 'well behaved' (i.e. ones that this equation works for...).

For a fixed mass of gas at a constant temperature:

$$\text{pressure} \times \text{volume} = \text{constant} \implies pV = \text{constant}$$

You can also write the equation as:

$$p_1V_1 = p_2V_2$$

(where p_1 and V_1 are your starting conditions and p_2 and V_2 are your final conditions).

Writing it like that is much more useful a lot of the time.

> Example: A gas at a pressure of 250 kilopascals is compressed from a volume of 300 cm³ down to a volume of 175 cm³. The temperature of the gas does not change. Find the new pressure of the gas, in kilopascals.
>
> Answer: $p_1V_1 = p_2V_2$, so $250 \times 300 = p_2 \times 175$
>
> $p_2 = (250 \times 300) \div 175 = 429$ kPa (to 3 s.f.)

At Constant Volume "p/T = Constant"

In a sealed container (i.e. at constant volume):

$$\frac{\text{pressure}}{\text{temperature (in K)}} = \text{constant} \implies \frac{p}{T} = \text{constant}$$

You can also write the equation as

$$p_1/T_1 = p_2/T_2$$

(where p_1 and T_1 are your starting conditions and p_2 and T_2 are your final conditions).

> Example: 30 litres of gas are placed in a sealed container. The gas is at a pressure of 100 kPa and a temperature of 290 K. Find the new pressure if the temperature is increased to 315 K.
>
> Answer: $p_1/T_1 = p_2/T_2$, so $100 \div 290 = p_2 \div 315$
>
> $p_2 = 315 \times (100 \div 290) = 109$ kPa (to 3 s.f.)

NB: The temperatures in this formula must always be in kelvins, so if they give you the temperatures in °C, convert to kelvins FIRST (by adding 273). Always keep the pressure units the same as they are in the question (in this case, kPa).

EXAM TIP

You can use the equations sheet to help jog your memory

There are lots of formulas in IGCSE Physics. You'll need to know most of them off by heart, but some of the trickier ones will be given to you on an equations sheet in the exams. So it's worth getting to know what is on the equations sheet and what isn't — there's a copy of it on p.165.

Specific Heat Capacity

The <u>temperature</u> of something <u>isn't quite the same</u> thing as the <u>energy</u> stored in the substance's thermal energy store. That's where specific heat capacity comes in...

Specific Heat Capacity Relates Temperature and Energy

1) <u>Heating</u> a substance <u>increases</u> the <u>energy</u> in its <u>thermal energy store</u>. You may see this referred to as the <u>internal energy</u> of a substance.

2) So <u>temperature</u> is a way of measuring the <u>average internal energy</u> of a substance.

3) However, it takes <u>more energy</u> to <u>increase the temperature</u> of some materials than others. E.g. you need <u>4200 J</u> to warm 1 kg of <u>water</u> by 1 °C, but only <u>139 J</u> to warm 1 kg of <u>mercury</u> by 1 °C.

4) Materials that need to <u>gain</u> lots of energy to <u>warm up</u> also <u>release</u> loads of energy when they <u>cool down</u> again. They <u>store</u> a lot of energy for a given change in temperature.

5) The <u>change in the energy</u> stored in a substance when you heat it is related to the change in its <u>temperature</u> by its <u>specific heat capacity</u>. The <u>specific heat capacity</u> of a substance is the <u>energy</u> required to change the <u>temperature</u> of an object by <u>1 °C</u> per <u>kilogram</u> of mass. E.g. water has a specific heat capacity of <u>4200 J/kg°C</u> (that's pretty high).

6) You need to know how to use the <u>equation</u> relating energy, mass, specific heat capacity and temperature.

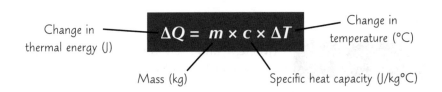

Change in thermal energy (J)

$$\Delta Q = m \times c \times \Delta T$$

Change in temperature (°C)

Mass (kg)

Specific heat capacity (J/kg°C)

The symbol 'Δ' is Greek letter <u>delta</u>. Δ just means 'change in'.

> <u>Example:</u> Calculate the change in temperature when <u>12 600 J</u> of energy is transferred to the thermal energy stores of <u>0.5 kg</u> of water. The specific heat capacity of water is <u>4200 J/kg °C</u>.
>
> <u>Answer:</u> $\Delta Q = m \times c \times \Delta T$,
> so $\Delta T = \Delta Q \div (m \times c)$
> $= 12\ 600 \div (0.5 \times 4200) = 6$ °C

Specific heat capacity = how hard it is to heat something up

The equation relating <u>energy</u>, <u>mass</u>, <u>specific heat capacity</u> and <u>temperature</u> is quite a tricky one. So get plenty of <u>practice</u> at using it — including <u>rearranging</u> it and checking that all your data is in the right <u>units</u>. That way you'll be more confident if you get a question on it in your exam.

Paper 2

Specific Heat Capacity

PRACTICAL

You can use the practical on this page to find the specific heat capacity of a material...

You can Find the **Specific Heat Capacity** of a **Liquid**...

You can use this experiment to find the specific heat capacity of water — or any liquid for that matter. You should use a thermally insulated container for this experiment to reduce the amount of energy that's transferred to the surroundings.

1) Use a mass balance to measure the mass of the insulating container.

2) Fill the container with water and measure the mass again. The difference in mass is the mass of the water in the container.

3) Set up the experiment as shown — make sure the joulemeter reads zero and place a lid on the container if you have one.

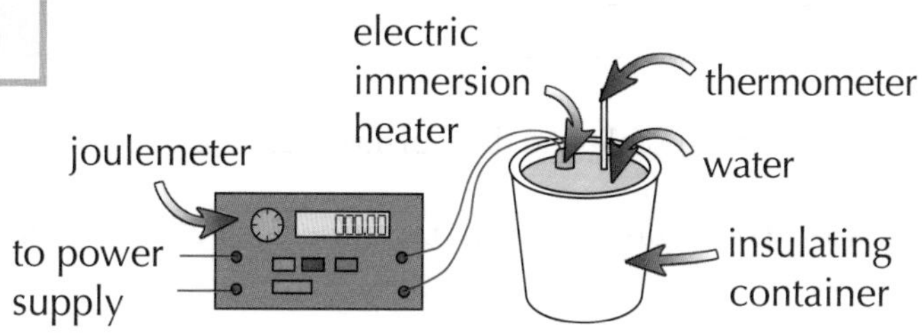

4) Measure the temperature of the water, then turn on the power.

5) Keep an eye on the thermometer. When the temperature has increased by e.g. ten degrees, switch off the power and record this temperature increase and the energy on the joulemeter.

6) You can then calculate the specific heat capacity of the water by rearranging the equation $\Delta Q = m \times c \times \Delta T$ and plugging in your measurements.

7) Repeat the whole experiment at least three times, then calculate an average of the specific heat capacity.

You could use a voltmeter and ammeter instead of a joulemeter. Time how long the heater was on for, then calculate the energy supplied using the equation energy transferred = current × voltage × time (see page 43).

Your experimental value for the specific heat capacity will probably be a bit too high, since some of the heat supplied will be lost to the environment.

...or of a **Solid**

You can use a similar method to find the specific heat capacity of a solid. Make sure the block of material you use has two holes in it for the heater and thermometer, and wrap it up with an insulating layer before starting. When you have switched off the power and finished timing, wait until the temperature has stopped increasing before recording the highest final temperature — this gives the energy from the heater time to spread through the solid block.

Paper 2

Paper 2

PRACTICAL TIP

Think about how you could improve your experiments...

You need to be able to evaluate the method used for an investigation and suggest improvements to make the results more accurate. For example, if you saw a method for this practical using a beaker to hold the liquid, you could suggest changing it to a thermally insulated container.

Warm-Up & Exam Questions

You know the drill by now — time to put all the lovely information you've just absorbed to good use.

Warm-Up Questions

1) The temperature in kelvins of a certain volume of air increases by a factor of three. How will the kinetic energy of the air particles change, and by what factor?

2) Use particle theory to explain how gas particles create pressure in a sealed container.

3) What is meant by the specific heat capacity of a substance?

Exam Questions

1   The Kelvin scale and the Celsius scale are two scales that can be used to measure temperature.

(a)   (i)   A gas is cooled. Describe what effect this has on the average speed of its particles.

[1 mark]

(ii) Explain why there is a minimum possible temperature that any substance can reach, known as the absolute zero of temperature.

[2 marks]

(iii) Give the numerical value of the absolute zero of temperature in degrees Celsius.

[1 mark]

(b)   Temperature can be converted between the Kelvin and Celsius scales.

(i)   Convert 10 K into °C.

[1 mark]

(ii) Convert 631 °C into K.

[1 mark]

PAPER 2

2   The graph below shows the temperature of a substance against time as it is heated.

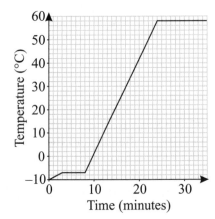

(a)   Describe what is happening during the period 3-8 minutes from the beginning of heating.

[1 mark]

(b)   Give the melting and boiling points of the substance.

[2 marks]

Exam Questions

3 A sealed container with a fixed volume is fitted with internal temperature and pressure gauges. The gauges show that the temperature is 288 K and the pressure is 107 kPa inside the container.

The container is heated so that the temperature of the gas inside it becomes 405 K.
Calculate the pressure that will be shown on the pressure gauge.

[3 marks]

4 A cylinder sealed with a piston contains 0.014 m³ of gas at a pressure of 98 kPa.

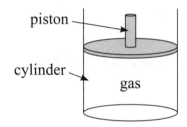

(a) (i) The piston is squeezed in and the volume containing the gas decreases.
State the effect on the gas pressure inside the cylinder.
Explain your answer in terms of particle theory.

[3 marks]

(ii) The gas is compressed to a volume of 0.013 m³. The temperature of the gas remains constant.
Calculate the pressure inside the cylinder after the compression.

[3 marks]

(b) The cylinder is heated while the piston remains in place to keep its volume constant.
State and explain what happens to the pressure inside the cylinder.

[3 marks]

PAPER 2   **PRACTICAL**

5 A student uses the equipment listed below to investigate the specific heat capacity of different liquids.

- Insulated flask
- Thermometer
- Mass balance
- Power supply
- Joulemeter
- Immersion heater

Describe how the student could use this apparatus to calculate the specific heat capacity of a liquid.

[5 marks]

Section 5 — Solids, Liquids and Gases

Revision Questions for Section 5

Section 5, over and out — time to put yourself to the test and find out how much you really know.
- Try these questions and tick off each one when you get it right.
- When you've done all the questions under a heading and are completely happy with it, tick it off.

Density and Pressure (p.101-102) ☑

1) What is the relationship between the density, mass and volume of a substance?

2) *If the density of water = 1000 kg/m³, calculate the volume in m³ of 2 kg of water.

3) How would you measure the density of an unknown cube of material in the lab?

4) Draw a formula triangle containing pressure, force and area.

5) *What pressure does a woman weighing 600 N exert on the floor if her high-heeled shoes have an area of 5 cm² touching the floor?

Changes of State (p.103-104) ☑

6) Describe how the particles are arranged and move in:
   a) a liquid,   b) a gas.

7) Explain what happens to particles in a substance during:
   a) melting,   b) boiling,   c) evaporation.

Temperature, Pressure and Particle Theory (p.106-109) ☑

8) A substance is heated, and its temperature rises until it melts from a solid to a liquid.
   The substance then rises in temperature again until it begins to boil.
   Sketch a temperature-time graph to show this.

9) On which temperature scale is the numerical value of 'absolute zero' actually equal to 0?

10) How does the temperature of a gas in kelvins relate to the
    energy in the kinetic energy stores of its particles?

11) What happens to the pressure of a gas in a sealed container if you increase the temperature?

12) *500 cm³ of a fixed mass of gas at 50 kPa is forced into a 100 cm³ container.
    What is the new pressure of the gas (assuming the temperature is kept constant)?

13) *Another 500 cm³ of gas is kept sealed in its container at 50 kPa, but is then heated from
    a temperature of 290 K to 300 K. What is the new pressure of the gas?

Specific Heat Capacity (p.110-111) ☑

14) What equation relates energy, mass, specific heat capacity and temperature?

15) *110 J of energy is supplied to a substance to heat it from a temperature of 21 °C to 45 °C.
    The substance has a mass of 0.25 kg. Calculate the specific heat capacity of the substance.

16) Describe an experiment that can be used to find the specific heat capacity of a solid.

*Answers on page 212.

Magnets and Magnetic Fields

I think magnetism is an <u>attractive</u> subject, but don't get <u>repelled</u> by the exam — <u>revise</u>.

Magnets Produce Magnetic Fields

1) All magnets have <u>two poles</u> — north and south.

2) A <u>magnetic field</u> is a <u>region</u> where <u>magnetic materials</u> (e.g. iron) experience a <u>force</u>.

3) <u>Magnetic field lines</u> (or "lines of force") are used to show the size and direction of magnetic fields. They <u>always</u> point from <u>north</u> to <u>south</u>.

4) Placing the north and south poles of <u>two</u> permanent bar magnets <u>near</u> each other creates a <u>uniform field between</u> the two magnets.

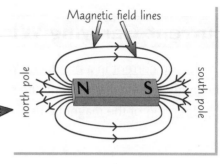

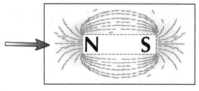

You Can See Magnetic Field Patterns Using Compasses

1) Compasses and iron filings <u>align</u> themselves with <u>magnetic fields</u>.

2) You can use <u>multiple compasses</u> to see the magnetic field lines coming out of a bar magnet or between two bar magnets.

PRACTICAL

You shouldn't put the compasses too close to each other. Compasses also produce magnetic fields — you need to make sure you're measuring the field of the magnet rather than the compasses nearby.

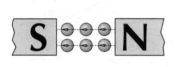

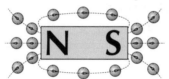

If you don't have lots of compasses, you can just use one and move it around (trace its position on some paper before each move if it helps).

3) You could also use <u>iron filings</u> to see magnetic field patterns. Just put the magnet(s) under a piece of paper, <u>scatter</u> the iron filings on top, and <u>tap</u> the paper until the iron filings form a <u>clear pattern</u>.

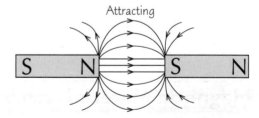

Magnetism Can Be Induced

1) Magnets affect <u>magnetic materials</u> and other <u>magnets</u>.

2) Like poles <u>repel</u> each other and opposite poles <u>attract</u>.

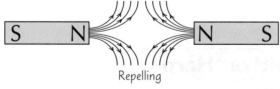

3) Both poles <u>attract</u> magnetic materials (that aren't magnets).

4) When magnetic materials are brought <u>near</u> to a magnet (into its <u>magnetic field</u>), that material acts as a <u>magnet</u>.

5) This magnetism has been <u>induced</u> by the original magnet.

6) The <u>closer</u> the magnet and the magnetic material get, the <u>stronger</u> the induced magnetism will be.

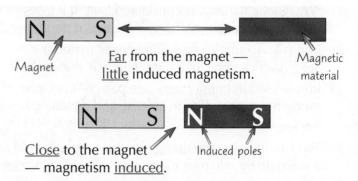

Electromagnetism

Permanent magnets are great, but it would be <u>really</u> handy to be able to turn a magnetic field <u>on</u> and <u>off</u>. Well, it turns out that when <u>electric current</u> flows it <u>produces a magnetic field</u> — problem solved.

A **Current-Carrying Wire** Creates a **Magnetic Field**

1) An <u>electric current</u> in a <u>conductor</u> produces a <u>magnetic field</u> around it.
2) The <u>larger</u> the electric current, the <u>stronger</u> the magnetic field.
3) The <u>direction</u> of the <u>magnetic field</u> depends on the <u>direction</u> of the <u>current</u>.

The Magnetic Field Around a **Straight Wire**

1) There is a magnetic field around a <u>straight</u>, <u>current-carrying wire</u>.
2) The field is made up of <u>concentric circles</u> with the wire in the centre.

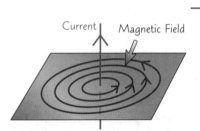

Current   Magnetic Field

The Magnetic Field Around a **Flat Circular Coil**

1) The magnetic field in the <u>centre</u> of a flat circular coil of wire is similar to that of a <u>bar magnet</u>.
2) There are concentric <u>ellipses</u> (stretched circles) of magnetic field lines <u>around</u> the coil.

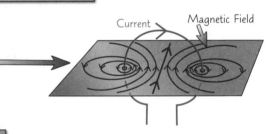

Current   Magnetic Field

The Magnetic Field Around a **Solenoid**

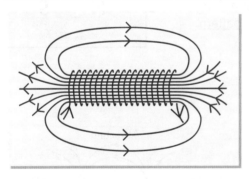

1) The magnetic field <u>inside</u> a current-carrying <u>solenoid</u> (a coil of wire) is <u>strong</u> and <u>uniform</u>.
2) <u>Outside</u> the coil, the field is just like the one around a <u>bar magnet</u>.
3) This means that the <u>ends</u> of a solenoid act like the <u>north pole</u> and <u>south pole</u> of a bar magnet. This type of magnet is called an <u>electromagnet</u>.

Magnetic Materials can be **'Soft'** or **'Hard'**

1) A magnetic material is considered '<u>soft</u>' if it <u>loses</u> its induced magnetism quickly, or '<u>hard</u>' if it keeps it <u>permanently</u>.
2) <u>Iron</u> is an example of a <u>soft</u> magnetic material. <u>Steel</u> is an example of a <u>hard</u> magnetic material.
3) Iron is used in <u>transformers</u> (see page 64) because of this property — it needs to magnetise and demagnetise 50 times a second (mains electricity in the UK runs at 50 Hz).
4) You can increase the <u>strength</u> of the magnetic field around a solenoid by adding a magnetically "<u>soft</u>" iron core through the middle of the coil.

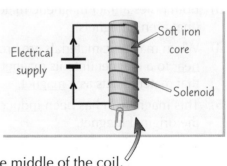

Soft iron core

Electrical supply

Solenoid

Paper 2

The Motor Effect

The <u>motor effect</u> happens when you put a <u>current-carrying wire</u> in a <u>magnetic field</u>. Read on for more...

A **Current** in a **Magnetic Field** Experiences a **Force**

When a <u>current-carrying</u> wire is put between magnetic poles, the two <u>magnetic fields</u> affect one another. The result is a <u>force</u> on the wire. This can cause the <u>wire</u> to <u>move</u>. This is called the <u>motor effect</u>.

This is because <u>charged particles</u> (e.g. electrons in a current) moving through a magnetic field will experience a <u>force</u>, as long as they're not moving parallel to the field lines.

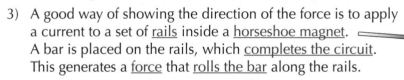

This is an aerial view.
The red dot represents a
wire carrying current "out
of the page" (towards you).

Resulting Force

N   S

→ Normal magnetic field of wire
→ Normal magnetic field of magnets
→ Deviated magnetic field of magnets

1) To experience the <u>full force</u>, the <u>wire</u> has to be at <u>90°</u> to the <u>magnetic field</u>. If the wire runs <u>along</u> the <u>magnetic field</u>, it won't experience <u>any force at all</u>. At angles in between, it'll feel <u>some</u> force.

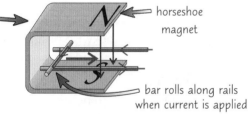

2) The force always acts in the <u>same direction</u> relative to the <u>magnetic field</u> of the magnets and the <u>direction of the current</u> in the wire.

3) A good way of showing the direction of the force is to apply a current to a set of <u>rails</u> inside a <u>horseshoe magnet</u>. A bar is placed on the rails, which <u>completes the circuit</u>. This generates a <u>force</u> that <u>rolls the bar</u> along the rails.

horseshoe
magnet

4) The magnitude (strength) of the force <u>increases</u> with the strength of the <u>magnetic field</u>. The force also <u>increases</u> with the amount of <u>current</u> passing through the conductor.

bar rolls along rails
when current is applied

5) <u>Reversing</u> the current <u>or</u> the magnetic field also reverses the direction of the <u>force</u>.

Fleming's Left-Hand Rule Tells You **Which Way** the Force Acts

1) They could test if you can do this, so <u>practise it</u>.

2) Using your <u>left hand</u>, point your <u>First finger</u> in the direction of the <u>Field</u> and your <u>seCond finger</u> in the direction of the <u>Current</u>.

3) Your <u>thuMb</u> will then point in the direction of the <u>force</u> (Motion).

thuMb
Motion

First finger
Field

seCond finger
Current

<u>Example:</u> Which <u>direction</u> is the <u>force</u> on this wire?

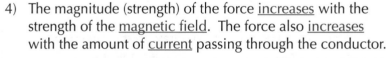

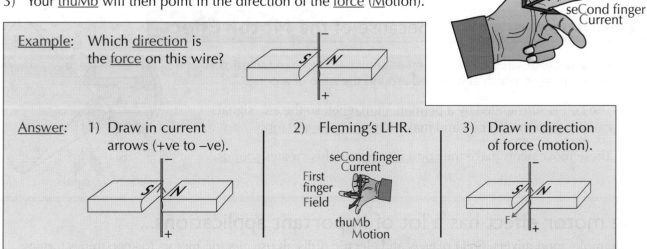

<u>Answer:</u> 1) Draw in current arrows (+ve to –ve). 2) Fleming's LHR. 3) Draw in direction of force (motion).

seCond finger
Current

First
finger
Field

thuMb
Motion

Electric Motors and Loudspeakers

Electric motors use the motor effect to get them moving (and to keep them moving).

A Simple D.C. Electric Motor

Four factors that will speed it up:
1) More current
2) More turns on the coil
3) Stronger magnetic field
4) A soft iron core in the coil

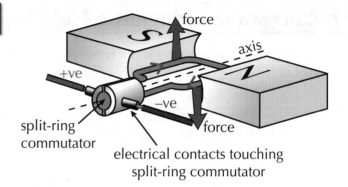

force
axis
+ve
−ve
force
split-ring commutator
electrical contacts touching split-ring commutator

1) The diagram shows the forces acting on the two side arms of the coil.
2) These forces are just the usual forces which act on any current in a magnetic field.
3) Because the coil is on a spindle and the forces act one up and one down, it rotates.
4) The split-ring commutator is a clever way of swapping the contacts every half turn to keep the motor rotating in the same direction.
5) The direction of the motor can be reversed either by swapping the polarity of the d.c. supply or swapping the magnetic poles over.
6) The speed can be increased by adding more turns to the coil, increasing the current, increasing the strength of the magnetic field or by adding a soft iron core.
7) You can use Fleming's left-hand rule to work out which way the coil will turn.

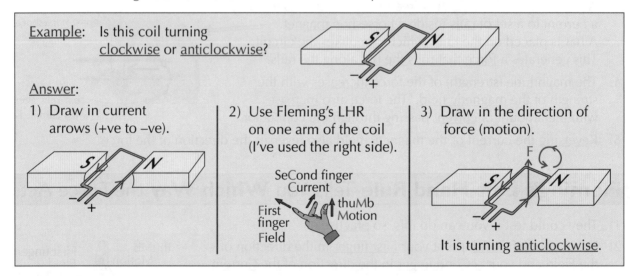

Example: Is this coil turning clockwise or anticlockwise?

Answer:

1) Draw in current arrows (+ve to −ve).

2) Use Fleming's LHR on one arm of the coil (I've used the right side).

SeCond finger Current
First finger Field
thuMb Motion

3) Draw in the direction of force (motion).

F

It is turning anticlockwise.

Loudspeakers Work Because of the Motor Effect

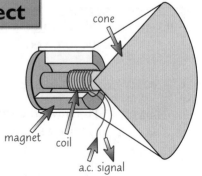

cone

1) The a.c. electrical signals from an amplifier are fed to a coil of wire in the speaker, which is wrapped around the base of a cone.

2) The coil is surrounded by a permanent magnet, so the a.c. signals cause a force on the coil and make it move back and forth.

3) These movements make the cone vibrate and this creates sounds.

magnet   coil

a.c. signal

The motor effect has a lot of important applications...

For example, food mixers, DVD players and electric drills all use electric motors to keep things turning.

Warm-Up & Exam Questions

It's time for another page of questions to check your knowledge. If you can do the warm-up questions without breaking into a sweat, then see how you get on with the exam questions.

Warm-Up Questions

1) Draw a diagram to show the magnetic field around a single bar magnet.
2) True or false? The further a magnet and a magnetic material are from each other, the stronger the induced magnetism will be.
3) Iron is a soft magnetic material. What does this mean?
4) If you are using Fleming's left-hand rule, in which direction should your second finger point?

Exam Questions

1   A student arranges two magnets as shown below.

   (a)   Describe the magnetic field in the shaded region between the dotted lines.

   [1 mark]

   (b)   State whether there will be a force of attraction, repulsion, or no force
         between the two magnets. Explain your answer.

   [2 marks]

PRACTICAL

2   A student draws the magnetic field lines between four bar magnets, as shown in the diagram.

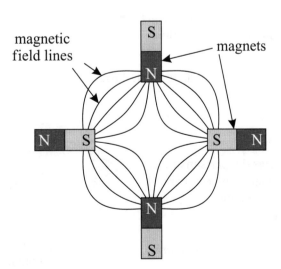

   Describe an experiment that the student could have done to show this magnetic field pattern.

   [2 marks]

Exam Questions

3   An electromagnet is used by a crane to lift, move and drop iron and steel.

  (a)   The electromagnet contains a solenoid. State what is meant by a **solenoid**.

[1 mark]

  (b)   Describe the shape of the magnetic field that a solenoid produces.
        You may use a sketch to help with your answer.

[2 marks]

  (c)   When a current is passed through the electromagnet, an iron bar on the ground nearby
        is attracted to it. When the current is stopped, the bar drops back to the ground.
        Explain why this happens.

[4 marks]

  (d)   The crane's electromagnet contains a magnetically soft iron core.

        Explain why putting a magnetically hard core in the electromagnet
        would cause the crane to not work properly.

[2 marks]

4   A student is building a simple
     d.c. motor. He starts by putting a loop
     of current-carrying wire into a magnetic
     field. The wire loop is free to rotate
     about an axis, as shown in the diagram.

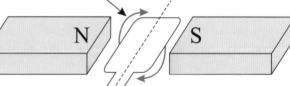

direction of rotation   axis of rotation

N   S

  (a)   Copy the diagram and add an arrow to show
        the direction of the current in the wire.

[1 mark]

  (b)   The starting position of the loop is shown in the diagram. Explain why the motor will
        stop rotating in the same direction after 90° of rotation from its start position.

[1 mark]

  (c)   Suggest and explain how the student could get the
        motor to keep rotating in the same direction.

[2 marks]

  (d)   Give **one** way the motor could be made to rotate faster.

[1 mark]

5   The diagram on the right shows the parts inside an
     earphone. Sound waves are caused by mechanical
     vibrations. Explain how the earphone uses an a.c.
     supply to produce sound waves.

[4 marks]

coil of wire

cone

permanent
magnet

base of the cone

to a.c. supply

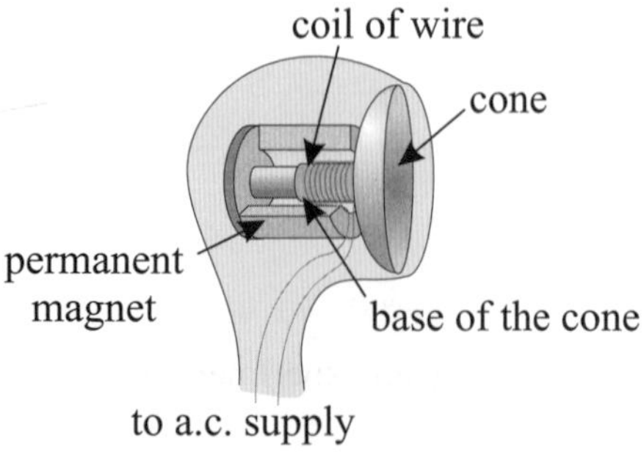

Electromagnetic Induction

Generators use a pretty cool piece of physics to make electricity from the movement of a turbine.
It's called electromagnetic (EM) induction — which basically means making electricity using a magnet.

Electromagnetic induction: The creation of a voltage (and maybe
current) in a wire which is experiencing a change in magnetic field.

The Dynamo Effect — Move the Wire or the Magnet

1) Using electromagnetic induction to generate electricity using energy from kinetic energy stores
   is called the dynamo effect. (In a power station, this energy is provided by the turbine.)

2) There are two different situations where you get EM induction:

   a) An electrical conductor (a coil of wire is often used) moves through a magnetic field.

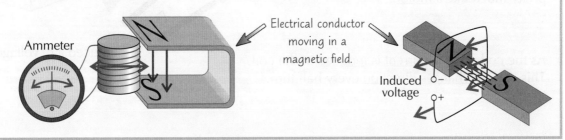

Ammeter

Electrical conductor
moving in a
magnetic field.

Induced
voltage

   b) The magnetic field through
      an electrical conductor
      changes (gets bigger or
      smaller or reverses).

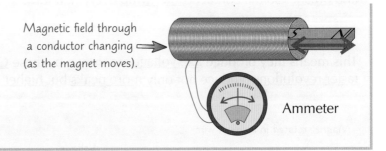

Magnetic field through
a conductor changing
(as the magnet moves).

Ammeter

3) You can test this by connecting an ammeter to a conductor and moving the
   conductor through a magnetic field (or moving a magnet through the conductor).
   The ammeter will show the magnitude and direction of the induced current.

4) If the direction of movement is reversed, then the induced voltage/current will be reversed too.

To get a bigger voltage, you can increase...
1) The strength of the magnet
2) The number of turns on the coil
3) The speed of movement

Think about the simple electric motor — you've got a current in the wire and a magnetic field,
which causes movement. A generator works the opposite way round — you've got a magnetic field
and movement, which induces a current.

Electromagnetic induction transfers energy from kinetic energy stores...

...to electrical energy stores. In a power station, a turbine moves — electromagnetic induction is then
used to transfer energy from the kinetic energy store of the turbine to electrical energy stores.

Electromagnetic Induction

Power stations use a.c. generators to produce electricity — it's just a matter of turning a coil in a magnetic field.

A.C. Generators — Just Turn the Coil and There's a Current

You've already met generators and electromagnetic induction —
this is a bit more detail about how a simple generator works.

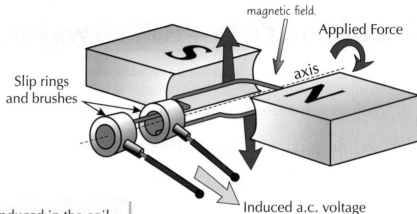

1) Generators rotate a coil in a magnetic field (or a magnet in a coil).

2) Their construction is pretty much like a motor.

3) As the coil spins, a current is induced in the coil. This current changes direction every half turn.

4) Instead of a split-ring commutator, a.c. generators have slip rings and brushes so the contacts don't swap every half turn.

5) This means they produce a.c. voltage, as shown by these CRO displays. Note that faster revolutions produce not only more peaks but higher overall voltage too.

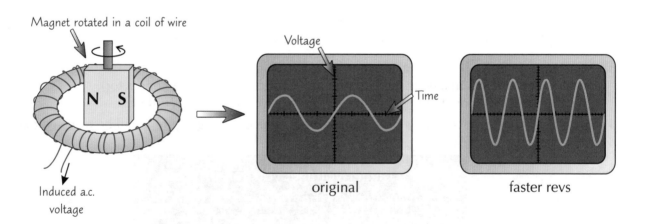

6) Power stations use a.c. generators to produce electricity — they just get the energy needed to turn the coil or magnetic field in different ways.

EM induction works whether the coil or the field is moving

EM induction's not as tough as it might look: when you have a conductor, a magnetic field and some movement, you get a voltage (and a current if there's a circuit). So you have no excuse not to learn it.

Transformers

Transformers only work with an alternating current. Try using a d.c. battery and you'll be there for days.

Transformers Change the Voltage (but only Alternating Voltages)

1) Transformers change the size of the voltage of an alternating current.
2) They all have two coils, the primary and the secondary, joined with an iron core.
3) When an alternating voltage is applied across the primary coil, the magnetically soft (iron) core magnetises and demagnetises quickly. This induces an alternating voltage in the secondary coil.
4) The ratio between the primary and secondary voltages is the same as the ratio between the number of turns on the primary and secondary coils.

Step-up transformers increase the voltage. They have more turns on the secondary coil than the primary coil.

Step-down transformers decrease the voltage. They have more turns on the primary coil than the secondary.

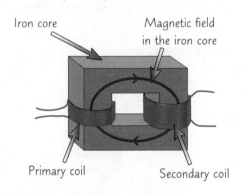

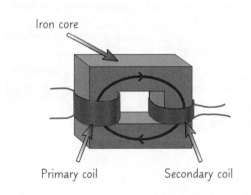

The Transformer Equation — Use it Either Way Up

1) You can calculate the output voltage from a transformer from the input voltage and the number of turns on each coil.

$$\frac{\text{Input (Primary) Voltage}}{\text{Output (Secondary) Voltage}} = \frac{\text{Number of turns on Primary}}{\text{Number of turns on Secondary}}$$

$$\frac{V_P}{V_S} = \frac{N_P}{N_S}$$

OR

$$\frac{V_S}{V_P} = \frac{N_S}{N_P}$$

2) This equation can be used either way up — there's less rearranging to do if you put whatever you're trying to calculate (the unknown) on the top.
3) The number of turns on the secondary coil divided by the number of turns on the primary coil is called the turns ratio.

Step-up transformers increase the voltage...

If you're struggling to remember the difference between step-up and step-down transformers, try to think about what's changing from the primary coil (input) to the secondary coil (output). If the number of turns is increasing, the voltage will also increase across the transformer — both things have been "stepped up" (increased), so it's a step-up transformer.

Transformers

Transformers are needed to change the voltage of electricity produced in <u>power stations</u>, before it can be transported through the <u>National Grid</u> to be used at <u>home</u> or in <u>factories</u>.

Transformers are Nearly **100% Efficient**, so **Power In = Power Out**

The formula for <u>power supplied</u> is: <u>Power = Voltage × Current</u> or: $P = V \times I$.

So you can rewrite <u>input power = output power</u> as:

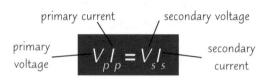

primary current   secondary voltage

primary voltage $V_p I_p = V_s I_s$ secondary current

Transformers Make **Transmitting** Mains Electricity **More Efficient**

Step-up and step-down <u>transformers</u> are used when transmitting electricity across the country:

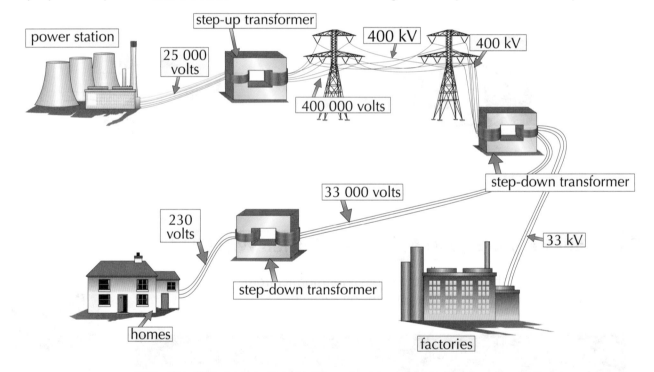

1) The voltage produced by power stations is too <u>low</u> to be <u>transmitted</u> efficiently. Power = $V \times I$, so the <u>lower</u> the voltage the <u>higher</u> the current for a given amount of power, and <u>current</u> causes wires to <u>heat up</u>.

2) A <u>step-up</u> transformer is used to <u>boost</u> the voltage before it is transmitted.

3) <u>Step-down</u> transformers are used at the <u>end</u> of the journey to <u>reduce</u> the voltage so it's more <u>useful</u> and <u>safer</u> to use.

The national grid — it's a powerful thing...

Electricity is transmitted across the national grid at a <u>low current</u> to reduce <u>energy losses by heating</u>. In order to transmit the power at a low current, a <u>high voltage</u> must be used. To get high voltage and low current, a <u>step-up transformer</u> is used to transfer the electricity from the power station to the national grid.

Warm-Up & Exam Questions

There were lots of new ideas in that section, not to mention the transformer equation. Better have a go at these questions so you can tell what's gone in and what you might need to go over again.

Warm-Up Questions

1) What is electromagnetic induction?
2) True or false? An a.c. generator uses a split-ring commutator.
3) How does a step-up transformer differ from a step-down transformer?

Exam Questions

1 Which of these is **not** an example of electromagnetic induction?

  ☐ **A** A coil turned in a magnetic field generates a current in the coil.

  ☐ **B** A magnet moved in and out of a solenoid creates a voltage in the solenoid.

  ☐ **C** A current-carrying wire placed between two magnets experiences a force.

  ☐ **D** A rotating bicycle wheel generates electricity by turning a magnet in a coil.

  [1 mark]

2 A student uses the rotation of a hamster wheel to power a battery charger.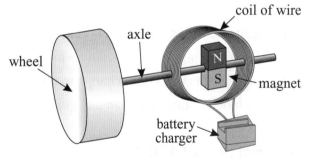

  (a) Explain how rotating the wheel creates a voltage across the battery charger.

  [2 marks]

  (b) Give **two** ways the voltage created across the battery charger could be increased.

  [2 marks]

PAPER 2

3 The National Grid is a network that transmits electricity around the country. The diagram shows a step-up transformer used in the National Grid. The secondary coil has 16 times more turns on it than the primary coil.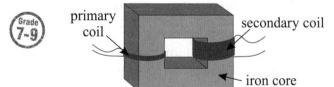

  (a) Explain how transformers are used in the National Grid to transmit electricity from power stations efficiently and supply the electricity to the consumer safely.

  [3 marks]

  (b) (i) State the equation linking the number of turns on the primary and secondary coils of a transformer and the voltages across the primary and secondary coils.

  [1 mark]

  (ii) The voltage across the primary coil is 25 000 V. Calculate the voltage across the secondary coil.

  [4 marks]

Revision Questions for Section 6

That wraps up Section 6 — take a deep breath and then motor on through these revision questions.
- Try these questions and tick off each one when you get it right.
- When you've done all the questions under a heading and are completely happy with it, tick it off.

Magnets and Magnetic Fields (p.115) ☑

1) What is a magnetic field? ☑
2) Sketch a diagram showing how you can produce a uniform magnetic field using two bar magnets. ☑
3) What happens when a magnetic material is brought into the magnetic field of a magnet? ☑

Electromagnetism, Motors and Loudspeakers (p.116-118) ☑

4) Sketch the magnetic field produced by:
   a) A straight wire.   b) A flat loop of wire. ☑
5) What is an electromagnet? ☑
6) Give one example of a hard magnetic material. ☑
7) What's the motor effect? ☑
8) What will happen to a charged particle moving through a magnetic field? ☑
9) Name two factors that increase the strength of the
   force on a current-carrying wire in a magnetic field. ☑
10) What's a split-ring commutator used for in an electric motor? ☑
11) Sketch a labelled diagram of a loudspeaker. ☑

Electromagnetic Induction (p.121-122) ☑

12) Briefly describe how a voltage can be induced using a coil of wire and a magnet. ☑
13) Give three factors you could change to increase the size of an induced voltage. ☑
14) Sketch a labelled diagram of an a.c. generator and briefly explain how it works. ☑

Transformers (p.123-124) ☑

15) What kind of transformer has more turns on the primary coil than the secondary coil? ☑
16) Sketch a diagram of a step-up transformer. ☑
17) Explain how a transformer changes the voltage of an electricity supply. ☑
18) *A transformer has 10 turns on the primary coil and 50 turns on the secondary coil.
    If the primary voltage is 30 V, what will the secondary voltage be? ☑
19) *The power output of a transformer is 6000 W.
    If the input voltage is 30 000 V, what is the input current? ☑

*Answers on page 213.

Atoms and Isotopes

Before you get stuck into <u>nuclear radiation</u>, you need to know a bit about <u>atoms</u> and <u>isotopes</u>.

At the **Centre** of Every **Atom** is a **Nucleus**

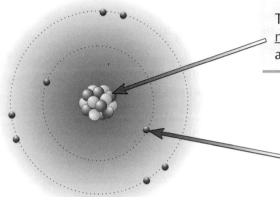

The <u>nucleus</u> of an atom contains <u>protons</u> and <u>neutrons</u>. It makes up most of the <u>mass</u> of the atom, but takes up <u>virtually no space</u> — it's <u>tiny</u>.

The <u>electrons</u> are <u>negatively charged</u> and really really <u>small</u>.
They whizz around the <u>outside</u> of the atom.
Their <u>paths take up a lot of space</u>, giving the atom its <u>overall size</u> (though it's <u>mostly empty space</u>).

1) The number of <u>protons</u> in the nucleus is called the <u>atomic number</u>, or <u>proton number</u>.

2) Atoms are <u>neutral</u>, so the <u>number of protons = the number of electrons</u>.

3) The <u>total</u> number of <u>protons and neutrons</u> in the nucleus is called the <u>mass number</u>, or <u>nucleon number</u>.

Protons and electrons have an equal but opposite charge.

Isotopes are Atoms with **Different Numbers** of **Neutrons**

1) Many elements have a few different <u>isotopes</u>. Isotopes are atoms with the <u>same</u> number of <u>protons</u> (i.e. the <u>same</u> atomic number) but a <u>different</u> number of <u>neutrons</u> (so a <u>different</u> mass number).

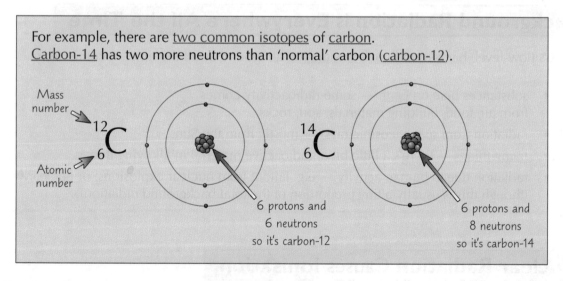

For example, there are <u>two common isotopes</u> of <u>carbon</u>.
<u>Carbon-14</u> has two more neutrons than 'normal' carbon (<u>carbon-12</u>).

Mass number $\rightarrow$ $^{12}_{6}C$ $\leftarrow$ Atomic number

6 protons and 6 neutrons so it's carbon-12

6 protons and 8 neutrons so it's carbon-14

2) Usually each element only has one or two <u>stable isotopes</u> — like carbon-12. The other isotopes tend to be <u>radioactive</u> — the nucleus is <u>unstable</u>, so it <u>decays</u> (breaks down) and emits <u>radiation</u>. Carbon-14 is an <u>unstable isotope</u> of carbon.

You can get different isotopes of the same element

This isotope business can be confusing at first, but remember... it's the number of <u>protons</u> which decides what <u>element</u> it is, then the number of <u>neutrons</u> decides what <u>isotope</u> of that element it is.

Radioactivity

The <u>nuclei</u> of <u>unstable</u> isotopes can <u>decay</u> and <u>emit radiation</u>. Although you can't see it, nuclear radiation is <u>all around us</u> all the time. And that's what this page is all about.

Radioactive Decay is a Random Process

1) The nuclei of <u>unstable</u> isotopes break down at <u>random</u>. If you have 1000 unstable nuclei, you can't say when any <u>one of them</u> is going to decay, and you can't do anything at all to <u>make a decay happen</u>.

2) Each nucleus just decays quite <u>spontaneously</u> in its <u>own good time</u>. It's completely unaffected by <u>physical</u> conditions like <u>temperature</u> or by any sort of <u>chemical bonding</u> etc.

3) When the nucleus <u>does</u> decay it <u>spits out</u> one or more types of radiation — <u>alpha</u> (α), <u>beta</u> (β^-), gamma (γ) (see next page) or <u>neutrons</u> (n) (see page 130).

4) In the process, the <u>nucleus</u> often <u>changes</u> into a <u>new element</u>.

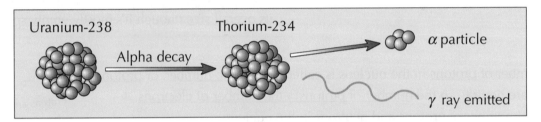

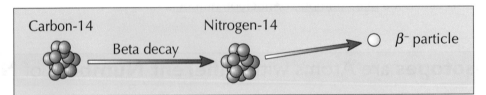

Background Radiation is Everywhere All the Time

There's (low-level) <u>background nuclear radiation</u> all around us all the time. It comes from:

- substances here on <u>Earth</u> — some radioactivity comes from air, food, building materials, soil, rocks...
- radiation from <u>space</u> (cosmic rays) — mostly from the Sun,
- <u>living things</u> — there's a little bit of radioactive material in all living things,
- radiation due to <u>human activity</u> — e.g. fallout from nuclear explosions, or nuclear waste (though this is usually a tiny proportion of the total background radiation).

Nuclear Radiation Causes Ionisation

1) Nuclear radiation causes <u>ionisation</u> by <u>bashing into atoms</u> and <u>knocking electrons off</u> them. Atoms (with <u>no overall charge</u>) are turned into <u>ions</u> (which are <u>charged</u>) — hence the term "<u>ionisation</u>".

2) There's a pattern: the <u>further</u> the radiation can <u>penetrate</u> before hitting an atom and getting stopped, the <u>less damage</u> it will do along the way and so the <u>less ionising</u> it is.

3) Ionising radiation can be detected using either a <u>Geiger-Müller detector</u> (see page 131) or <u>photographic film</u>.

There's more about ionising radiation coming up on the next page.

Alpha, Beta and Gamma Radiation

Alpha, beta and gamma are three types of ionising radiation. You need to remember <u>what</u> they are, how well they <u>penetrate</u> materials, and their <u>ionising</u> power.

Alpha Particles are Helium Nuclei ← $^4_2$He

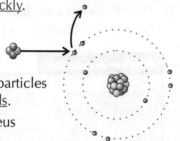

1) Alpha (α) particles are made up of <u>2 protons and 2 neutrons</u>. They're <u>big</u>, <u>heavy</u> and <u>slow-moving</u>.

2) They therefore <u>don't penetrate</u> far into materials but are <u>stopped quickly</u>.

3) Because of their size they're <u>strongly ionising</u>, which means they <u>bash into a lot of atoms</u> and <u>knock electrons off</u> them before they slow down, which creates lots of ions.

4) Because they're electrically <u>charged</u> (with a positive charge), alpha particles are <u>deflected</u> (their <u>direction changes</u>) by <u>electric</u> and <u>magnetic fields</u>.

5) Emitting an alpha particle <u>decreases</u> the <u>atomic</u> number of the nucleus by <u>2</u> and the <u>mass</u> number by <u>4</u> (see next page for more).

Beta Particles are Electrons ← $^0_{-1}$e$^-$

There's more on penetrating power on the next page.

1) A beta (β) particle is an <u>electron</u> which has been emitted from the <u>nucleus</u> of an atom when a <u>neutron</u> turns into a <u>proton</u> and an <u>electron</u>.

2) When a <u>beta particle</u> is emitted, the number of <u>protons</u> in the nucleus increases by 1. So the <u>atomic</u> number <u>increases</u> by <u>1</u> but the <u>mass</u> number <u>stays the same</u> (see next page for more).

3) They move <u>quite fast</u> and they are <u>quite small</u>.

4) They <u>penetrate moderately</u> before colliding and are <u>moderately ionising</u> too.

5) Because they're <u>charged</u> (negatively), beta particles are <u>deflected</u> by electric and magnetic fields.

Gamma Rays are Very **Short** Wavelength **EM Waves**

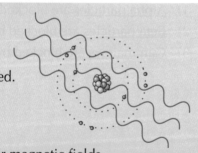

1) In a way, gamma (γ) rays are the <u>opposite of alpha particles</u>. They have <u>no mass</u> — they're just <u>energy</u> (in the form of an EM wave — see page 55).

2) They can <u>penetrate a long way</u> into materials without being stopped.

3) This means they are <u>weakly ionising</u> because they tend to <u>pass through</u> rather than collide with atoms. But eventually they <u>hit something</u> and do <u>damage</u>.

4) Gamma rays have <u>no charge</u>, so they're <u>not deflected</u> by electric or magnetic fields.

5) Gamma emission <u>always</u> happens after alpha or beta decay. You <u>never</u> get <u>just gamma rays</u>.

6) Gamma ray emission has <u>no effect</u> on the atomic or mass numbers of the isotope (see next page for more). If a nucleus has <u>excess energy</u>, it loses this energy by emitting a gamma ray.

Alpha particles are more ionising than beta particles...

... and <u>beta particles</u> are <u>more ionising</u> than <u>gamma rays</u>. Make sure you've got that clearly memorised, as well as what makes up each type of <u>radiation</u>, since this isn't the last you'll see of this stuff...

Radioactivity and Nuclear Equations

Some stuff on <u>nuclear equations</u> (well it is <u>Physics</u> — there was bound to be an equation somewhere...), and then back to how well the three types of ionising radiation <u>penetrate materials</u> (including <u>air</u>).

Balancing Nuclear Equations

1) You can write <u>equations</u> for <u>nuclear reactions</u> — just like you can for chemical reactions.

2) The overall <u>charge</u> and <u>mass</u> have to <u>be the same</u> after a nuclear reaction as they were <u>before</u>.

3) The charge on a nucleus or particle is <u>equal to</u> the atomic number, and its mass is <u>equal to</u> the mass number. So the totals of the <u>atomic</u> and <u>mass</u> numbers <u>must</u> be the <u>same</u> on <u>both sides</u> of the equation:

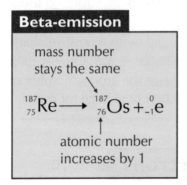

Alpha-emission

mass number decreases by 4

$$^{226}_{88}\text{Ra} \longrightarrow {}^{222}_{86}\text{Rn} + {}^{4}_{2}\text{He}$$

atomic number decreases by 2

Beta-emission

mass number stays the same

$$^{187}_{75}\text{Re} \longrightarrow {}^{187}_{76}\text{Os} + {}^{0}_{-1}\text{e}$$

atomic number increases by 1

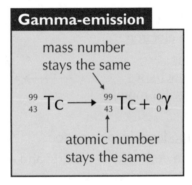

Gamma-emission

mass number stays the same

$$^{99}_{43}\text{Tc} \longrightarrow {}^{99}_{43}\text{Tc} + {}^{0}_{0}\gamma$$

atomic number stays the same

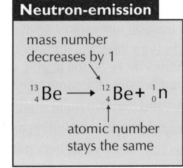

Neutron-emission

mass number decreases by 1

$$^{13}_{4}\text{Be} \longrightarrow {}^{12}_{4}\text{Be} + {}^{1}_{0}\text{n}$$

atomic number stays the same

Neutron radiation is a type of radiation where neutrons are emitted. It's ionising too, but you don't need to know its properties — only how to balance neutron decay equations.

You Can **Identify** the **Type of Radiation** by its **Penetrating Power**

1) <u>Alpha particles</u> are blocked by <u>paper</u>, <u>skin</u>, or a few cm of <u>air</u>.

2) <u>Beta particles</u> are blocked by <u>thin metal</u>.

3) <u>Gamma rays</u> are blocked by <u>thick lead</u> or <u>very thick concrete</u>.

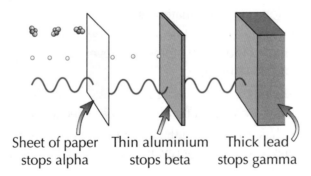

Sheet of paper stops alpha   Thin aluminium stops beta   Thick lead stops gamma

Like chemical equations, nuclear equations should be balanced

EXAM TIP If you're completing a <u>nuclear equation</u> in an exam, do a quick check when you've finished. Make sure the <u>totals</u> of the <u>atomic numbers</u> and <u>mass numbers</u> of everything on the right are <u>the same</u> as the <u>atomic number</u> and <u>mass number</u> of the thing on the left. If they aren't, something's wrong.

Investigating Radioactivity

You can see for yourself how <u>penetrating</u> the different kinds of radiation are by carrying out the following <u>experiment</u>. It's super-important to be aware of the safety precautions first though.

You can **Investigate** the **Penetration** of Radiation

1) You can <u>detect</u> ionising radiation with a <u>Geiger-Müller detector</u>. A Geiger-Müller detector gives a <u>count rate</u> — the number of <u>radioactive particles</u> reaching it per second.

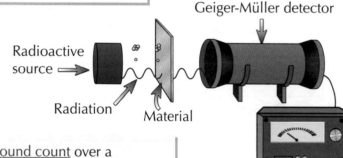

2) Set up the equipment as shown on the right, so that when nothing is placed between the source and detector, the counter records a <u>high count rate</u>.

3) Remove the source to measure the <u>background count</u> over a time period (e.g. 30 seconds). <u>Divide</u> your count by the time period to get a <u>background count</u> rate (in counts per second). Do this three times and find the mean. <u>Subtract</u> this from all your results.

4) <u>Replace</u> the source and measure the count rate (<u>minus</u> the background count rate) with <u>no material present</u> three times and take a mean. Then insert <u>different materials</u> between the source and detector. Record the count rate for each material three times and find the mean.

5) If the count rate remains about <u>the same</u> when the material is inserted, then the radiation can <u>penetrate</u> the material. If it <u>drops</u> by a large amount, then the radiation is being <u>absorbed</u> and blocked by the material. If it drops to <u>zero</u> after the background count is subtracted, the radiation is being <u>completely absorbed</u>.

6) Repeat this experiment with <u>different sources</u> to investigate the penetrations of different kinds of radiation.

You can also investigate this using a computerised radiation simulator. Doing it in the lab requires lots of work with dangerous radioactive sources, so you might have simulated it in class instead.

Radioactive Sources Can Be **Dangerous**

Radioactive sources can be dangerous if you don't use them properly (see page 138).
- Radioactive sources should be kept in a <u>lead-lined box</u> when not in use.
- They should only be picked up using <u>long-handled tongs</u> or <u>forceps</u>.
- Take care not to <u>point</u> them at anyone, and keep a <u>safe distance</u> from them.

Always handle radioactive sources safely

OK, so it might be incredibly obvious, but <u>radiation</u> can be <u>so harmful</u> that it's worth saying: if you're doing an experiment that involves using a <u>radioactive source</u>, make sure that you know <u>all</u> of the <u>safety measures</u> that you should be taking — and then make sure that you <u>take them</u>.

Warm-Up & Exam Questions

Well, it's time to test what you know. If you've learnt everything on the previous few pages, you should be able to answer every single one of these questions. Better get started...

Warm-Up Questions

1) What is the nucleon number of a nucleus?
2) What is the name of an atom that has been ionised?
3) Explain why alpha radiation is so strongly ionising.
4) Name the type of nuclear radiation whose particles are electrons.
5) Name the type of nuclear radiation that is a type of electromagnetic wave.

Exam Questions

1 Iodine-131 ($^{131}_{53}I$) is an unstable isotope of iodine. Grade 4-6

   (a) (i) Copy and complete the table for an atom of iodine-131.

Particle	Charge	Number present in an atom of iodine-131
Proton	positive	
Neutron	zero	
Electron		53

   [3 marks]

   (ii) Name the particle(s) found in the nucleus of an atom.

   [1 mark]

   (b) What is meant by the term **isotopes**?

   ☐ **A** atoms with the same atomic number but a different mass number

   ☐ **B** atoms with the same mass number but a different atomic number

   ☐ **C** atoms with the same proton number but a different atomic number

   ☐ **D** atoms with the same number of neutrons but a different number of electrons

   [1 mark]

   (c) Iodine-131 is a waste product of some power plants and it contributes to the low level of radiation that is present around us all the time.

   (i) Give the name of this low level of radiation.

   [1 mark]

   (ii) Give **two** natural sources of this low level of radiation.

   [2 marks]

   (d) Name **four** types of radiation that can be given out when unstable nuclei decay.

   [4 marks]

Exam Questions

PRACTICE

2   A student is doing an investigation to identify the radiation produced by three unknown radioactive sources. The sources were used to pass radiation through thin sheets of paper and aluminium. A detector was used to measure if radiation had passed through the sheets. The results are shown below.

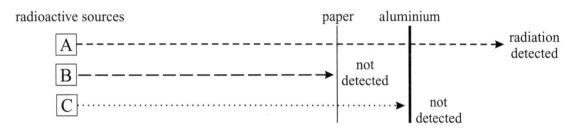

(a)   Suggest the type of radiation that source C produces. Explain your answer.

[2 marks]

(b)   The student uses a Geiger-Müller counter to detect the radiation.
Name **one** other detector that can be used to detect radiation.

[1 mark]

(c)   Explain why the student subtracts the background radiation count from all the readings shown on the detector before she analyses her results.

[2 marks]

3   Nuclear equations show what is produced when unstable nuclei decay.

(a)   Copy and complete the symbol for neutron radiation: $\overset{\cdots}{\underset{\cdots}{}}$ n

[1 mark]

(b)   Copy and complete this nuclear equation, which shows a polonium isotope decaying by alpha and gamma emission.

An alpha particle can be written as He or α. $\overset{\cdots}{\underset{\cdots}{}}$ Po $\longrightarrow$ $\overset{195}{\underset{82}{}}$ Pb $+$ $\overset{\cdots}{\underset{\cdots}{}}$ α $+$ $\overset{\cdots}{\underset{\cdots}{}}$ γ

[4 marks]

4   The unstable isotope lead-212 ($^{212}_{82}$Pb) decays by emitting nuclear radiation. After the three stages of decay described below, it becomes a different isotope of lead.

    1.   Lead-212 decays by beta decay to become an isotope of bismuth.
    2.   The bismuth isotope decays by alpha and gamma decay to become an isotope of thallium.
    3.   The thallium isotope decays by beta decay into a different isotope of lead.

(a)   Describe what happens to the atomic number and the mass number of a nucleus when it undergoes gamma decay.

[2 marks]

(b)   State the mass number of the lead isotope that is reached in stage 3. Explain your answer.

[4 marks]

Half-Life

Half-life is the time it takes for a radioactive material to lose half of its radioactivity. Simple really.

The **Radioactivity** of a Sample Always **Decreases** Over Time

1) This is pretty obvious when you think about it. Each time a decay happens and an alpha or beta particle or gamma ray is given out, it means one more radioactive nucleus has disappeared.

2) Obviously, as the unstable nuclei all disappear, the activity (the number of decays in a given time) will decrease. So the older a sample becomes, the less radiation it will emit.

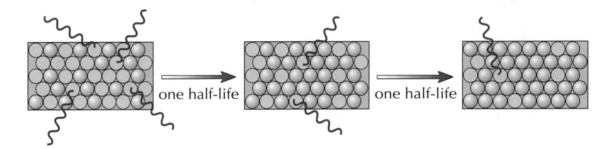

3) How quickly the activity drops off varies a lot. For some isotopes it takes just a few hours before nearly all the unstable nuclei have decayed, whilst others last for millions of years.

4) The problem with trying to measure this is that the activity never reaches zero, which is why we have to use the idea of half-life to measure how quickly the activity drops off.

5) Learn this important definition of half-life:

> Half-life is the time taken for half of the radioactive atoms now present to decay.

6) Another definition of half-life is:
   "The time taken for the activity (or count rate) to fall by half". Use either.

7) A short half-life means the activity falls quickly, because lots of the nuclei decay quickly.

8) A long half-life means the activity falls more slowly because most of the nuclei don't decay for a long time — they just sit there, basically unstable, but kind of biding their time.

For any particular isotope, the half-life is always the same.

Make sure you've learnt a definition of half-life

Isotopes can have very different half-lives. For example, uranium-235 (used in nuclear power stations) has a half-life of 700 million years, while the half-life of fluorine-18 (used in hospitals) is less than 2 hours.

Half-Life

This page is about <u>how to tackle</u> the two main types of half-life questions.

Do **Half-Life** Questions **Step by Step**

Half-life is maybe a little confusing, but the calculations are <u>straightforward</u>
so long as you do them carefully, <u>step by step</u>. Like this one:

> <u>Example:</u>   The <u>activity</u> of a radioactive isotope is <u>640 Bq</u>.
> <u>Two hours later</u> it has fallen to <u>40 Bq</u>.
> Find the <u>half-life</u> of the sample.
>
> *Radioactivity is measured in becquerels (Bq).*
> *1 Bq is 1 decay per second.*
>
> <u>Answer:</u>   To answer, go through it in <u>short simple steps</u> like this:
>
> | INITIAL count: | (÷2)→ | after ONE half-life: | (÷2)→ | after TWO half-lives: | (÷2)→ | after THREE half-lives: | (÷2)→ | after FOUR half-lives: |
> |---|---|---|---|---|---|---|---|---|
> | 640 | | 320 | | 160 | | 80 | | 40 |
>
> It takes <u>four half-lives</u> for the activity to fall from 640 to 40.
> This means that <u>two hours</u> represents four half-lives, so the half-life is (2 hours ÷ 4) = 30 minutes.

Measuring the **Half-Life** of a Sample Using a Graph

1) This can <u>only be done</u> by taking <u>several readings</u>
   of a source's activity, usually using
   a <u>Geiger-Müller (G-M) detector</u>.
   The results can then be <u>plotted</u> as a <u>graph</u>,
   which will <u>always</u> be shaped like this.

2) The <u>half-life</u> is found from the graph,
   by finding the <u>time interval</u> on the
   <u>bottom axis</u> corresponding to a <u>halving</u>
   of the <u>activity</u> on the <u>vertical axis</u>.

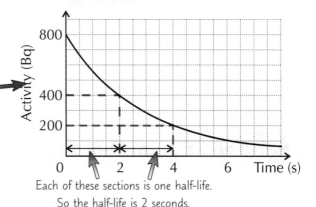

Each of these sections is one half-life.
So the half-life is 2 seconds.

You need to make sure you've <u>subtracted</u>
the <u>background count</u> from your readings
before you plot the graph. If you
don't, you'll get an <u>incorrect value</u> for
half-life, and it'll be <u>different</u> for each
measurement you take from the graph.

Realistically, the only difficult bit is actually
<u>remembering</u> about that for your exam,
should they ask you about it. They could
also test that idea in a <u>calculation</u> question.

Background still included — no
use for working out half-life

Background subtracted —
can now obtain consistent
results for half-life

Show your working on the graph

Don't just estimate the time at which the activity reaches a certain value — get out your ruler
and draw some lines between the axes and the graph line to find it accurately. This will also
show the examiner that you know what you're doing and have followed the correct method.

Uses of Nuclear Radiation

Nuclear radiation can be <u>really</u> useful — but you've got to be careful about what <u>isotope</u> you use.

Medical Tracers Use Beta or Gamma Radiation

Beta and gamma will <u>penetrate</u> the skin and other body tissues.
This makes them suitable as <u>medical tracers</u>:

1) A source which emits beta or gamma radiation is <u>injected</u> into the patient (or <u>swallowed</u>). The radiation penetrates the body tissues and can be <u>detected externally</u>.

2) As the source moves around the body, the radiographer uses a <u>detector</u> and a <u>computer</u> to monitor its progress on a display.

3) Doctors use this method to check whether the <u>organs</u> of the body are working as they should.

4) The radioactive source has to have a <u>short half-life</u>, so that the initial levels are high enough to be easily <u>detected</u>, but the radioactivity inside the patient <u>quickly disappears</u>.

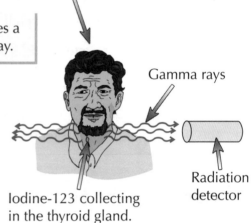

Gamma rays

Radiation detector

Iodine-123 collecting in the thyroid gland.

5) An <u>alpha</u> source would be <u>worse than useless</u> as a medical tracer — <u>useless</u> because it would be stopped by the body's tissues, so you'd never detect it externally, and <u>worse</u> than useless because its <u>strong ionising</u> power makes alpha radiation really <u>harmful</u> if it gets <u>inside</u> you (see page 138).

Food and Equipment can be Sterilised Using Gamma Rays

1) <u>Food</u> can be <u>irradiated</u> (see page 138) with a <u>high dose</u> of <u>gamma rays</u> to <u>kill</u> all <u>microbes</u>, so that it doesn't go bad as quickly as it would do otherwise.

2) Similarly, <u>medical equipment</u> can be <u>sterilised</u> using gamma rays.

3) <u>Irradiation</u> is a particularly good method of sterilisation because, unlike boiling, it doesn't involve <u>high temperatures</u>. So <u>fresh fruit</u> or <u>plastic instruments</u> can be <u>sterilised</u> without being <u>damaged</u>.

4) The radioactive source used for this needs to be a <u>very strong</u> emitter of <u>gamma rays</u> with a <u>reasonably long half-life</u> (at least several months) so that it doesn't need <u>replacing</u> too often.

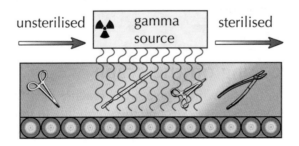

unsterilised → gamma source → sterilised

More Uses of Nuclear Radiation

Yep, there are <u>even more ways</u> in which nuclear radiation has proved itself useful. Take a look...

Radiation is Also Used to **Treat Cancer**

1) You'll see on the next page that <u>ionising radiation</u> can kill or damage cells and tissues — and this can cause <u>cancer</u>. But once the cancer's started, ionising radiation can <u>also</u> be used to <u>treat</u> it.

2) <u>Radiotherapy</u> kills the cancer cells and stops them dividing — it involves using a <u>high</u> dose of gamma rays, carefully directed to zap the cells in the <u>tumour</u> while minimising the dose to the rest of the body.

Radiation is Used in Industry for **Tracers** and **Thickness Gauges**

Gamma Radiation in Industrial Tracers

1) <u>Gamma emitting tracers</u> are used in <u>industry</u> to detect <u>leaks</u> in <u>underground pipes</u>.

2) The source is allowed to flow down the pipe and a <u>detector</u> is used above ground. Gamma is used because it can pass through any <u>rocks or earth</u> surrounding the pipe.

3) If there's a <u>crack</u> in the pipe, more radiation will collect outside the pipe, and the detector will show <u>extra high</u> radioactivity at that point.

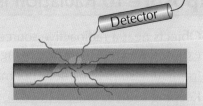

4) It should have a <u>short half-life</u> so as not to cause a long-term <u>hazard</u> if it collects somewhere.

Beta Radiation in Thickness Gauges

1) <u>Beta radiation</u> is used in <u>thickness control</u>.

2) You direct radiation through the stuff being made (e.g. paper), and put a detector on the other side, connected to a control unit. When the <u>detected</u> radiation level changes, it means the paper is coming out too thick or too thin, so the control unit adjusts the rollers to give the correct thickness.

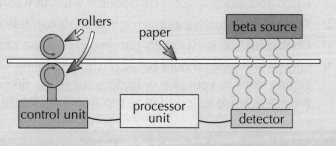

3) It needs to be a <u>beta</u> source, because then the paper will <u>partly block</u> the radiation (see page 130). If it <u>all</u> goes through (or <u>none</u> of it does), then the reading <u>won't</u> <u>change</u> at all as the thickness changes.

Choose your source carefully

To make use of radiation, you've got to match the <u>requirements</u> of the <u>job</u> to your <u>source's properties</u>. If the radiation needs to go through any kind of material, then an alpha source won't be any good to you.

Risks from Nuclear Radiation

Radiation's dangerous and useful at the same time — it can both <u>cause</u> and <u>cure</u> cancer, for instance.

Ionising Radiation Can **Damage Cells** and **Tissues**

1) <u>Beta</u> and <u>gamma</u> can penetrate the skin and soft tissues to reach the delicate <u>organs</u> inside the body. This makes beta and gamma sources more hazardous than alpha when <u>outside</u> the body. If they get <u>inside</u> (e.g. <u>swallowed</u> or <u>breathed in</u>), their radiation mostly <u>passes straight out</u> without doing much damage.

The properties of alpha, beta and gamma are on page 129.

2) <u>Alpha radiation</u> can't penetrate the skin, but it's very dangerous if it gets inside the body. Alpha sources do all their damage in a <u>very localised area</u>.

3) When radiation enters your body, it will <u>collide</u> with molecules in your cells. These collisions cause <u>ionisation</u>, which <u>damages</u> or <u>destroys</u> the molecules. The <u>extent</u> of the harmful effects depends on <u>how much exposure</u> you have to the radiation, and its <u>energy</u> and <u>penetration</u>.

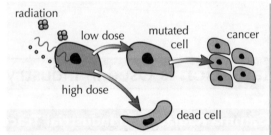

4) <u>Lower</u> doses tend to cause <u>minor</u> damage without <u>killing</u> the cell. This can cause <u>mutations</u> in cells which then <u>divide uncontrollably</u> — this is <u>cancer</u>.

5) <u>Higher</u> doses tend to <u>kill cells</u> completely, causing <u>radiation sickness</u> if a large part of your body is affected at the same time.

Exposure to Radiation is called **Irradiation**

1) Objects <u>near</u> a radioactive source are <u>irradiated</u> by it. This simply means they're <u>exposed</u> to it (we're <u>always</u> being irradiated by <u>background radiation</u> sources).

2) <u>Irradiating</u> something does <u>not</u> make it <u>radioactive</u>.

3) Keeping sources in <u>lead-lined boxes</u>, standing behind <u>barriers</u> or being in a <u>different room</u> and using <u>remote-controlled arms</u> are all ways of reducing the risk of <u>irradiation</u>.

Contamination is Radioactive Particles **Getting onto Objects**

1) If <u>unwanted radioactive atoms</u> get onto or into an object, the object is said to be <u>contaminated</u>. E.g. if you <u>touch</u> a radioactive source without wearing <u>gloves</u>, your hands would be <u>contaminated</u>.

2) These <u>contaminating atoms</u> might then decay, releasing <u>radiation</u> which could cause you <u>harm</u>.

3) Contamination is especially dangerous because radioactive particles could get <u>inside your body</u>.

4) <u>Gloves</u> and <u>tongs</u> should be used when handling sources, to avoid particles getting stuck to your <u>skin</u> or <u>under your nails</u>. Some industrial workers wear <u>protective suits</u> and <u>masks</u> to stop them <u>breathing in</u> particles.

Radioactive Waste is **Difficult** to Dispose of **Safely**

1) Most <u>radioactive waste</u> from nuclear power stations and hospitals is '<u>low-level</u>' (slightly radioactive) — e.g. clothing, syringes, etc. This kind of waste can be disposed of by <u>burying</u> it in secure landfill sites.

2) <u>High-level</u> waste is the <u>really dangerous</u> stuff — a lot of it stays highly radioactive for <u>tens of thousands</u> of years, and so has to be treated very carefully. It's often sealed into <u>glass blocks</u>, which are then sealed in <u>metal canisters</u>. These <u>could</u> then be buried <u>deep</u> underground.

3) However, it's difficult to find <u>suitable places</u> to bury high-level waste. The site has to be <u>geologically stable</u> (e.g. not suffer from earthquakes), since big movements in the rock could disturb the canisters and allow radioactive material to <u>leak out</u>. If this material gets into the <u>groundwater</u>, it could contaminate the soil, plants, rivers, etc., and get into our <u>drinking water</u>.

Nuclear Fission

Most power stations get the energy they need to drive the generators by <u>burning fuel</u> (e.g. coal) or from the <u>natural motion</u> of something (e.g. waves, tides). <u>Nuclear</u> power stations do it a bit differently...

Nuclear Power Stations use **Nuclear Fission Chain Reactions**

1) <u>Nuclear fission</u> is the <u>splitting</u> of an atom, which releases <u>energy</u>. It can be <u>spontaneous</u>, but in a nuclear reactor it's made to happen — e.g. to <u>uranium-235</u>.

2) If a <u>slow-moving neutron</u> is absorbed by a uranium-235 nucleus, the nucleus can <u>split</u>.

3) Each time this happens, it spits out a <u>small number of neutrons</u>. These might go on to hit other uranium-235 nuclei, causing them to split also... and so on and so on. This is a <u>chain reaction</u>.

4) When uranium-235 splits in two it will form <u>two</u> new <u>daughter nuclei</u>, both <u>lighter elements</u> than uranium.

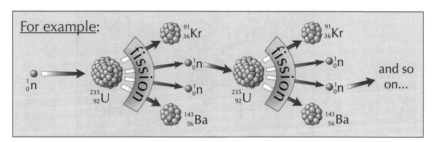

For example:

5) These new nuclei are usually <u>radioactive</u>. This is the <u>big problem</u> with nuclear power — <u>radioactive waste</u>.

6) Each nucleus <u>splitting</u> gives out <u>a lot of energy</u> — this energy is in the <u>kinetic energy stores</u> of the <u>fission products</u> (the daughter nuclei and the neutrons).

7) In a reactor, this energy is transferred to <u>thermal energy stores</u> to produce <u>steam</u> to drive a <u>turbine</u> (see below).

Nuclear Reactors Have to Work **Safely**

1) The <u>neutrons</u> released by fission reactions in a nuclear reactor have <u>a lot</u> of energy. In order to be <u>absorbed</u> by uranium nuclei and <u>sustain</u> the chain reaction, they need to be <u>slowed down</u>.

2) The <u>moderator</u>, usually graphite or water, <u>slows</u> down <u>neutrons</u>.

3) <u>Control rods</u>, often made of <u>boron</u>, limit the rate of fission by <u>absorbing</u> excess neutrons.

4) The <u>high-energy</u> neutrons and <u>gamma rays</u> (energy) released in fission are highly penetrating <u>ionising radiation</u>. <u>Shielding</u> has to be used to <u>absorb</u> the ionising radiation. The shielding is usually a <u>thick concrete</u> structure, which may also contain <u>lead</u> or other metals.

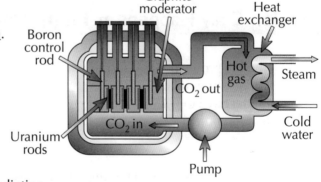

5) A substance (e.g. CO_2) pumped round the reactor <u>transfers</u> the energy (by heating) to the water in the <u>heat exchanger</u>. The water turns to <u>steam</u>, which turns a <u>turbine</u>, which turns a <u>generator</u> and generates <u>electricity</u>.

Nuclear power releases a lot of energy, but it has its downsides

Nothing to it really: throw in some <u>neutrons</u>, split some <u>atoms</u>, get some <u>heat</u>, make some <u>steam</u>, turn a <u>turbine</u>, drive a <u>generator</u> and there you have it — some <u>electricity</u>. But the big problem is how to <u>dispose of the waste</u> — the products left over are generally <u>radioactive</u>, so they can't just be <u>thrown away</u>.

Nuclear Fusion

Nuclei can be <u>joined together</u>, as well as split apart. But power stations <u>can't</u> take advantage of this (yet).

Nuclear **Fusion** — **Joining Small Nuclei**

1) <u>Nuclear fusion</u> is the opposite of nuclear fission. In nuclear fusion, two <u>light nuclei collide</u> at high speed and <u>join</u> (fuse) to create a <u>larger</u>, heavier nucleus.

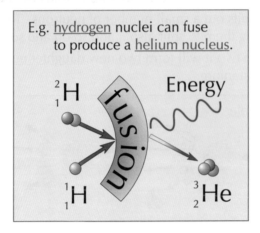

E.g. <u>hydrogen</u> nuclei can fuse to produce a <u>helium nucleus</u>.

2) This <u>heavier</u> nucleus doesn't have as much <u>mass</u> as the two <u>separate</u>, lighter nuclei did. Some of the mass of the lighter nuclei is converted to <u>energy</u> (<u>don't panic</u>, you don't need to know <u>how</u>). This energy is then <u>released</u> as radiation.

3) Fusion releases <u>a lot</u> of energy (more than fission for a given mass of fuel) — all the energy released in <u>stars</u> comes from fusion.

Fusion Only Happens at **High Temperatures** and **Pressures**

1) The <u>big problem</u> is that fusion only happens at <u>really high pressures</u> and <u>temperatures</u> (about <u>10 000 000 °C</u>). This is because the <u>positively charged</u> nuclei have to get <u>very close</u> to fuse, so they need to be moving <u>very fast</u> to overcome the strong <u>force</u> due to <u>electrostatic repulsion</u> (see page 45).

2) So far, scientists haven't found a way of using fusion to generate energy for us to use. The <u>temperatures</u> and <u>pressures</u> needed for fusion are so <u>high</u> that fusion reactors are really <u>hard</u> and <u>expensive</u> to build.

Why do we even bother?

Building a working <u>fusion</u> reactor is a real headache. It's <u>expensive</u>, <u>difficult</u> and no one's got it quite right yet. So what's the point? Well, it releases loads of <u>energy</u>. And the main waste produce is <u>helium</u>, which is <u>neither radioactive nor a greenhouse gas</u>. So some people believe it could solve the <u>current energy crisis</u>.

Warm-Up & Exam Questions

Here we go again — time to test your knowledge with some specially selected questions.
The warm-up questions should ease you in. Try them out before you dive into the exam questions.

Warm-Up Questions

1) What units is radioactivity measured in?
2) Name the two types of radiation that can be used in medical tracers.
3) How could you use gamma rays to detect a leak in an underground pipe?
4) Why is it important that sites where high-level radioactive waste is buried are geologically stable?

Exam Questions

1 A sample of a radioactive isotope has a half-life of 40 seconds. *(Grade 6-7)*

(a) (i) The initial activity of the sample is 8000 Bq. Calculate the activity after 2 minutes.

[2 marks]

(ii) Calculate the number of whole minutes it would take for the activity to fall below 200 Bq from its initial activity.

[3 marks]

(b) Which of the following statements about half-life are true?

1. Two samples of the same size but of different isotopes would have the same half-life.

2. Two samples of the same size but of different isotopes would have different half-lives.

3. Two samples of the same isotope of different sizes would have the same half-life.

4. Two samples of the same isotope of different sizes would have different half-lives.

☐ **A**   2 and 3 only

☐ **B**   4 only

☐ **C**   2 and 4 only

☐ **D**   None of the statements

[1 mark]

2 A scientist is concerned about contamination and irradiation in her lab. *(Grade 6-7)*

(a) State what is meant by **contamination**.

[1 mark]

(b) The scientist is using a low activity radioactive sample.
Give **one** example of how she can protect herself from irradiation and **one** example of how she can protect herself from contamination.

[2 marks]

Exam Questions

3 Iodine-123 is a gamma emitter commonly used as a tracer in medicine.

    (a) Describe how iodine-123 can be used to detect whether the thyroid gland is absorbing iodine as it normally should do.

[2 marks]

    (b) Explain why alpha emitters cannot be used as tracers in medicine.

[4 marks]

    (c) This table shows the properties of three other radioisotopes.

       State which of these would be best to use as a medical tracer.

       Explain your answer.

Radioisotope	Half-life	Type of emission
technetium-99m	6 hours	gamma
phosphorus-32	14 days	beta
cobalt-60	5 years	beta/gamma

[2 marks]

4 Nuclear fission takes place in nuclear reactors. The diagram shows the basic structure of a gas-cooled nuclear reactor.

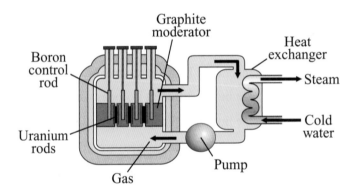

    (a) Give **one** fuel that can be used in a nuclear reactor.

[1 mark]

    (b) (i) Describe what happens during a single nuclear fission event and state the products formed.

[4 marks]

       (ii) Explain how nuclear fission can be used to produce energy continuously in a nuclear reactor, and how part of the nuclear reactor is designed to help this happen.

[3 marks]

    (c) Explain the purpose of the control rods in a nuclear reactor.

[1 mark]

5 Two protons are fired at each other and combine to form a hydrogen-2 nucleus. Describe the conditions required for this reaction to occur and explain why they are needed.

[3 marks]

Revision Questions for Section 7

That's <u>Section 7</u> over and done with — time to find out <u>how much of it you can remember</u>.

- Try these questions and <u>tick off each one</u> when you <u>get it right</u>.
- When you've done <u>all the questions</u> under a heading and are <u>completely happy</u> with it, tick it off.

Isotopes and Nuclear Radiation (p.127-131) ☑

1) What is the atomic number of a nucleus? ☑
2) What is the mass number of a nucleus? ☑
3) What are atoms with the same number of protons but different numbers of neutrons called? ☑
4) Briefly describe what background radiation is and where it comes from. ☑
5) Describe what alpha, beta and gamma radiation are. ☑
6) Which is the most ionising out of alpha, beta and gamma radiation? ☑
7) Which is the most penetrating out of alpha, beta and gamma radiation? ☑
8) Describe how the mass and atomic numbers of an atom change if it emits an alpha particle. ☑
9) In what type of nuclear decay does a neutron change into a proton within the nucleus? ☑
10) What type of nuclear decay doesn't change the mass or charge of the nucleus? ☑
11) What type of radiation is stopped by paper? ☑
12) What quantities need to be the same on each side of a nuclear equation? ☑

Half-Life (p.134-135) ☑

13) What is meant by the 'activity' of a radioactive source? ☑
14) Define half-life. ☑
15) True or false? A short half-life means a small proportion of the atoms are decaying per second. ☑

Uses and Risks of Nuclear Radiation (p.136-138) ☑

16) Briefly describe two uses of nuclear radiation in medicine. ☑
17) Explain why alpha radiation could not be used to check the thickness of metal sheets. ☑
18) Other than thickness gauges, give one other use of nuclear radiation in industry. ☑
19) Why is nuclear radiation dangerous to living organisms? ☑
20) Explain why radioactive waste is difficult to dispose of safely. ☑

Fission and Fusion (p.139-140) ☑

21) What are the products of the nuclear fission of uranium-235? ☑
22) True or false? The fission products of uranium-235 are also radioactive. ☑
23) What job does shielding do in a nuclear reactor? ☑
24) What is the name of the process in which two light nuclei collide
    at high speed and join together? ☑

The Universe

There's all sorts of exciting stuff in the universe... Our whole solar system is just part of a huge galaxy. And there are billions upon billions of galaxies. Which should tell you that the universe is pretty big...

We are Part of the **Milky Way Galaxy**

1) The universe is a large collection of billions of galaxies.

2) A galaxy is a large collection of stars.

3) Our Sun is just one of many billions of stars which form the Milky Way galaxy. Our Sun is about halfway along one of the spiral arms of the Milky Way.

You are here.

4) The distance between neighbouring stars in the galaxy is often millions of times greater than the distance between planets in our solar system.

5) The force which keeps the stars together in a galaxy is gravity, of course. And like most things in the universe, galaxies rotate — a bit like a Catherine wheel.

6) Galaxies themselves are often millions of times further apart than the stars are within a galaxy.

7) So the universe is mostly empty space and is really, really big.

Our Solar System has **One** Star — The **Sun**

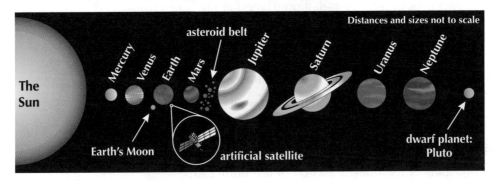

Distances and sizes not to scale

The Sun — Mercury — Venus — Earth — Mars — asteroid belt — Jupiter — Saturn — Uranus — Neptune

Earth's Moon — artificial satellite — dwarf planet: Pluto

Our solar system is all the stuff that orbits the Sun. This includes things like:

1) Planets — these are large objects that orbit a star. The eight planets in our solar system are, in order (from the Sun outwards): Mercury, Venus, Earth, Mars, Jupiter, Saturn, Uranus and Neptune.

2) Dwarf planets, like Pluto. These are planet-like objects that aren't big enough to be planets.

3) Moons — these orbit planets with almost circular orbits. They're a type of natural satellite (i.e. they're not man-made).

A satellite is an object that orbits a second, more massive object.

4) Artificial satellites (ones humans have built) that usually orbit the Earth in fairly circular orbits.

5) Asteroids — lumps of rock and metal that orbit the Sun. They're usually found in the asteroid belt.

6) Comets — lumps of ice and dust that orbit the Sun. Their orbits are usually highly elliptical (a very stretched out circle) — some travel from near to the Sun to the outskirts of our solar system.

Gravity and Orbits

The structure of the Solar System is determined by orbits — the paths that objects take as they move around each other in space. I bet you can't wait to find out more. Well, read on...

Gravity Provides the Force That Creates Orbits

1) The planets move around the Sun in almost circular orbits (same goes for the Moon around the Earth).

2) If an object is travelling in a circle it is constantly changing direction (and so constantly accelerating), which means there must be a force acting on it.

3) The force causing this is a centripetal force. It acts towards the centre of the circle.

4) This force would cause the object to just fall towards whatever it was orbiting, but as the object is already moving, it just causes it to change its direction.

5) The object keeps accelerating towards what it's orbiting but the instantaneous velocity (which is at a right angle to the acceleration) keeps it travelling in a circle.

6) The force that makes this happen is provided by the gravitational force (gravity). The gravitational attraction of the Sun keeps the planets and comets in their orbits around it.

7) Satellites are kept in their orbits around planets by the gravitational attraction of the planet.

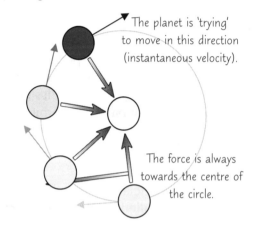

The planet is 'trying' to move in this direction (instantaneous velocity).

The force is always towards the centre of the circle.

Gravity leads to orbits that are either circles or ellipses (see next page).

The Force due to Gravity Depends on Mass and Distance

1) Back on page 5 you saw that the weight (i.e. the force on an object due to gravity) of any object varies depending on the strength (g) of the gravitational field that it is in.

2) Gravitational field strength depends on the mass of the body creating the field. The larger the mass of the body, the stronger its gravitational field. (The Earth is more massive than the Moon, so an object would weigh more on Earth than it would on the Moon.)

3) Gravitational field strength also varies with distance. The closer you get to a star or planet, the stronger the gravitational force is.

4) The stronger the force, the larger the instantaneous velocity needed to balance it.

5) So the closer to a star or planet you get, the faster you need to go to remain in orbit.

6) For an object in a stable orbit, if the speed of the object changes, the size (radius) of its orbit must do so too. Faster moving objects will move in a stable orbit with a smaller radius than slower moving ones.

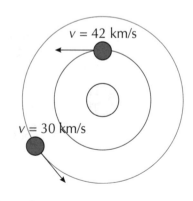

v = 42 km/s

v = 30 km/s

The fact that different planets orbit the Sun at different speeds means that the distances between planets vary over time.

Gravity and Orbits

There are Different Types of Orbit

1) The orbits of moons and planets are usually slightly elliptical.

2) Comets orbit the Sun, but have very elliptical (elongated) orbits with the Sun at one focus (near one end of the orbit).

3) Comets have orbital periods much longer than the Earth, as they travel from the outer edges of our solar system. A comet travels much faster when it's nearer the Sun than it does in the more distant parts of its orbit. That's because the increased pull of gravity makes it speed up the closer it gets to the Sun.

4) Some artificial Earth satellites have an orbital period of exactly one day. They're called geostationary satellites, and are useful in communications because they're always over the same part of the planet.

You can Calculate Orbital Speeds

1) You can calculate the speed of an orbit using the formula from page 1:

$$\text{speed} = \frac{\text{distance}}{\text{time}}$$

2) For a circular orbit, the distance travelled is the circumference of the orbit, which is given by the formula:
distance = 2 × π × radius of orbit

3) So the formula for the speed of an orbit is:

$$\text{orbital speed} = \frac{2 \times \pi \times \text{orbital radius}}{\text{time period}} \qquad v = \frac{2\pi r}{T}$$

Remember: 'r' is the distance between the centre of the planet or star and the object that is orbiting around it.

Example: Calculate the speed in m/s of a satellite that is orbiting above the Earth's surface at an altitude of 600 km. The radius of the Earth is 6400 km and the satellite takes 200 min to orbit the Earth once.

Answer: First calculate r in m: r = 6400 + 600 = 7000 km = 7 000 000 m
Then find the time period in seconds, T = 200 × 60 = 12 000 s

So orbital speed = $\frac{2 \times \pi \times 7\,000\,000}{12\,000}$

= 3665.191... m/s = 3700 m/s (to 2 s.f.)

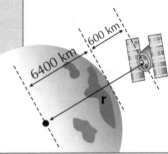

Pay close attention to the units of values you're given...

The values you get given in the question may not be in units you want for the equation, especially when it's large values like orbital radius in the question above. Make sure you convert them first.

Warm-Up & Exam Questions

Astronomy has some pretty cool stuff, but that doesn't mean you can escape a few practice questions...

Warm-Up Questions

1) Name the galaxy where our solar system is located.
2) Give two factors that affect the strength of the gravitational force on an object orbiting a planet.
3) A planet orbits a star at a distance of 55 000 000 km. It takes 1800 hours to orbit the star. Assuming its orbit is circular, find the planet's orbital speed in m/s.

Exam Questions

1 Which of the following correctly describes a galaxy? *(Grade 3-4)*

☐ **A** a star surrounded by orbiting planets

☐ **B** a collection of billions of stars

☐ **C** a collection of billions of universes

☐ **D** a collection of 5 to 10 stars

[1 mark]

2 The diagrams below represent the orbits of four different objects in space. *(Grade 6-7)*

(a) Which of the objects, A, B, C or D, is most likely to be a comet? Explain your answer.

[2 marks]

(b) Objects A and D have the same time period and orbital radius. Object D has an orbital speed of 1.2 km/s. What is the orbital speed of object A? Give a reason for your answer.

[1 mark]

(c) Object B has an orbital radius of 42 000 km and a time period of 24 hours. Calculate the orbital speed of object B in m/s.

[3 marks]

3 A comet orbits a star with a varying orbital radius and speed. It completes one orbit in 72.0 years and its orbital speed is 48.1 km/s at the fastest point in its orbit. *(Grade 6-7)*

(a) Calculate the time period of the comet's orbit in seconds. Assume there are 365 days in a year.

[1 mark]

(b) At which point in the comet's orbit will its speed be greatest? Explain your answer.

[2 marks]

(c) A planet travels in a circular orbit around the same star. It has the same orbital period as the comet and a constant orbital speed of 7.4 km/s. Calculate the orbital radius of this planet in metres.

[3 marks]

Stellar Evolution

Stars go through some <u>dramatic transformations</u> during their life cycle.

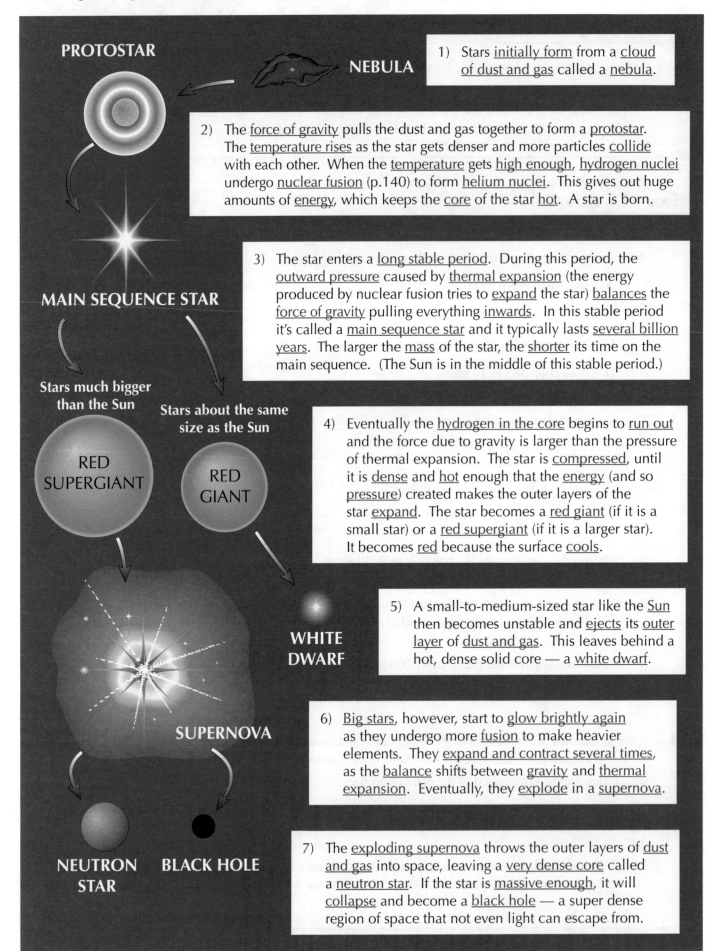

PROTOSTAR

NEBULA

1) Stars <u>initially form</u> from a <u>cloud of dust and gas</u> called a <u>nebula</u>.

2) The <u>force of gravity</u> pulls the dust and gas together to form a <u>protostar</u>. The <u>temperature rises</u> as the star gets denser and more particles <u>collide</u> with each other. When the <u>temperature</u> gets <u>high enough</u>, <u>hydrogen nuclei</u> undergo <u>nuclear fusion</u> (p.140) to form <u>helium nuclei</u>. This gives out huge amounts of <u>energy</u>, which keeps the <u>core</u> of the star <u>hot</u>. A star is born.

MAIN SEQUENCE STAR

3) The star enters a <u>long stable period</u>. During this period, the <u>outward pressure</u> caused by <u>thermal expansion</u> (the energy produced by nuclear fusion tries to <u>expand</u> the star) <u>balances</u> the <u>force of gravity</u> pulling everything <u>inwards</u>. In this stable period it's called a <u>main sequence star</u> and it typically lasts <u>several billion years</u>. The larger the <u>mass</u> of the star, the <u>shorter</u> its time on the main sequence. (The Sun is in the middle of this stable period.)

Stars much bigger than the Sun

Stars about the same size as the Sun

RED SUPERGIANT

RED GIANT

4) Eventually the <u>hydrogen in the core</u> begins to <u>run out</u> and the force due to gravity is larger than the pressure of thermal expansion. The star is <u>compressed</u>, until it is <u>dense</u> and <u>hot</u> enough that the <u>energy</u> (and so <u>pressure</u>) created makes the outer layers of the star <u>expand</u>. The star becomes a <u>red giant</u> (if it is a small star) or a <u>red supergiant</u> (if it is a larger star). It becomes <u>red</u> because the surface <u>cools</u>.

WHITE DWARF

5) A small-to-medium-sized star like the <u>Sun</u> then becomes unstable and <u>ejects</u> its <u>outer layer</u> of <u>dust and gas</u>. This leaves behind a hot, dense solid core — a <u>white dwarf</u>.

SUPERNOVA

6) <u>Big stars</u>, however, start to <u>glow brightly again</u> as they undergo more <u>fusion</u> to make heavier elements. They <u>expand and contract several times</u>, as the <u>balance</u> shifts between <u>gravity</u> and <u>thermal expansion</u>. Eventually, they <u>explode</u> in a <u>supernova</u>.

NEUTRON STAR

BLACK HOLE

7) The <u>exploding supernova</u> throws the outer layers of <u>dust and gas</u> into space, leaving a <u>very dense core</u> called a <u>neutron star</u>. If the star is <u>massive enough</u>, it will <u>collapse</u> and become a <u>black hole</u> — a super dense region of space that not even light can escape from.

Classifying Stars

We need to be able to <u>categorise</u> and <u>compare</u> stars, so we can better understand our universe.

Stars can be Classified by their Colours

1) The <u>colour</u> of a star depends on the <u>visible light</u> it <u>emits</u>. <u>All</u> stars emit visible light, but <u>how much</u> light of each <u>frequency</u> a star emits will depend on its <u>surface temperature</u>.

2) This means we can <u>classify</u> stars based on their <u>colour</u>. We use <u>red</u>, <u>orange</u>, <u>yellow</u>, <u>white</u> and <u>blue</u>. All stars of a <u>similar colour</u> will be of a <u>similar temperature</u>.

3) The <u>hotter</u> the star, the <u>more</u> light of <u>higher frequencies</u> it will emit.

4) A <u>cool star</u> will emit most of its visible light at the <u>lowest frequency</u> of visible light (i.e. <u>red light</u> — see page 55), and so it will appear <u>red</u>.

5) <u>Orange</u> stars are <u>hotter</u> than <u>red</u> stars, <u>yellow</u> stars are <u>hotter</u> than <u>orange</u> stars, and <u>white</u> stars are <u>hotter</u> than <u>yellow</u> stars. White stars emit <u>all frequencies</u> of visible light roughly <u>equally</u>.

6) <u>Blue</u> stars are <u>hotter</u> than white stars. They emit more <u>high frequency</u> light (blue, indigo and violet) than lower frequency light (red and orange), and so they appear <u>blue</u>.

Colour	Surface Temperature
Blue	Hottest
White	↑
Yellow	
Orange	
Red	Coolest

You can Compare Brightness using Absolute Magnitude

1) A star's <u>brightness</u> depends on its <u>size</u> and <u>temperature</u>. In general, the <u>bigger</u> and <u>hotter</u> the star, the <u>brighter</u> it is.

2) <u>Classifying</u> stars by brightness can be difficult, since the brightness they appear from Earth also depends on their <u>distance from Earth</u>. The <u>closer</u> the star, the <u>brighter</u> it appears.

3) If we just looked at brightness, we may end up classifying stars that are <u>very far away</u> but <u>very bright</u> in the same group as a star that is <u>relatively dim</u>, but <u>nearby</u>, which wouldn't be very useful.

4) To deal with this, we use a value called 'absolute magnitude'.

5) Absolute magnitude is a measure of how bright a given star would appear to be if it was a <u>fixed distance from Earth</u> (around 3.1×10^{17} m). This allows us to <u>compare</u> the brightness of stars without worrying about their relative distances from Earth.

6) Confusingly, the <u>lower the absolute magnitude</u>, the <u>brighter</u> the star. Very bright stars have a <u>negative</u> value for their absolute magnitudes. For example, the <u>Sun</u> has an absolute magnitude of around <u>+5</u>, while the <u>Pole Star</u>, one of the brightest looking stars in the night sky, has an absolute magnitude of around <u>−4</u>.

Bigger and hotter stars are brighter than smaller and cooler ones...

Blue stars are <u>brighter</u> than red stars of the <u>same size</u> because they're <u>hotter</u>, but many red stars are <u>brighter</u> than <u>hotter</u> stars because they are much <u>bigger</u> — e.g. red giants are much brighter than white dwarfs.

Paper 2

Classifying Stars and Red-Shift

The **Hertzsprung-Russell Diagram** Shows Different Types of Star

1) The Hertzsprung-Russell diagram is a graph of absolute magnitude against temperature for many stars.

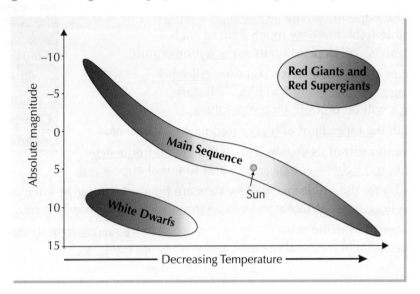

2) There are clear groups on the graph that correspond to different periods in a star's life cycle.

3) Red giants and red supergiants are in the top-right.
They are cool, but very large, and so are very bright.

4) White dwarfs are found in the bottom-left. They are very hot, but small, so are dim.

5) Main sequence stars span the whole range of the graph diagonally from top-left to bottom-right. Since all main sequence stars are roughly the same size, the brighter the star, the higher the temperature.

Waves are Affected by the **Motion** of the **Source**

1) As you saw on page 53, when a source of waves is moving relative to the observer, the waves will undergo an change in frequency and wavelength when they are observed, compared to when they were emitted — this is the Doppler effect.

2) This happens with all types of waves, including light.

3) If the light source is moving away from you, the light it emits will be shifted towards the red end (i.e. the lower frequency end) of the visible part of the EM spectrum — this is red-shift.

4) Astronomers see this happening with the light that reaches us from distant galaxies. This light is red-shifted — we observe light with a longer wavelength (lower frequency) than we would expect these galaxies to emit. The galaxies must be moving away from the Earth.

Make sure you can draw a basic Hertzsprung-Russell diagram...

Remember that the axes on a Hertzsprung-Russell diagram are back to front — temperature decreases as you go along the x-axis, and absolute magnitude decreases as you go up the y-axis.

More on Red-Shift

Knowing <u>how much</u> the light from <u>galaxies</u> is <u>red-shifted</u> means you can <u>calculate</u> their <u>velocities</u>.

Light from **Galaxies** is **Red-shifted**

Most <u>galaxies</u> seem to be <u>moving away</u> from each other. There's good evidence for this:

1) Different elements <u>absorb</u> different <u>frequencies</u> (or wavelengths) of light.

2) When light is passed through a sample of an element, a <u>pattern</u> of <u>dark lines</u> is produced — with a dark line at each of the frequencies in the visible part of the EM spectrum that the element <u>absorbs</u>.

An absorption spectrum showing dark lines measured on Earth.

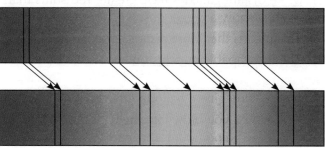

The same absorption spectrum measured from light from a distant galaxy. The dark lines in this spectrum are red-shifted.

3) When we look at <u>light from distant galaxies</u> we see the <u>same patterns</u> but at <u>slightly lower frequencies</u> (and so <u>longer wavelengths</u>) than they should be.

4) The patterns have been <u>shifted</u> towards the <u>red end</u> of the spectrum — <u>red-shift</u>.

Calculating Red-shift

You need to be able to make <u>calculations</u> involving red-shift.
The <u>amount</u> by which light from a galaxy is <u>red-shifted</u> is determined by the following formula:

$$\frac{\text{change in wavelength}}{\text{reference wavelength}} = \frac{\text{velocity of a galaxy}}{\text{speed of light}} \qquad \frac{\lambda - \lambda_0}{\lambda_0} = \frac{\Delta \lambda}{\lambda_0} = \frac{v}{c}$$

The 'reference wavelength' means the wavelength of the light when it was emitted, before it was red-shifted.

Example: A galaxy emits light with a <u>wavelength</u> of 410×10^{-9} m. The light is observed on Earth with a wavelength of 425×10^{-9} m. Calculate the <u>velocity</u> of the galaxy.

Answer: Rearrange the equation for velocity: The speed of light is 3.00×10^8 m/s.

$$v = \frac{\lambda - \lambda_0}{\lambda_0} \times c = \frac{(425 \times 10^{-9}) - (410 \times 10^{-9})}{410 \times 10^{-9}} \times 3.00 \times 10^8 = 1.0975... \times 10^7$$
$$= 1.10 \times 10^7 \text{ m/s (to 3 s.f.)}$$

You'll find standard form all over the place...

Physics covers everything from tiny particles to giant stars. That means dealing with <u>huge numbers</u> and with <u>tiny numbers</u>. So, unless you want to spend all day writing zeros, you've got to get used to using <u>standard form</u>. After all, writing 3.00×10^8 m/s is easier than writing 300 000 000 m/s.

Paper 2

The Big Bang

'How did it all begin?' is a tricky question. The most <u>widely-accepted theory</u> now is the <u>Big Bang theory</u>.

Red-shift Suggests the Universe is Expanding

1) <u>Measurements</u> of the red-shift suggest that <u>all the distant galaxies</u> are <u>moving away from us</u> very quickly — and it's the <u>same result</u> whichever direction you look in.

2) <u>More distant</u> galaxies have <u>greater</u> red-shifts than nearer ones — they show a <u>bigger</u> observed <u>increase</u> in <u>wavelength</u>.

3) This means that more distant galaxies are <u>moving away faster</u> than nearer ones.

4) The inescapable <u>conclusion</u> appears to be that the whole universe (space itself) is <u>expanding</u>.

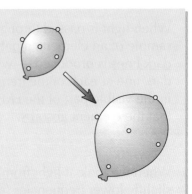

- Imagine a <u>balloon</u> covered with <u>pompoms</u>.
- As you <u>blow</u> into the balloon, it <u>stretches</u>. The pompoms move <u>further away</u> from each other.
- The balloon represents the <u>universe</u> and each pompom is a <u>galaxy</u>. As time goes on, <u>space stretches</u> and expands, moving the galaxies away from each other.
- This is a <u>simple model</u> (balloons only stretch <u>so far</u>) but it shows how the <u>expansion</u> of space makes it look like galaxies are <u>moving away</u> from us.

There's Microwave Radiation from All Directions

This is another <u>observation</u> that scientists made. It's not super interesting in itself, but the model that explains it definitely is.

1) Scientists can detect <u>low frequency microwave radiation</u> coming from <u>all directions</u> and <u>all parts</u> of the universe.

2) It's known as the <u>Cosmic Microwave Background (CMB) radiation</u>.

3) For complicated reasons this background radiation is strong evidence for an initial <u>Big Bang</u> (see below). As the universe <u>expands and cools</u>, this background radiation '<u>cools</u>' and <u>drops in frequency</u>.

This Evidence Suggests the Universe Started with a Bang

The galaxies are moving away from each other at great speed — suggesting something must have got them <u>going</u> from a <u>single starting point</u>. That 'something' was probably a <u>big explosion</u> — the <u>Big Bang</u>:

1) Initially, all the matter in the universe occupied <u>a single point</u>.
2) This tiny space was very <u>dense</u> and very <u>hot</u>.
3) This single point then '<u>exploded</u>' — the Big Bang.
4) Space started expanding, and the <u>expansion</u> is still going on.

According to the Big Bang model, <u>CMB</u> radiation is the <u>leftover radiation</u> from this initial explosion.

We can't say for sure if the Big Bang theory is correct...

...it's just the <u>best theory</u> that we have <u>at the moment</u> — but <u>new evidence</u> might mean it needs adapting.

Warm-Up & Exam Questions

You're so close to the end of the section. Time for just a few more questions before you can take a break, have a brew and give yourself a pat on the back for making it this far.

Warm-Up Questions

1) True or false? The larger the mass of a star, the more time it spends on the main sequence.
2) Explain why very hot stars appear blue.
3) Give one reason why a dim star might look as bright as a very bright star when seen from Earth.
4) What does red-shift suggest about the motion of galaxies?

Exam Questions

1 The diagram below shows the life cycle of a star. *(Grade 4-6)*

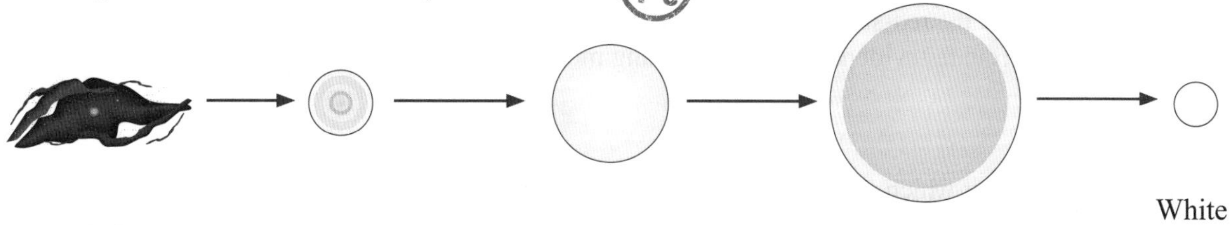

| Nebula | Protostar | Main sequence star | X | White dwarf |

(a) What is the name of the life cycle stage marked X?

☐ **A** red supergiant   ☐ **B** red giant   ☐ **C** red dwarf   ☐ **D** neutron star

[1 mark]

(b) State what is meant by a **nebula**.

[1 mark]

(c) Name the force responsible for 'pulling together' a nebula as it begins to form a star.

[1 mark]

2 The table below shows some properties of a number of stars. *(Grade 4-6)*

(a) Which of the following shows the stars in the correct order of hottest to coolest?

☐ **A** Megrez, Alkaid, Pollux
☐ **B** Alkaid, Pollux, Megrez
☐ **C** Pollux, Megrez, Alkaid
☐ **D** Alkaid, Megrez, Pollux

Star	Absolute Magnitude	Colour
Megrez	+1.3	White
Pollux	+1.1	Orange
Alkaid	−0.6	Blue

[1 mark]

PAPER 2

(b) State and explain which of the stars in the table is the brightest.

[2 marks]

Exam Questions

3   The table shows a list of galaxies and their distance from Earth in light years.

Galaxy	Distance From Earth (light years)
Cigar Galaxy	12 million
Black Eye Galaxy	24 million
Sunflower Galaxy	37 million
Tadpole Galaxy	420 million

1 light year ≈ 9.5×10^{15} m

The light from the galaxies in the table shows red-shift.

(a)   From which of the galaxies in the table would you expect the light to show the greatest red-shift? Explain your answer.

[3 marks]

(b)   Explain how the red-shift of light from distant galaxies provides evidence for the Big Bang model.

[4 marks]

4   Betelgeuse is a star which is much more massive than our Sun.

Describe the life cycle of a massive star like Betelgeuse, beginning from a cloud of dust and gas.

[6 marks]

5   An astronomer is analysing the light received from a distant galaxy, known as Hoag's Object.

To do this, she compares the absorption lines of helium observed in the light from Hoag's Object with the known absorption spectrum of helium on Earth. Part of the known absorption spectrum of helium is shown below.

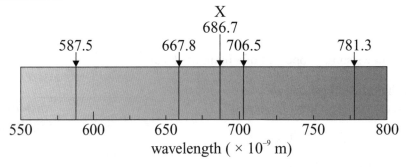

The astronomer notices that the absorption line for light with a reference wavelength, λ_0, of 587.5×10^{-9} m in the known spectrum appears to correspond to a wavelength of 612.5×10^{-9} m in the light received from Hoag's Object. The speed of light in free space, $c = 3.0 \times 10^8$ m/s.

(a)   Calculate the velocity of Hoag's Object.

[3 marks]

(b)   Calculate the wavelength at which the absorption line marked X in the spectrum above will appear in the light received from Hoag's Object.

[3 marks]

Revision Questions for Section 8

Stellar job, you've finished <u>Section 8</u> — now stop gazing at stars and shift your attention to some questions...
- Try these questions and <u>tick off each one</u> when you <u>get it right</u>.
- When you've done <u>all the questions</u> under a heading and are <u>completely happy</u> with it, tick it off.

Galaxies, Our Solar System and Orbits (p.144-146) ☑

1) How many galaxies are in the universe?
2) What force causes the orbits of moons, planets, comets and satellites?
3) How do the orbits of comets differ from the orbits of moons and planets?
4) Write down the formula that you would use to calculate the orbital speed of an object, assuming that its orbit was circular and that you knew its orbital radius and time period.

The Life Cycle of Stars (p.148) ☑

5) What causes the rise in temperature that leads to nuclear fusion in a protostar?
6) What causes a main sequence star to remain stable for a long time?
7) What happens to a star about the same size as our Sun when it's core begins to run out of hydrogen?
8) What is a white dwarf and how is it made?
9) True or false? The Sun will eventually turn into a black hole.

Classification of Stars, Red-shift and the Big Bang (p.148-152) ☑

10) What colour of star has the lowest surface temperature?
11) True or false? The higher the absolute magnitude, the brighter the star.
12) Sketch the Hertzsprung-Russell diagram and label the regions of the graph corresponding to white dwarfs, main sequence stars, red giants and red supergiants.
13) What is red-shift?
14) *A galaxy is moving away from Earth at a velocity of 7.8×10^6 m/s. The light from the galaxy is red-shifted by 15×10^{-9} m when observed from the Earth. Calculate the original wavelength of the light emitted by the galaxy.
15) True or false? Very distant galaxies are moving away faster than ones closer to us.
16) What does CMB stand for?
17) Briefly describe the ideas that make up the Big Bang theory.

*Answer on page 215.

Experimental Know-How

Scientists need to know how to plan and carry out experiments. They also need to know how to interpret and evaluate the data they collect. Unluckily for you, the examiners think you should be able to do the same. But don't worry — that's what this topic is all about...

You Might Get Asked Questions on Reliability and Validity

1) RELIABLE results come from experiments that give similar data:

- each time the experiment is repeated (by you),
- each time the experiment is reproduced by other scientists.

2) VALID results are both reliable AND come from experiments that were designed to be a fair test.

In the exam, you could be asked to suggest ways to improve the reliability or validity of some experimental results. If so, there are a couple of things to think about:

Controlling Variables Improves Validity

1) A variable is something that has the potential to change, e.g. mass.
In a lab experiment you usually change one variable and measure how it affects another variable.

> Example: you might change only the mass of a toy car travelling down a ramp and measure how this affects its average speed.

2) To make it a fair test, everything else that could affect the results should stay the same — otherwise you can't tell if the thing you're changing is causing the results or not.

> Example continued: you need to keep the angle of the ramp the same, otherwise you won't know whether any change in average speed is caused by the change in angle of the ramp or the difference in mass of the car.

3) The variable you CHANGE is called the INDEPENDENT variable.
The variable you MEASURE is called the DEPENDENT variable.
The variables that you KEEP THE SAME are called CONTROL variables.

> Example continued:
> Independent variable = mass of toy car
> Dependent variable = average speed of toy car
> Control variables = angle of ramp, position of car release, material of ramp etc.

4) Make sure you think about how you'll control these variables, e.g. you could use a ruler to make sure you release the car from the same position each time.

5) Because you can't always control all the variables, you often need to use a control experiment — an experiment that's kept under the same conditions as the rest of the investigation, but doesn't have anything done to it. This is so you can see what happens when you don't change anything.

Carrying Out Repeats Improves Reliability

1) There will usually be differences between any sets of measurements you take, so you should make sure you repeat your measurements at least three times and calculate the mean (average).

2) Repeats with small differences between them show that your measurements are reliable — that they are similar and can be repeated.

Experimental Know-How

Thought you knew <u>everything</u> there was to know about experiments? <u>Think again</u> my friend...

You Might Have to **Suggest Ways** to Make an **Experiment Safer**

1) It's important that experiments are safe. If you're asked to suggest ways to make an experiment safer, you'll first need to identify what the <u>potential hazards</u> might be. Hazards include things like:

> <u>Light sources</u>, e.g. if a laser is directed into the eye, this can cause blindness.
> <u>Radiation</u>, e.g. radiation from radioactive sources can cause cancer.
> <u>Fire</u>, e.g. an unattended heater is a fire hazard.
> <u>Electricity</u>, e.g. faulty electrical equipment could give you a shock.

2) Then you'll need to suggest ways of <u>reducing</u> the <u>risks</u> involved with the hazard, e.g.:

> If you're working with <u>springs</u>, always wear <u>safety goggles</u>. This will reduce the risk of the spring hitting your eye if the spring snaps.
>
> If you're using a <u>heater</u> to raise the temperature of something, stand the apparatus on a <u>heatproof mat</u>. This will reduce the risk of starting a fire.

You can find out about potential hazards by looking in textbooks, doing some internet research, or asking your teacher.

You Could be Asked About **Accuracy**...

1) It's important that results are <u>accurate</u>. Accurate results are those that are <u>very close</u> to the <u>true answer</u>.
2) The accuracy of your results usually depends on your <u>method</u>.

> <u>Example</u>: Say you want to estimate the <u>volume</u> of an irregularly shaped solid. Working out its volume by <u>measuring its sides</u> isn't very accurate, because this won't include any gaps in the object. You'd get a <u>more accurate</u> result by submerging the object in a <u>eureka can</u> filled with water (see page 101) and measuring the volume of water that it displaces.

3) To make sure your results are as <u>accurate</u> as possible, make sure you're measuring the <u>right thing</u> and that you <u>don't miss</u> anything, or <u>include</u> anything that shouldn't be included in the measurements.

> <u>Example continued</u>: if you're using a eureka can to measure the volume of an object, make sure the object is <u>completely submerged</u> before measuring the volume of the displaced water. Otherwise your result will be <u>too small</u>.

...And **Precision**

Results also need to be <u>precise</u>. Precise results are ones where the data is <u>all really close</u> to the <u>mean</u> (average) of your repeated results (i.e. not spread out).

Sometimes, results are described as precise if they've been taken using sensitive instruments that can measure in small increments, e.g. using a ruler with a millimetre scale gives more precise data than a ruler with a scale in centimetres.

Repeat	Data set 1	Data set 2
1	12	11
2	14	17
3	13	14
Mean	13	14

Data set 1 is more precise than data set 2.

Safety is the most important thing in any experiment...

If you're planning an <u>experiment</u> (or answering a <u>question</u> about an experiment in an exam), you'll need to be able to spot any <u>hazards</u> and suggest <u>safety measures</u> you could take to reduce the <u>risks</u>.

Anomalous Results and Processing Data

Once you've collected your data, you might need to _process_ it — that just means doing things like finding the _average_ of your repeated readings. You'll need to watch out for _anomalous results_ too.

You Should Be Able to Identify **Anomalous Results**

1) Most results vary a bit, but any that are _totally different_ are called _anomalous results_.

2) They're usually _caused_ by _human errors_, e.g. by a mistake made when measuring, or by not setting up a piece of equipment properly.

3) You could be asked to _identify_ an anomalous result in the exam and suggest what _caused_ it — just look for a result that _doesn't fit in_ with the rest (e.g. it's _too high_ or _too low_) then try to figure out what could have _gone wrong_ with the experiment to have caused it.

4) If you're calculating an _average_, you can _ignore_ any anomalous results.

You Might Have to **Process Your Data**

1) When you've done repeats of an experiment you should always calculate the _mean_ (a type of average). To do this _add together_ all the data values and _divide_ by the number of repeats.

2) You might also need to calculate the _range_ (how spread out the data is). To do this find the _largest_ number and _subtract_ the _smallest_ number from it.

Ignore anomalous results when calculating these.

Example: The table below shows the results of an experiment to find the _extension_ of two _springs_ when a certain _force_ was applied to both of them.

Calculate the _mean_ and _range_ for the extension for both springs.

Spring	Repeat 1 (mm)	Repeat 2 (mm)	Repeat 3 (mm)
A	28	37	31
B	47	52	60

Answer: Spring A: mean = (28 + 37 + 31) ÷ 3 = 32 mm   range = 37 − 28 = 9 mm

Spring B: mean = (47 + 52 + 60) ÷ 3 = 53 mm   range = 60 − 47 = 13 mm

Don't forget your calculator...

EXAM TIP

In the exam you could be given some _data_ and be expected to _process it_ in some way. Make sure that you remember to _write down your working_ and _check your answer_ when you've finished.

Drawing Graphs

Presenting your results in a <u>chart</u> or <u>graph</u> can help you to <u>spot patterns</u> in your data...

Bar Charts can be Used to Show Different Types of Data

<u>Bar charts</u> are used to display:

1) <u>Categoric data</u> — data that comes in <u>distinct categories</u>, e.g. solid, liquid, gas.

2) <u>Discrete data</u> — data that can be counted in <u>chunks</u>, where there's no in-between value, e.g. number of protons is discrete because you can't have half a proton.

3) <u>Continuous data</u> — <u>numerical</u> data that can have any <u>value</u> in a <u>range</u>, e.g. length, volume, temperature.

There are some <u>golden rules</u> you need to follow for <u>drawing</u> bar charts:

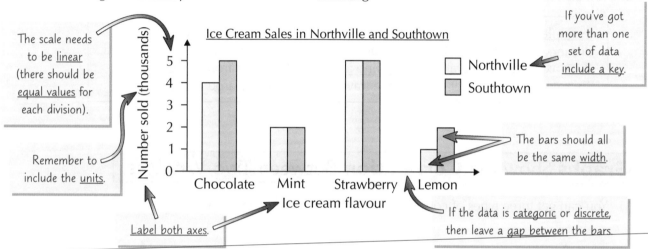

The scale needs to be <u>linear</u> (there should be <u>equal values</u> for each division).

If you've got more than one set of data <u>include a key</u>.

Remember to include the <u>units</u>.

The bars should all be the same <u>width</u>.

<u>Label both axes</u>.

If the data is <u>categoric</u> or <u>discrete</u>, then leave a <u>gap between the bars</u>.

Graphs can be Used to Plot Continuous Data

Whether you're drawing a bar chart or a graph, make it <u>nice and big</u> — it should cover <u>at least half</u> of the graph paper).

1) If both variables are <u>continuous</u> you should use a <u>graph</u> to display the data.

2) Here are the rules for plotting points on a graph:

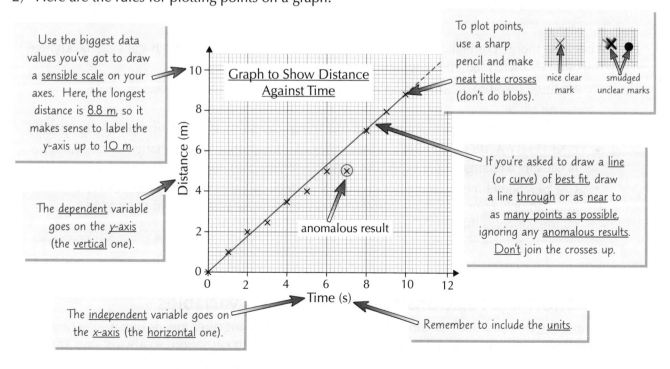

Use the biggest data values you've got to draw a <u>sensible scale</u> on your axes. Here, the longest distance is <u>8.8 m</u>, so it makes sense to label the y-axis up to <u>10 m</u>.

The <u>dependent</u> variable goes on the <u>y-axis</u> (the <u>vertical</u> one).

To plot points, use a sharp pencil and make <u>neat little crosses</u> (don't do blobs).

nice clear mark

smudged unclear marks

If you're asked to draw a <u>line</u> (or <u>curve</u>) of <u>best fit</u>, draw a line <u>through</u> or as <u>near</u> to as <u>many points as possible</u>, ignoring any <u>anomalous results</u>. <u>Don't</u> join the crosses up.

anomalous result

The <u>independent</u> variable goes on the <u>x-axis</u> (the <u>horizontal</u> one).

Remember to include the <u>units</u>.

Describing Experiments

Interpreting Results

Graphs aren't just fun to plot — they're also really useful for showing <u>trends</u> in your data...

You Need to be Able to **Interpret** Graphs

1) A graph is used to show the <u>relationship</u> between two variables —
   you need to be able to look at a graph and <u>describe</u> this relationship.

> <u>Example</u>: The graph on the previous page shows
> that <u>as time goes on</u>, <u>the distance increases</u> and
> that the distance is <u>directly proportional</u> to time.

A relationship is directly proportional if one variable increases at the same rate as the other variable. E.g. if one variable doubles, the other also doubles. This is only true if the line is straight and goes through the origin (O, O).

2) You also need to be able to <u>read information</u> from a graph.

> <u>Example</u>: On the graph on the previous page, if you wanted to know the
> distance travelled after <u>8.2 s</u>, you'd draw a <u>vertical line up</u> to the graph line from
> the x-axis at <u>8.2 s</u> and a <u>horizontal line across</u> to the y-axis from the graph line.
> This would tell you that the distance travelled in <u>8.2 s</u> was around <u>7.2 m</u>.

Graphs Show the **Correlation** Between Two Variables

1) You can get <u>three</u> types of <u>correlation</u> (relationship) between variables:

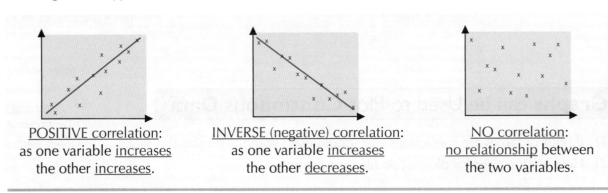

<u>POSITIVE</u> correlation:
as one variable <u>increases</u>
the other <u>increases</u>.

<u>INVERSE (negative)</u> correlation:
as one variable <u>increases</u>
the other <u>decreases</u>.

<u>NO</u> correlation:
<u>no relationship</u> between
the two variables.

1) Just because there's correlation, it doesn't mean the change in one variable is <u>causing</u> the change
   in the other — there might be <u>other factors</u> involved.

2) There are <u>three possible reasons</u> for a correlation:

- <u>CHANCE</u>: It might seem strange, but two things can show a correlation purely by <u>chance</u>.
- <u>LINKED BY A 3RD VARIABLE</u>: A lot of the time it may <u>look</u> as if a change in one variable
  is causing a change in the other, but it <u>isn't</u> — a <u>third variable links</u> the two things.
- <u>CAUSE</u>: Sometimes a change in one variable does <u>cause</u> a change in the other.
  You can only conclude that a correlation is due to cause when you've <u>controlled</u>
  <u>all the variables</u> that could, just could, be affecting the result.

A correlation is a relationship between two variables

It's <u>really important</u> that you don't assume that two things changing together means one is affecting the
other — examiners really won't like it if you confuse <u>correlation</u> with <u>causation</u>, so always stop and think.

Calculating Rates from Graphs

You can work out rates of change using graphs — but you have to know how to find the gradients of lines.

Graphs Can Give You a Lot of Information About Your Data

If you have a graph of distance against time, the gradient (slope) of the graph will be equal to the speed — the steeper the slope, the faster the speed. The gradient of a straight line is given by the equation:

gradient = change in y ÷ change in x

Example: The graph on the right shows the distance travelled by a bike against time. Here's how you find the bike's speed:

1) Find two points on the line that are easy to read the x and y values of (ones that pass through grid lines).

2) Draw a line straight down from the higher point and straight across from the lower one to make a triangle.

3) The height of your triangle = change in y
   The base of your triangle = change in x
   Change in y = 32 − 10 = 22   Change in x = 6.5 − 2 = 4.5

4) Use the formula to work out the gradient, and therefore the speed.
   Gradient = change in y ÷ change in x = 22 ÷ 4.5 = 4.9 m/s (to 2 s.f.)

   The units of the gradient are (units of y)/(units of x).

You can use this method to calculate other rates from a graph, not just the rate of change of distance (which is speed).

Draw a Tangent to Find the Gradient of a Curve

1) If your graph is a curve, the gradient, and therefore rate, is different at different points along the curve.

2) To find the gradient of the graph at a certain point, you'll have to draw a tangent at that point.

3) A tangent is just a line that touches the curve and has the same gradient as the line at that point.

4) To draw a tangent, place a ruler on the line of best fit at the point you're interested in, so you can see the whole curve. Adjust the ruler so the space between the ruler and the curve is the same on both sides of the point. Draw a line along the ruler to make the tangent.

5) The rate at that point is then just the gradient of the tangent.

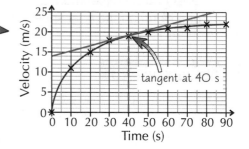

tangent at 40 s

Example: Look at the graph below, which shows the velocity of a vehicle, measured at regular intervals. Here's how you'd find the acceleration of the vehicle at 60 seconds:

1) Position a ruler on the graph at the point where you want to know the rate — here it's 60 s.

2) Adjust the ruler until the space between the ruler and the curve is equal on both sides of the point.

3) Draw a line along the ruler to make the tangent. Extend the line right across the graph.

4) Pick two points on the line that are easy to read. Use them to calculate the gradient of the tangent — this is the acceleration (see page 2):

   gradient = change in y ÷ change in x
   = (22 − 14) ÷ (100 − 40) = 8 ÷ 60 = 0.13 m/s² (to 2 s.f.)
   So the acceleration of the vehicle at 60 seconds was 0.13 m/s²

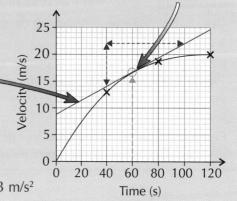

Planning Experiments

In the exam, you could be asked to <u>describe</u> how you'd <u>carry out</u> an experiment. It might be one you've already come across, or you might be asked to come up with an <u>experiment of your own</u>.

Experiments Test Hypotheses

1) A <u>hypothesis</u> is a possible <u>explanation</u> for something that you've observed.

2) You can use experiments to <u>test</u> whether a hypothesis might be <u>right or not</u>. This involves making a <u>prediction</u> based on the hypothesis and testing it by <u>gathering evidence</u> (i.e. data) from <u>investigations</u>. If <u>evidence</u> from <u>experiments</u> backs up a prediction, you're a step closer to figuring out if the hypothesis is true.

You Need to Be Able to Plan a Good Experiment

Here are some <u>general tips</u> on what to include when planning an experiment:

1) Say <u>what</u> you're <u>measuring</u> (i.e. what the <u>dependent variable</u> is going to be).

Even if you can't remember all the details of a method you've learned about, you could still get marks for describing things like the independent and dependent variables.

2) Say <u>what</u> you're <u>changing</u> (i.e. what the <u>independent variable</u> is going to be) and describe <u>how</u> you're going to change it.

3) Describe the <u>method</u> and the <u>apparatus</u> you'd use.

4) Describe what <u>variables</u> you're keeping <u>constant</u> — and <u>how</u> you're going to do it.

5) Say that you need to <u>repeat</u> the experiment at least three times, to make the results <u>more reliable</u>.

6) Say whether you're using a <u>control</u> or not.

Here's an <u>idea</u> of the sort of thing you might be asked in the exam and what you might write as an answer...

Exam-style Question:

1 Describe an experiment to investigate the effect of changing the angle of a ramp on the final speed of a toy car released at the top of it. (6 marks)

Example Answer:

In this experiment you should change the angle of the ramp. You can see what effect this has by measuring the average speed of the toy car on a flat section of track at the bottom of the ramp.

Measure the angle of the ramp with a protractor. Set up a flat runway at the bottom of the ramp, then put one light gate near the start of the runway and one light gate near the end of it. Measure the distance between the light gates with a ruler. Ensure the light gates are connected to a computer with data-logging software to record the time taken for the car to pass between them. Hold the car still at the top of the ramp, then let go so that it rolls down the ramp onto the runway. Record the time taken for the car to pass between the gates. Calculate the final speed of the car by dividing the distance between the gates by this time.

Carry out the experiment again with the ramp at different angles (e.g. 35°, 30°, 25° and 20°).

A line should be marked on the ramp to ensure that the car is released from the same position each time. The same car should be used each time and the car should not be changed in any way. The same ramp and runway should be used each time.

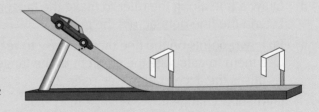

Repeat the experiment three times for each angle of the ramp and calculate an average speed for each angle.

Drawing Conclusions

Once you've carried out an experiment and processed your data, it's time to work out <u>what it shows</u>.

You Can **Only Conclude** What the Data Shows and **No More**

1) Drawing conclusions might seem pretty straightforward — you just <u>look at your data</u> and <u>say what pattern or relationship you see</u> between the dependent and independent variables.

> <u>Example</u>: A Geiger-Müller counter is set up to measure the <u>count rate</u> a set distance away from a gamma radiation source (see page 131). The table shows the count rate <u>before</u> and <u>after</u> a sheet of paper is placed between the source and the counter:
>
> | Obstacle | Count rate in counts per second (cps) |
> |----------|---------------------------------------|
> | None | 15 |
> | Paper sheet | 15 |
>
> <u>Conclusion</u>:
> Gamma radiation is able to pass through a paper sheet.

2) But you've got to be really careful that your conclusion <u>matches the data</u> you've got and <u>doesn't go any further</u>.

> <u>Example continued</u>: You <u>can't</u> conclude that <u>every</u> type of radiation can pass through paper — the results might be completely different for other radiation types.

3) You also need to be able to <u>use your results</u> to <u>justify your conclusion</u> (i.e. back up your conclusion with some specific data).

> <u>Example continued</u>: The <u>same amount</u> of radiation passed through to the counter both before and after the paper was inserted, as the count rates were both the same at <u>15 cps</u>.

4) When writing a conclusion you need to <u>refer back</u> to the original hypothesis and say whether the data <u>supports it</u> or not:

> <u>Example continued</u>: The hypothesis for this experiment might have been that gamma radiation can pass through a paper sheet. If so, the data <u>supports</u> the hypothesis.

Your conclusions have to be consistent with your evidence

That means you have to be <u>careful</u> you're only writing things based on your experiment's results — you need to be able to <u>back up</u> anything you say using your data. And remember, your data might not match the original hypothesis. That's fine — just point this out in your <u>conclusion</u>.

Evaluations

Hurrah! The end of another investigation. Well, now you have to work out all the things you did <u>wrong</u>. That's what <u>evaluations</u> are all about I'm afraid. Best get cracking with this page...

Evaluations — Describe **How** Investigations Could be **Improved**

An evaluation is a <u>critical analysis</u> of the whole investigation.

1) You should comment on the <u>method</u> — was it <u>valid</u>?
   Did you control all the other variables to make it a <u>fair test</u>?

2) Comment on the <u>quality</u> of the <u>results</u> — was there <u>enough evidence</u> to reach a valid <u>conclusion</u>? Were the results <u>reliable</u>, <u>valid</u>, <u>accurate</u> and <u>precise</u>?

3) Were there any <u>anomalous</u> results? If there were <u>none</u> then <u>say so</u>.
   If there were any, try to <u>explain</u> them — were they caused by <u>errors</u> in measurement?
   Were there any other <u>variables</u> that could have <u>affected</u> the results?

4) All this analysis will allow you to say how <u>confident</u> you are that your conclusion is <u>right</u>.

5) Then you can suggest any <u>changes</u> to the <u>method</u> that would <u>improve</u> the quality of the results, so that you could have <u>more confidence</u> in your conclusion. For example, you might suggest <u>changing</u> the way you controlled a variable, or <u>increasing</u> the number of <u>measurements</u> you took. Taking more measurements at <u>narrower intervals</u> could give you a <u>more accurate result</u>.

> <u>Example</u>: <u>Springs</u> stop returning to their original shape when they are stretched past their <u>elastic limit</u>. Say you do an <u>experiment</u> to find the elastic limit of a certain type of spring by taking measurements for applied forces of 1 N, 2 N, 3 N, 4 N and 5 N. The results of this experiment tell you that the elastic limit is at <u>4 N</u>.
> You could then <u>repeat</u> the experiment using the same type of spring, but taking <u>more measurements around 4 N</u> to get a <u>more accurate</u> value for the elastic limit.

When suggesting improvements to an investigation, always make sure that you say why you think this would make the results better.

6) You could also make more <u>predictions</u> based on your conclusion, then <u>further experiments</u> could be carried out to test them.

 Always look for ways to improve your investigations

There are marks on offer in the exams for experimental skills — things like describing experiments, analysing data and evaluating methods. So make sure you're happy with everything in this section.

Equations Page

Here are some equations that might be useful when you're doing the practice papers — you'll be given these equations in the real exams. The first section is for both papers, the second section is just for Paper 2.

(final speed)^2 = (initial speed)^2 + (2 × acceleration × distance moved) $$v^2 = u^2 + (2 \times a \times s)$$	
energy transferred = current × voltage × time	$E = I \times V \times t$
frequency $= \dfrac{1}{\text{time period}}$	$f = \dfrac{1}{T}$
power $= \dfrac{\text{work done}}{\text{time taken}}$	$P = \dfrac{W}{t}$
power $= \dfrac{\text{energy transferred}}{\text{time taken}}$	$P = \dfrac{W}{t}$
pressure × volume = constant	$p_1 \times V_1 = p_2 \times V_2$
$\dfrac{\text{pressure}}{\text{temperature}} = \text{constant}$	$\dfrac{p_1}{T_1} = \dfrac{p_2}{T_2}$
orbital speed $= \dfrac{2\pi \times \text{orbital radius}}{\text{time period}}$	$v = \dfrac{2 \times \pi \times r}{T}$
Assume that acceleration due to gravity is $g = 10$ m/s^2.	

PAPER 2

force $= \dfrac{\text{change in momentum}}{\text{time taken}}$	$F = \dfrac{(mv - mu)}{t}$
change in thermal energy = mass × specific heat capacity × change in temperature $$\Delta Q = m \times c \times \Delta T$$	
$\dfrac{\text{change of wavelength}}{\text{wavelength}} = \dfrac{\text{velocity of a galaxy}}{\text{speed of light}}$ $$\dfrac{\lambda - \lambda_0}{\lambda_0} = \dfrac{\Delta \lambda}{\lambda_0} = \dfrac{v}{c}$$	

Candidate Surname	Candidate Forename(s)

Centre Number	Candidate Number

Edexcel
International GCSE

Physics
Paper 1P

Practice Paper
Time allowed: 2 hours

You must have:
*   A ruler.
*   A calculator.

Total marks:

Instructions to candidates
*   Use **black** ink to write your answers.
*   Write your name and other details in the spaces provided above.
*   Answer **all** questions in the spaces provided.
*   In calculations, show clearly how you worked out your answers.
*   You will need to answer some questions by placing a cross in a box, like this: ☒
    To change your answer, draw a line through the box like this: ☒
    Then mark your new answer as normal.

Information for candidates
*   The marks available are given in brackets at the end of each question.
*   There are 110 marks available for this paper.
*   You might find the equations on page 165 useful.

Advice for candidates
*   Read all the questions carefully.
*   Write your answers as clearly and neatly as possible.
*   Keep in mind how much time you have left.

Answer **all** questions

1   At the start of a roller coaster ride a carriage is raised by a chain lift through a vertical height of 40 m to point W, as shown in the diagram. It is stopped at point W and then released to follow the track through points X, Y and Z.

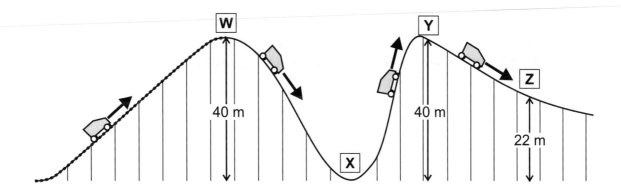

(a) (i) At which two points does the carriage have the same amount of energy in its gravitational potential energy store?

☐ **A** X and Z

☐ **B** W and Y

☐ **C** Y and Z

☐ **D** W and Z

[1]

(ii) At which point does the carriage have the most energy in its kinetic energy store?

☐ **A** W

☐ **B** X

☐ **C** Y

☐ **D** Z

[1]

Turn over ▶

(b)   The mass of the carriage and the people in it is 1500 kg.
       The Earth's gravitational field strength is 10 N/kg.

   (i) State the equation linking gravitational potential energy, mass, height and
        gravitational field strength.

        ....
                                                                                                            [1]

   (ii) Calculate the energy transferred to the gravitational potential energy store (in kJ)
         of a full carriage as it is raised by the chain lift to point W.

                                    Energy = ... kJ
                                                                                                            [2]

(c) (i) A different type of roller coaster uses a spring system to launch a carriage forward.
         State the energy store that energy is transferred from when a compressed spring is
         used to launch a roller coaster carriage.

        ....
                                                                                                            [1]

   (ii) State the equation linking efficiency, useful energy output and total energy output.

        ....
                                                                                                            [1]

   (iii) The spring system transfers 18.0 kJ of energy to the kinetic energy store of a carriage.
         However, the system also wastes 41.5 kJ of energy, transferred to useless thermal energy
         stores and carried away by sound. Calculate the efficiency of the spring system.
         Give your answer to an appropriate number of significant figures.

                                    Efficiency = ... %
                                                                                                            [3]
                                                                                          [Total 10 marks]

2   A swimmer swims one length of a 20 m swimming pool in a straight line.
The diagram below shows the distance-time graph of her motion.

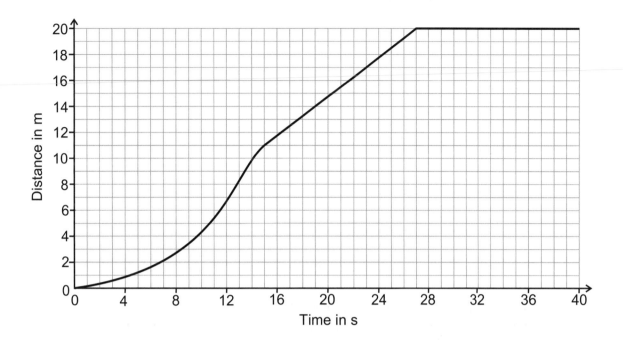

(a)   Determine the time it takes for the swimmer to complete the length.

Time = ... s

[1]

(b) (i)   For part of her swim, the swimmer is travelling at a constant speed.
Calculate the time she spends travelling at a constant speed.

Time = ... s

[1]

(ii)   State the resultant force on the swimmer when she is travelling
at a constant speed.

Force = ... N

[1]

(c)   Between which of the following **distances** was the swimmer travelling fastest?

☐   **A**   between 13 m and 14 m

☐   **B**   between 9 m and 10 m

☐   **C**   between 0 m and 1 m

☐   **D**   between 17 m and 18 m

[1]

Turn over ▶

A camera travels along the length of the pool to film the swimmer. It starts at the same time as the swimmer, travels at a constant speed, and reaches the end of the pool in 25 s.

(d) (i) State the equation which links speed, distance moved and time taken.

....

[1]

(ii) Calculate the speed of the camera.

Speed = ... m/s

[2]

(iii) On the diagram, draw a distance-time graph to represent the motion of the camera.

[2]

(e) The camera cannot film the swimmer if it is behind her.
Explain whether the camera will be able to film the swimmer for the whole length.
You should refer to the distance-time graphs in your answer.

....

....

....

....

[2]

[Total 11 marks]

3 A student wanted to model how the thickness of an insulating layer affects how quickly the water in a hot water tank cools.

To model this system in the lab, she carried out an investigation to test how the thickness of a cotton wool jacket affected the rate of cooling of a beaker of hot water.
The apparatus she used is shown in the diagram below.

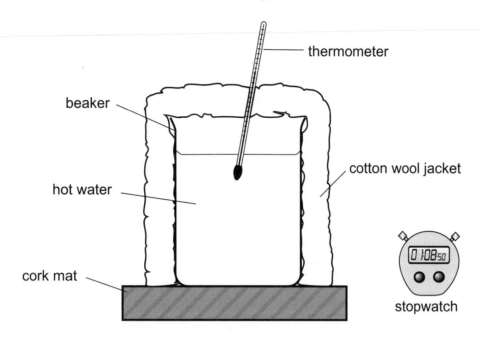

(a) State the independent variable in this investigation.

....

[1]

(b) State **one** control variable in this investigation.

....

....

[1]

(c) The cotton wool jacket traps tiny pockets of air between the beaker and its surroundings.
Explain how this reduces the rate of energy transfer away from the beaker by convection.

....

....

[2]

(d) The student decides to record the water's temperature after 3 minutes.
For each thickness of cotton wool jacket, she repeats this process three times.

   (i) Describe how the student could process her repeated results to get one value
for the final water temperature for each thickness of insulating layer.

....

....

[1]

Turn over ▶

(ii) The student's results are shown in the sketch below.

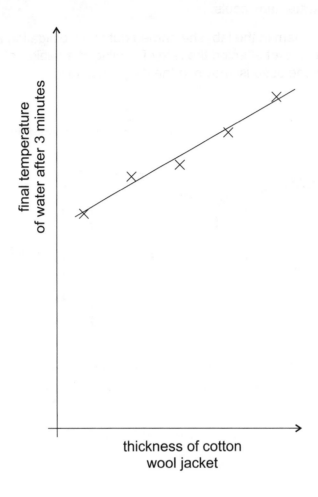

thickness of cotton
wool jacket

Use the graph to write a suitable conclusion for this investigation.

....

....

[1]

[Total 6 marks]

4   A driving instructor has been looking at the Highway Code. He has found the following data about thinking and braking distances for a car travelling on dry roads at various speeds.

Speed (m/s)	Thinking distance (m)	Braking distance (m)
9	6	6
13	9	14
18	12	24
22	15	38
27	18	55
31	21	75

(a)   Calculate the stopping distance for a speed of 13 m/s.

Stopping distance = ... m

[1]

(b)   The data in the table was obtained by observing a large number of vehicles and drivers. Explain why it was sensible to collect the data this way.

....

....

....

[2]

(c)   Describe **three** different factors, other than speed, that can increase the stopping distance of a car. State whether each one affects the thinking distance or the braking distance.

1. ....

....

2. ....

....

3. ....

....

[5]

[Total 8 marks]

Turn over ▶

5   An artificial satellite orbits the Earth in an almost circular path, as shown in the diagram. It takes 1 day to orbit the Earth.

(a)   Name the force that keeps the satellite in orbit around the Earth.

....

[1]

(b)   The satellite has an orbital speed of 3080 m/s. Calculate the radius of the satellite's orbit.

Radius = ... m

[3]

The Earth orbits the Sun. Another planet that orbits the Sun is Venus.
The gravitational field strength on Venus is approximately 9 N/kg.

(c)   Compare the weight of the same object on Venus and on Earth. Explain your answer.

....

....

....

[2]

The Sun is a main sequence star. Main sequence stars are fuelled by the nuclear fusion of hydrogen nuclei into helium nuclei. When the amount of hydrogen in the core of the Sun begins to run out, it will change into a different kind of star.

(d)   Name the kind of star the Sun will become when it begins to run out of hydrogen in its core.

....

[1]

[Total 7 marks]

6   A student investigates a material that emits ionising radiation. He uses a detector to measure the activity of a sample of the radioactive material every minute.
His results are shown in the table.

Time (minutes)	0	1	2	3	4	5	6
Activity (becquerels)	80	60	45	34	25	19	14

(a)   Give **two** dangers of exposure to ionising radiation.

1. ....

2. ....

[2]

(b)   Suggest **one** piece of equipment that could have been used to measure the activity of the sample.

....

[1]

(c) (i)   Plot the student's data on the grid below.

[3]

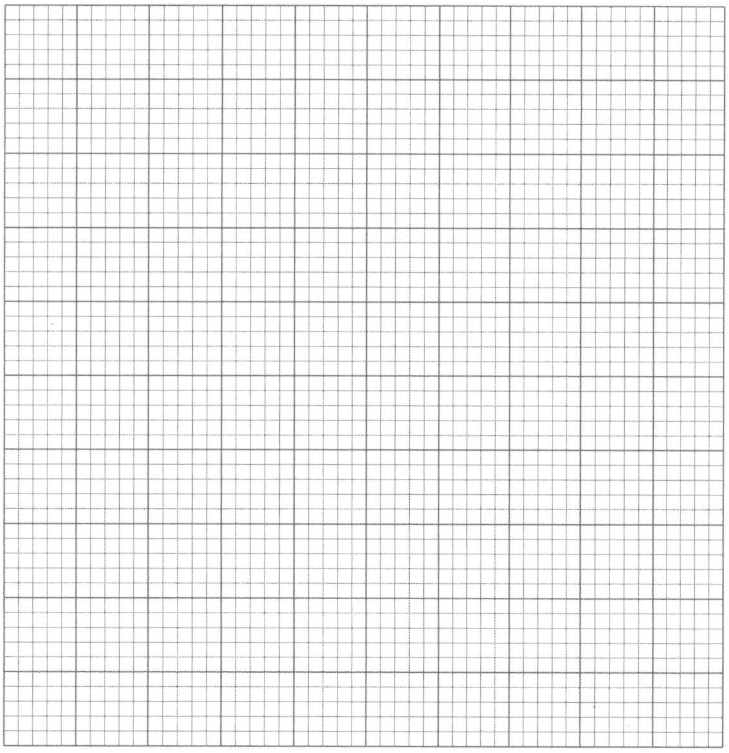

(ii)   Draw a curve of best fit on the graph.

[2]

(iii)   Use the graph to find the half-life of this radioactive material.

Half-life = ... min

[2]

Turn over ▶

(d)   After the experiment is finished, the radioactive sample is stored in another part of the building. The detector still picks up background radiation in the laboratory.

Give **one** source that may contribute to this background radiation.

....

....

[1]

(e) (i)   Another radioactive isotope, radium-226, decays by alpha emission.
Fill in the blanks in the reaction below to show the alpha emission.

$$^{226}_{88}Ra \rightarrow ^{222}_{.....}Rn + ^{.....}_{2}\alpha$$

[1]

(ii)   How many protons does the radium-226 (Ra) nucleus shown in part (i) have?

☐ **A**   226

☐ **B**   138

☐ **C**   88

☐ **D**   222

[1]

[Total 13 marks]

7   A student wanted to know how the current flowing through a filament lamp changes with the voltage across it. He set up this circuit.

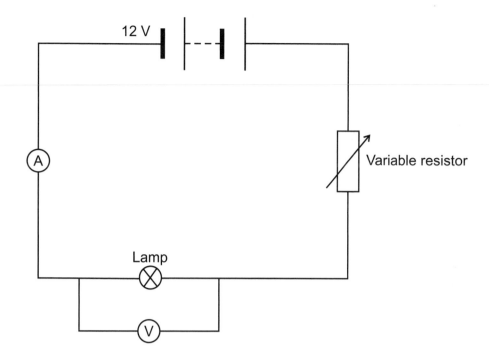

He used a variable resistor to change the voltage across the lamp.

Here is the graph he plotted of his results, along with his curve of best fit.

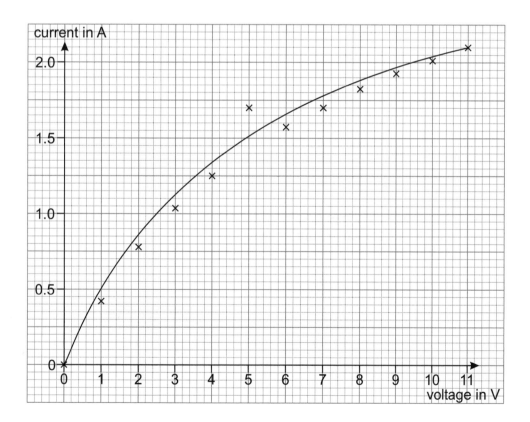

(a)   State the dependent variable in this experiment.

....

[1]

Turn over ▶

(b) (i) Describe what the student has done wrong when drawing the curve of best fit.

....

....

[1]

(ii) State the equation linking voltage, current and resistance.

....

[1]

(iii) The student corrects his curve of best fit and uses it to work out that when the voltage across the lamp is 5.0 V, the current through it is 1.4 A.
Calculate the resistance of the lamp when the voltage across it is 5.0 V.

Resistance = ... unit ....

[3]

(c) The student repeats the experiment with a fixed resistor in place of the filament lamp.
He again plots a graph of his results.

(i) Compare the shape of the graph the student would obtain for a fixed resistor with the graph for a filament lamp.

....

....

[1]

(ii) Explain why the shapes of these graphs are different.
You should refer to resistance in your answer.

....

....

[2]

[Total 9 marks]

8   An engineering student has made a simple electric motor as shown in the diagram.

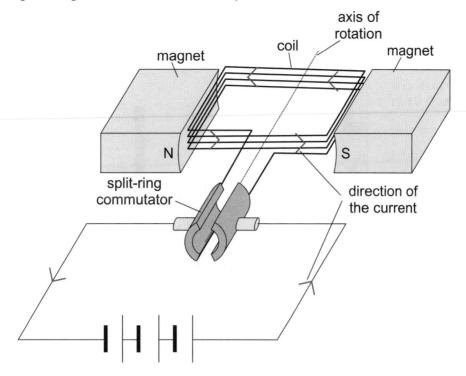

The split-ring commutator changes the direction of the current every half turn so that the motor will continue to rotate in the same direction.

(a)   The direction of the current is shown. State which direction the coil will rotate in.

....
                                                                                                            [1]

(b)   Explain what makes the coil of wire in a simple electric motor rotate.

....

....

....
                                                                                                            [2]

(c)   The engineering student decides to make some changes to her motor.

        Suggest **two** ways that she could speed up the rotation of the motor.

        1. ....

        ....

        2. ....

        ....
                                                                                                            [2]
                                                                                                 [Total 5 marks]

Turn over ▶

9 A hydraulic system is shown in the diagram below.

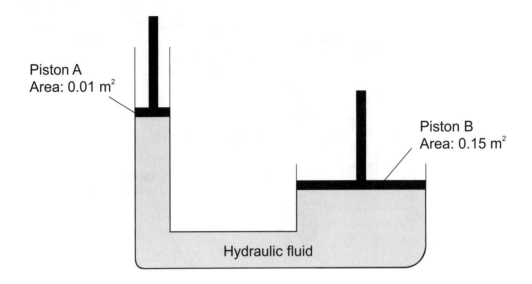

Piston A exerts a downwards force of 25 N.

(a) Calculate the pressure in the liquid due to this force.

Pressure = ... Pa
[2]

(b) Explain why there is a force on piston B when a force is applied to piston A.

....

....

....

....
[3]

(c) Show that the force on piston B is 375 N.

[2]

[Total 7 marks]

10   Optical fibres, such as the one shown below, are used in medicine.

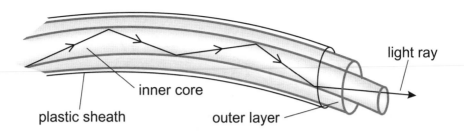

(a)   Explain why almost none of the light 'escapes' from an optical fibre as a light ray travels along it.

....

....

....

[2]

(b) (i) Describe an experiment to find the refractive index of a rectangular block of the material used to make the inner core of an optical fibre.

....

....

....

....

....

....

[4]

(ii) A student carries out the above experiment, using a laser as a light source. State **one** potential hazard involved with using a laser as a light source, and suggest **one** safety precaution that could be taken to minimise this hazard.

....

....

....

[2]

Turn over ▶

(c) The refractive index of a material used to make optical fibres is 1.5. Light is shone into a semicircular block of the material at different angles. As shown in the diagram, an angle, θ, is reached at which the light refracts along the flat boundary between the block and the air.

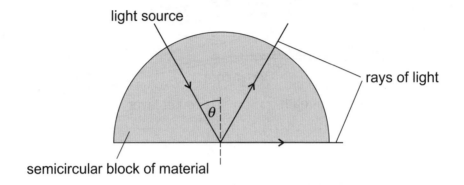

Calculate the angle θ.

θ = ... $^{\circ}$

[4]

[Total 12 marks]

11   This question is about velocity-time graphs.

(a)   The velocity-time graph below shows the motion of a vehicle as it travels along a flat, straight road before braking and stopping at a set of traffic lights.

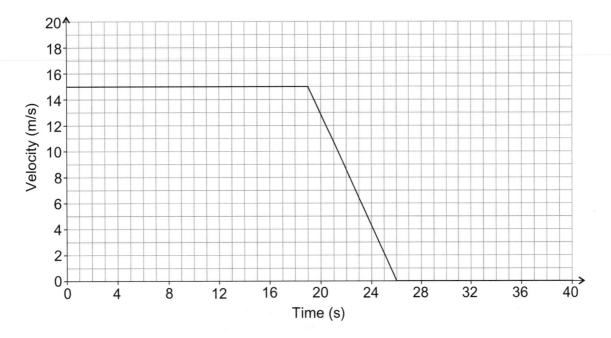

(i)   Calculate the total distance travelled by the car in the first 26 seconds.

Total distance travelled = ... m

[2]

(ii) The vehicle has a mass of 1000 kg.
Calculate the size of the force applied by the brakes to bring the vehicle to a stop.

Force = ... N

[4]

Turn over ▶

(b)   The velocity-time graph below shows the motion of a skydiver jumping from an aeroplane.

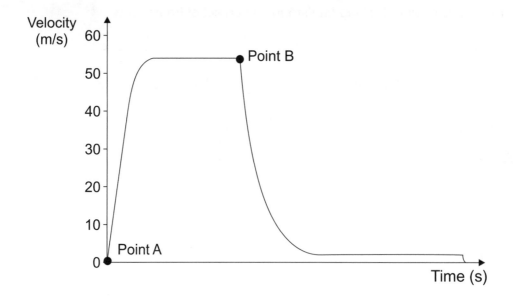

(i)   Describe the motion of the skydiver from point A to point B on the graph.
      Your answer should refer to ideas about the forces acting on him.

....

....

....

....

....

....

                                                                                                              [4]

(ii) At point B, the skydiver opens his parachute.
      Explain why this causes a change in his velocity.

....

....

....

                                                                                                              [2]
                                                                                                [Total 12 marks]

12   A microwave oven can be used for heating food quickly.

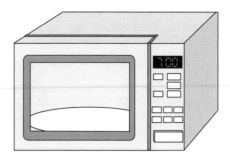

(a)   Describe how the microwave oven heats food.

....

....

....

....

[3]

(b) (i)   State the equation linking frequency, wavelength and speed.

....

[1]

(ii)   A microwave oven uses microwaves with a frequency of 2.5×10^9 Hz
that travel at 3.0×10^8 m/s. Calculate the wavelength of these microwaves.

Wavelength = ... m

[2]

(c) (i)   Mobile phones work by transmitting and receiving microwave signals.
Explain why some people are concerned about using microwaves in this way.

....

....

....

[2]

186

(ii) Radio waves can also be used in communications technology.
Explain why radio waves have fewer potentially harmful effects than microwaves.

....

....

....

[2]

[Total 10 marks]

[Total for paper 110 marks]

Candidate Surname		Candidate Forename(s)	

Centre Number		Candidate Number	

Edexcel
International GCSE

Physics
Paper 2P

Practice Paper
Time allowed: 1 hour 15 minutes

You must have:
*   A ruler.
*   A calculator.

Total marks:

Instructions to candidates
*   Use **black** ink to write your answers.
*   Write your name and other details in the spaces provided above.
*   Answer **all** questions in the spaces provided.
*   In calculations, show clearly how you worked out your answers.
*   You will need to answer some questions by placing a cross in a box, like this: $\boxed{\text{x}}$
    To change your answer, draw a line through the box like this: $\boxed{\text{x}}$
    Then mark your new answer as normal.

Information for candidates
*   The marks available are given in brackets at the end of each question.
*   There are 70 marks available for this paper.
*   You might find the equations on page 165 useful.

Advice for candidates
*   Read all the questions carefully.
*   Write your answers as clearly and neatly as possible.
*   Keep in mind how much time you have left.

Answer **all** questions

1   The body panels of a plane are painted with a spray gun that gives the paint droplets a negative static charge. The body panels are given a positive static charge.

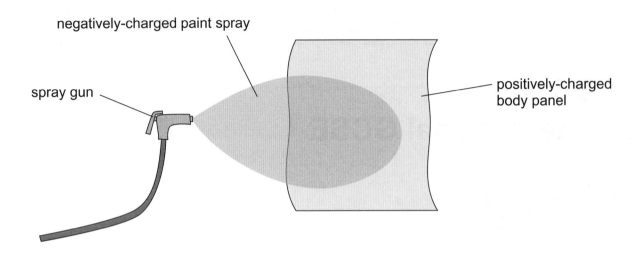

negatively-charged paint spray

spray gun

positively-charged body panel

(a) (i) The body panel is an electrical conductor.
Which of the following statements about electrical conductors is **incorrect**?

☐ **A** Electrical conductors conduct charge easily.

☐ **B** Metals are electrical conductors.

☐ **C** Current can flow through electrical conductors.

☐ **D** Plastic is an electrical conductor.

[1]

(ii) Explain why the spray gun produces a fine, even coverage of paint on the body panels, including areas that are not directly facing the spray gun.

....

....

....

....

....

....*[3]*

[3]

(b) When a plane is being refuelled, fuel is pumped into a tank in the wing of the plane. The tank and wing are made from metal and connected to earth.

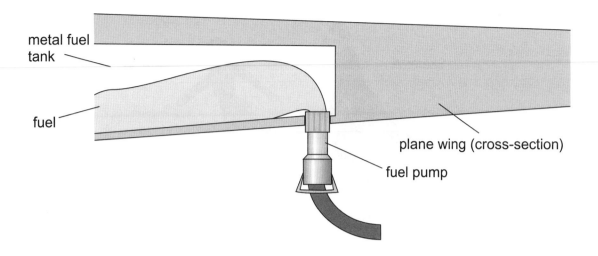

metal fuel tank

fuel

plane wing (cross-section)

fuel pump

(i) Describe, in terms of particle transfer, how a static charge could build up on the fuel tank during refuelling if the tank were made from an electrical insulator.

....

....

....

....

....

[2]

(ii) Explain why a build-up of static charge on the fuel tank could be dangerous.

....

....

[1]

[Total 7 marks]

Turn over ▶

2   Two skaters are taking part in a figure skating contest.
The diagram below shows their masses and their velocities at one point in their routine.

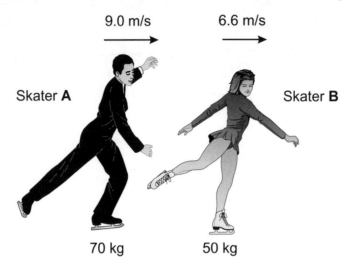

9.0 m/s   6.6 m/s

Skater **A**   Skater **B**

70 kg   50 kg

(a)   State the equation linking momentum, mass and velocity.

....

[1]

(b)   Complete the table below to show the momentum of each skater.

[2]

	Mass (kg)	Velocity (m/s to the right)	Momentum (kg m/s to the right)
Skater A	70	9.0	....
Skater B	50	6.6	....

(c)   The skaters continue at the same velocity until skater A catches up with skater B and holds on to her. They continue to move in the same direction.

Calculate their velocity immediately after skater A begins to hold skater B.

Velocity = ... m/s

[2]

(d)   During the routine, the skaters come to a stop.
      Skater A then pushes skater B away from him with a force of 100 N.

  (i)   Describe the reaction force that skater B exerts on skater A.

      ....

      ....
                                                                                                          [1]

  (ii) State the equation linking unbalanced force, mass and acceleration.

      ....
                                                                                                          [1]

  (iii) Calculate skater B's acceleration due to this force and state the correct unit.
        Assume there are no frictional forces acting on her.

                              Acceleration = ... unit ....
                                                                                                          [3]
                                                                                             [Total 10 marks]

3   The chart below shows the amount of electricity generated by different renewable energy resources in the UK each season between 2012 and 2015. A kilowatt-hour (kWh) is a unit of energy equal to 3.6×10^6 J.

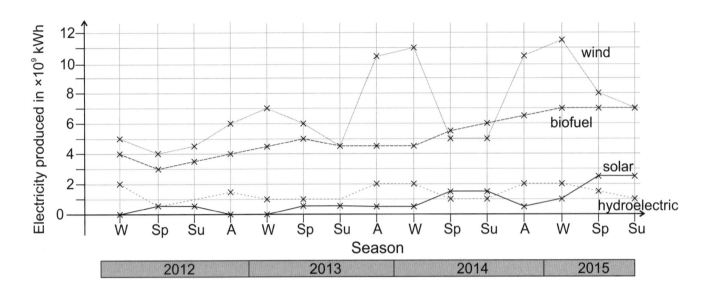

Key:
W — Winter   Sp — Spring   Su — Summer   A — Autumn

(a) (i) Using the chart, determine the amount of electricity generated by biofuels and by hydroelectric power in summer 2014.

Biofuels = ... kWh

Hydroelectric = ... kWh

[2]

(ii) Using the chart, suggest which renewable energy resource usually provides the largest amount of electricity to the UK.

....

[1]

(iii) The chart shows that the amount of electricity generated from solar power during summer is always larger than the amount generated during winter of the same year. Suggest a reason for this.

....

....

[1]

(b)   The majority of electricity in the UK is generated from non-renewable energy resources.
Give **one** advantage and **one** disadvantage of using non-renewable energy resources
to generate electricity.

Advantage: ....

....

Disadvantage: ....

....

[2]

This pie chart shows the proportions of another country's electricity
generated by different resources.

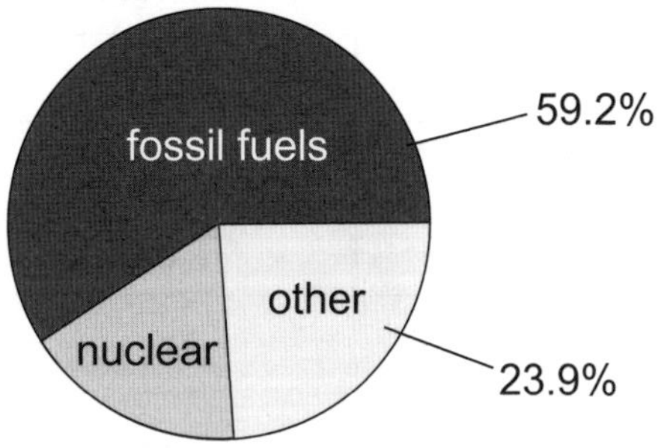

(c)   Calculate the proportion of the country's electricity that comes from nuclear power.

Proportion from nuclear power = ...%

[1]

(d)   Give **two** advantages and **two** disadvantages of using nuclear power
to generate electricity compared to burning fossil fuels.

Advantage 1: ....

....

Advantage 2: ....

....

Disadvantage 1: ....

....

Disadvantage 2: ....

....

[4]

[Total 11 marks]

Turn over ▶

194

4 A student performs an experiment to observe how the temperature of a solid changes when heated.

(a) She places an electric heater in a hole in the solid and places a thermometer in a second hole. She turns the heater on and records the temperature every 100 seconds. Her results are shown in the table below.

Time (s)	Temperature (°C)
0	20.0
100	27.5
200	36.0
300	45.0
400	53.5
500	57.0
600	57.0

(i) Name **one** control variable in the student's experiment.

....

[1]

(ii) Explain why control variables need to be kept constant in experiments such as this.

....

....

[1]

(b) (i) Use the grid to plot a graph of the results in the table.

[3]

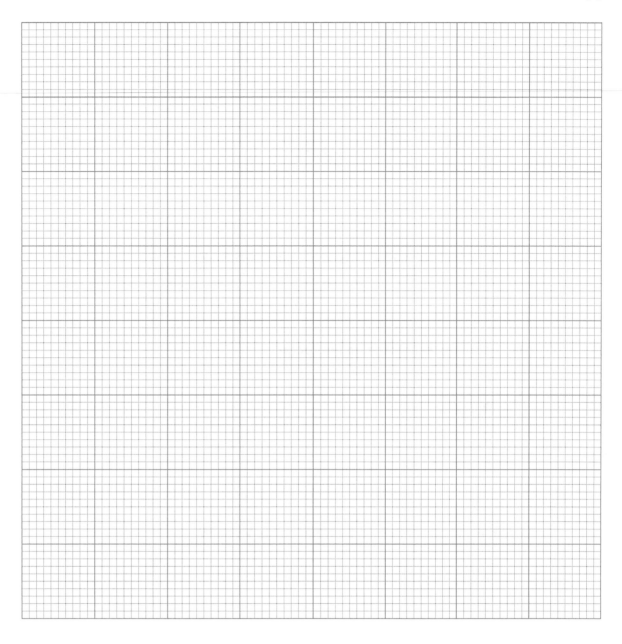

(ii) Draw a curve of best fit on the graph.

[2]

(c)   The student looked up the heating curve for the material in a textbook.
She found the following graph.

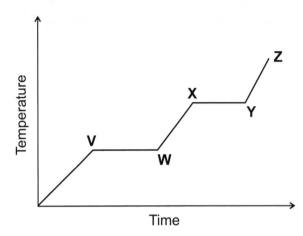

(i)   Identify the state of matter of the substance at point **Z**.

....

[1]

(ii) Which point represents the **boiling point**?

☐   **A**   V

☐   **B**   W

☐   **C**   X

☐   **D**   Z

[1]

(iii) Explain the shape of the line between points **V** and **W**.

....

....

....

....

[2]

(d)   The student does another experiment where she steadily heats a gas in a container with a changeable volume. She produces the following graph from her results. You can assume the pressure is constant.

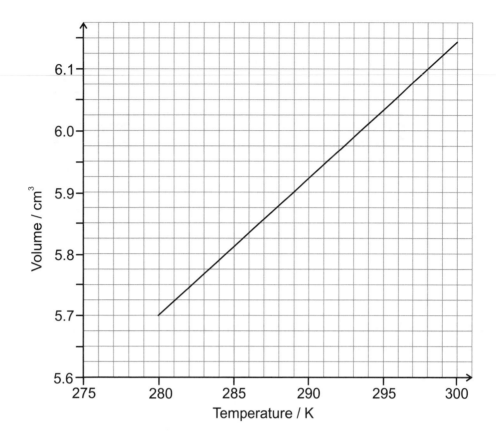

(i)   Using the graph, describe the relationship between the temperature and volume of the gas at a constant pressure.

....

....

[1]

(ii)   Use the graph to estimate the volume of the gas at 25 °C.

Volume of gas = ... cm³

[2]

[Total 14 marks]

5   The generator in a power station produces an alternating voltage of 25 kV.
This is changed to 400 kV by the transformer shown.

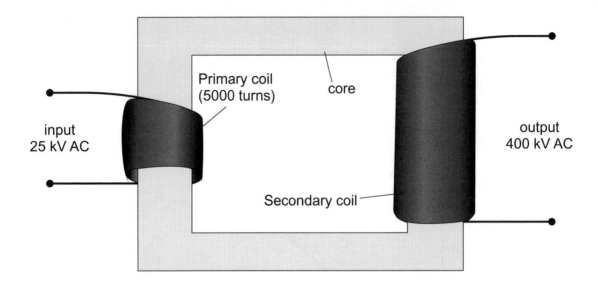

(a)   State whether the transformer shown in the diagram is a step-up transformer
or a step-down transformer. Justify your answer.

....

....

[1]

(b) (i) State the equation linking the number of turns on the primary coil, the number of turns on
the secondary coil, the input voltage and the output voltage for a transformer.

....

[1]

(ii) The primary coil has 5000 turns.
Calculate the number of turns on the secondary coil.

Number of turns = ...

[3]

(c) (i) State the equation linking the input power and the output power in terms of the current and voltage across each coil of a 100% efficient transformer.

....

[1]

(ii) The output current of this transformer is 250 A.
Calculate the input current, assuming the transformer is 100% efficient.

Input current = ... A

[2]

(d) Explain why the electricity produced by power stations is passed through a transformer before being transmitted through the national grid.

....

....

....

....

....

[2]

[Total 10 marks]

6 A construction worker is using a crane with an electromagnet to pick up a metal load.

(a) State what is meant by an **electromagnet**.

....

....

[1]

(b) The electromagnet is shown in the diagram.

(i) Sketch magnetic field lines to show the shape of the magnetic field around the electromagnet.

[1]

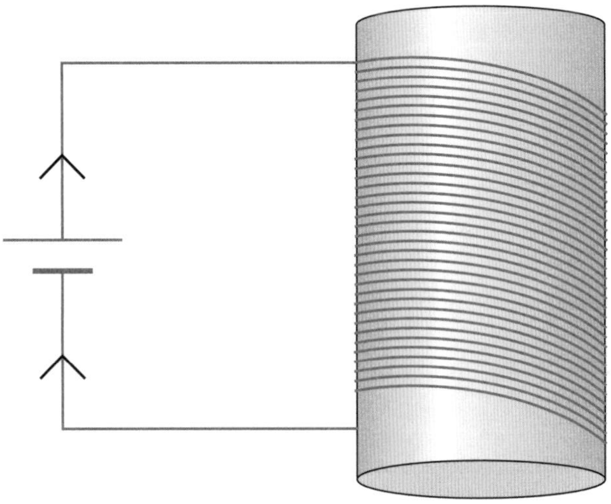

(ii) Explain why it is important for the core to be made from a magnetically soft material.

....

....

[1]

(c) The diagram shows all the forces acting on the crane as it carries a metal anvil. The crane is balanced.

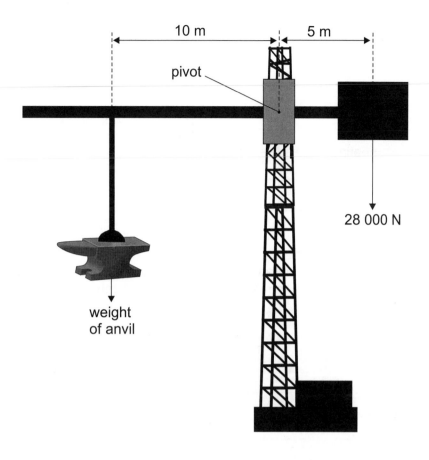

(i) State the equation linking the moment of a force, the force and the perpendicular distance from the line of action of the force to the pivot.

....

[1]

(ii) Calculate the weight of the anvil using the information on the diagram.

Weight = ... N

[3]

[Total 7 marks]

7   A student carried out an investigation into the specific heat capacity of liquids using the apparatus shown in the figure below. He used identical electric heating coils to heat a beaker of water and a beaker of oil. He used exactly 1 kg of each liquid.

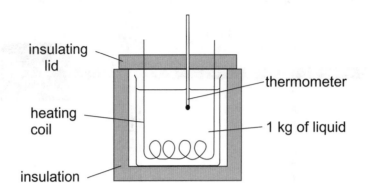

The student recorded the temperature of both the liquids before heating, and then again after ten minutes of heating. His results are shown in the table below.

	Water	Oil
Initial temperature in °C	18	18
Final temperature in °C	48	93

(a)   State what is meant by **specific heat capacity**.

....

....

                         [1]

(b)   The student used an insulating lid in the experiment.
         State and explain the effect this has on the accuracy of the results.

....

....

                         [2]

(c)   Explain why the student uses the same mass of each liquid.

....

....

....

....

[2]

(d)   During the experiment, the heating coil transferred 126 kJ of energy to each liquid.
       Calculate the specific heat capacity of the oil using the data from the experiment.

Specific heat capacity of oil = ... J/kg°C

[4]

(e)   Both oil and water can be used in heating systems.
       Explain why most heating systems use water rather than oil.
       You should refer to the specific heat capacities of oil and water in your answer.

....

....

....

[2]

[Total 11 marks]

[Total for paper 70 marks]

Answers

Section 1 — Forces and Motion

Pages 6-7
Warm-Up Questions
1) Velocity is a measure of how fast something is going, and in what direction. Speed is just a measure of how fast something is travelling.
2) time = distance/speed
   $$= 125 \div 6.50$$
   $$= \textbf{19.2 s (to 3 s.f.)}$$
3) m/s^2
4) acceleration
5) units of mass = kg, units of weight = N

Exam Questions
1 a) average speed = distance ÷ time
   $$= 1500 \div 300 = \textbf{5 m/s}$$
   [2 marks if answer correct, otherwise 1 mark for correct substitution of values into the equation.]

b) $a = \dfrac{(v - u)}{t}$

   $\Rightarrow t = \dfrac{(v - u)}{a} = \dfrac{(10 - 2)}{2.4} = 3.333... = \textbf{3.3 s (to 2 s.f.)}$
   [3 marks if answer correct, otherwise 1 mark for correct rearrangement of the equation and 1 mark for correct substitution of values into the equation.]

2 a) i) Weight = mass × gravitational field strength / $W = m \times g$
   [1 mark]

   ii) $W = m \times g \Rightarrow g = \dfrac{W}{m} = \dfrac{19.6}{2.0}$

   $= \textbf{9.8 N/kg (newtons per kilogram)}$
   [3 marks if answer correct, otherwise 1 mark for correct rearrangement of the equation and correct substitution of values into the equation, and 1 mark for correct unit.]

b) The weight would be smaller *[1 mark]* as the gravitational field strength, g, is lower on the Moon *[1 mark]*.

3 $v^2 = u^2 + 2as$, so $u^2 = v^2 - 2as$

$u = \sqrt{v^2 - 2as} = \sqrt{7^2 - (2 \times 2 \times 10)} = \sqrt{9} = \textbf{3 m/s}$
[3 marks if answer correct, otherwise 1 mark for correct rearrangement of the equation and 1 mark for correct substitution of values into the equation.]

4 a) 300 s *[1 mark]*

b) Yes — the gradient of the graph shows the student's speed *[1 mark]* and the gradient for this part of the journey is constant (it's a straight line) *[1 mark]*.

c) average speed = $\dfrac{\text{distance moved}}{\text{time taken}} = \dfrac{450}{300} = \textbf{1.5 m/s}$
   [3 marks if answer correct, otherwise 1 mark for using the correct equation and 1 mark for correct substitution of values in the equation.]

d) E.g.
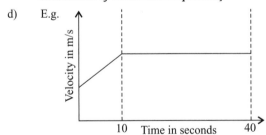
[3 marks available — 1 mark for a straight, sloped line showing the initial acceleration, 1 mark for a straight horizontal line showing the constant speed, and 1 mark for plotting a horizontal line for roughly 3 times the time the sloped line is plotted over.]

5 a) The car is slowing down/decelerating *[1 mark]*. The rate of deceleration of the car is increasing/changing *[1 mark]*.

b) Distance travelled = area under graph
   $$= (60 - 40) \times (20 - 0) = 20 \times 20$$
   $$= \textbf{400 m}$$
   [3 marks for the correct answer, otherwise 1 mark for attempting to find the area under the graph between 40 and 60 seconds, 1 mark for correctly showing $(60 - 40) \times 20$ or 20×20.]

c) Acceleration = gradient = $\dfrac{20 - 0}{40 - 0} = \textbf{0.5 m/s}^2$
   [3 marks for the correct answer, otherwise 1 mark for attempting to find the gradient, 1 mark for dividing a correct change in velocity by a correct change in time in the time range 0 – 40 s.]

d)
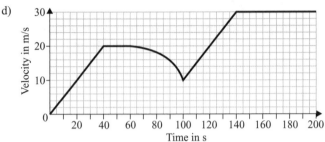
[1 mark for a straight line with a positive gradient between 100 and 140 seconds finishing at 30 m/s, 1 mark for a straight horizontal line at 30 m/s between 140 and 200 seconds.]

Page 11
Warm-Up Questions
1) Gravity/weight.
2) Forces of attraction or repulsion between two charged objects.
3) Friction between solid surfaces which are gripping.
4) The bikes would make the shape of the car less streamlined, which would increase the drag and reduce the top speed.

Exam Questions
1 a) i) In the opposite direction to the thrust *[1 mark]*.
   ii) As the speed increases, the resistance force increases *[1 mark]*.

b) E.g. reaction force *[1 mark]* (from the road) acting upwards on the truck *[1 mark]*. / Weight/gravitational force *[1 mark]* acting straight downwards *[1 mark]*.

2 a) Release the trolley so it can roll freely down the ramp. Use the light gates to record the time at which the trolley passes through them *[1 mark]*.
   The acceleration on the ramp can be found using: acceleration = change in velocity ÷ time taken *[1 mark]*.
   The time taken for the trolley to accelerate on the ramp is the time taken to pass between light gates A and B *[1 mark]*.
   Since the trolley started at rest just before light gate A, its initial speed is 0 m/s and the change in velocity between light gates A and B is equal to its speed between light gates B and C (ignoring any slowing down due to friction on the flat runway) *[1 mark]*.
   To find the trolley's speed on the runway, use the time taken for the trolley to pass from light gate B to light gate C, and the distance between them *[1 mark]*, to calculate the final speed of the trolley using: average speed = distance moved ÷ time taken *[1 mark]*.

b) The student has changed two variables (distance and ramp angle) at the same time *[1 mark]*, so he cannot conclude which one caused the speed of the trolley to increase *[1 mark]*. He should measure the speed of the trolley when only the distance is changed, and separately measure the speed of the trolley when only the ramp angle is changed *[1 mark]*.

Page 15
Warm-Up Questions

1) If all the forces on an object are balanced, then it will stay still, or else if it's already moving, it will continue to move at the same velocity.
2) Add the two forces together.
3) a) scalar b) vector c) vector d) scalar

Exam Questions

1 a) $F = m \times a \Rightarrow a = \dfrac{F}{m} = \dfrac{200}{2500} = 0.08$ m/s^2
[2 marks if answer correct, otherwise 1 mark for correct rearrangement of the equation and correct substitution of values into the equation.]

b) i) $F = m \times a = 10 \times 29 = 290$ N
[2 marks if answer correct, otherwise 1 mark for correct substitution of values into the equation.]

ii) 290 N *[1 mark]*

iii) $F = m \times a \Rightarrow a = \dfrac{F}{m} = \dfrac{290}{2500} = 0.116$ m/s^2
[2 marks if answer correct, otherwise 1 mark for correct rearrangement of the equation and correct substitution of values into the equation.]

2 a) Resultant force in the horizontal direction:
$1700 + 300 - 2000 = 0$ N
Resultant force in the vertical direction:
$800 - 300 = 500$ N *[1 mark]* down *[1 mark]*

b) i) $y - 400 = 0 \Rightarrow y = 400$ N *[1 mark]*

ii) $2000 - 500 - x = 0 \Rightarrow x = 2000 - 500 = 1500$ N *[1 mark]*

Pages 20-21
Warm-Up Questions

1) When the air resistance/drag on the falling object is equal to its weight.
2) A car full of people has a larger mass than a car that's less full, so with the same brakes it will take longer to stop. Other factors that increase stopping distance include any two from: e.g. how fast the vehicle is going / how good the brakes are / how good the grip is / tiredness of the driver / influence of alcohol/drugs on driver.
3) The total momentum after an event is the same as the total momentum before it (as long as no external forces act).

Exam Questions

1 a) i) Thinking distance *[1 mark]*.

ii) Any two from: e.g. tiredness / speed of the car / drug intake / alcohol intake / inexperience / old age.
[2 marks available — 1 mark for each correct answer.]

b) i) The distance the car travels during its deceleration whilst the brakes are being applied *[1 mark]*.

ii) Any two from: e.g. speed of the car / mass of the car / condition of the car's brakes / condition of the road surface / condition of the car's tyres / weather conditions.
[2 marks available — 1 mark for each correct answer.]

2 a) E.g. rain reduces the grip of the tyres on the road *[1 mark]*, increasing braking distance and stopping distance *[1 mark]*.

b) E.g. decrease their speed *[1 mark]*.

c) stopping distance = thinking distance + braking distance
thinking distance = stopping distance − braking distance
$= 37 - 28 = 9$ m
[2 marks if answer correct, otherwise 1 mark for correct substitution of values into the equation.]

3 a) i) momentum = mass × velocity / $p = m \times v$ *[1 mark]*

ii) $p = m \times v = 65 \times 14$
$= 910$ kg m/s (kilogram metres per second)
[3 marks if answer correct, otherwise 1 mark for correct substitution of values into the equation and 1 mark for correct unit.]

b) i) force = $\dfrac{\text{change in momentum}}{\text{time taken}}$ / $F = \dfrac{(mv - mu)}{t}$ *[1 mark]*

ii) force = $\dfrac{\text{change in momentum}}{\text{time taken}} = \dfrac{910}{1.3} = 700$ N
[2 marks if answer correct, otherwise 1 mark for correct substitution of values into the equation.]
You'll get full marks if an incorrect answer from part a) is used and the calculations are done correctly.

4 initial momentum of skater = $60 \times 5 = 300$ kg m/s
initial momentum of bag = 0
momentum of skater and bag = $(60 + \text{mass of bag}) \times 4.8$
momentum before = momentum after
$300 = (60 + \text{mass of bag}) \times 4.8$
mass of bag = $\dfrac{300}{4.8} - 60 = 2.5$ kg
[5 marks if answer correct, otherwise 1 mark for equating momentum before and after, 1 mark for correct substitution of values to calculate the initial momentum of the skater, 1 mark for correct rearrangement of the equation, and 1 mark for correct substitution of values into the equation to find the momentum of the skater and bag.]

5 a) $p = m \times v = 650 \times 15$
$= 9750$ kg m/s
[2 marks if answer correct, otherwise 1 mark for correct substitution of values into the equation.]

b) momentum before = momentum after
$(m_1 \times v_1) + (m_2 \times v_2) = ((m_1 + m_2) \times v_{after})$
$(650 \times 15) + (750 \times -10) = ((650 + 750) \times v_{after})$
$9750 - 7500 = 1400 \times v_{after}$
$v_{after} = \dfrac{2250}{1400}$
$v_{after} = 1.607... = 1.6$ m/s (to 2 s.f.)
[4 marks if answer correct, otherwise 1 mark for equating momentum before and after, 1 mark for correct substitution of values into the equations for momentum of each vehicle and 1 mark for correct rearrangement of the equation(s).]
You'll get full marks if an incorrect answer from part a) is used and the calculations are done correctly.

c) The crumple zone increases the time taken by the car to stop/change its velocity *[1 mark]*. The time over which momentum changes is inversely proportional to the force acting, so this reduces the force *[1 mark]*.

6 The ball with the lower weight, as it needs a smaller resistance/drag force to balance its weight *[1 mark]*. Air resistance increases with velocity *[1 mark]*, and the air resistance at any given velocity will be the same on each ball (because they're the same size), so air resistance will balance the weight of the lighter ball at a lower velocity *[1 mark]*.
If you answered the ball with the larger weight, you receive no marks for this question regardless of the reasoning.

Page 27
Warm-Up Questions

1) Suspend the shape and a plumb line from the same point, and wait until they stop moving. Draw a line along the plumb line. Repeat this, but suspend the shape from a different pivot point. The centre of gravity is where the two lines cross.
2) False
3) A material displays elastic behaviour if it returns to its original shape once the forces deforming it are removed.

Exam Questions

1 a) E.g. they have a straight-line relationship / they are directly proportional to each other *[1 mark]*.

b) No, it will not return to its original shape, because the spring's elastic limit has been passed *[1 mark]*.

2 B *[1 mark]*, because the force is acting at the furthest perpendicular distance from the pivot *[1 mark]*.

3 a) 20 cm = 0.2 m
moment = force × perpendicular distance from the pivot
= 2 × 0.2 = **0.4 Nm**
[3 marks if answer correct, otherwise 1 mark for
using the correct equation and 1 mark for correct
substitution of values into the equation.]

b) clockwise moments = anticlockwise moments
force$_C$ × perpendicular distance$_C$ = 0.4 + 0.8

perpendicular distance$_C$ = $\dfrac{0.4 + 0.8}{8}$ = **0.15 m**

[4 marks if answer correct, otherwise 1 mark for
referring to the moments in each direction being balanced,
1 mark for correct substitution of values into the equation
and 1 mark for correct rearrangement of the equation.]

You'll get full marks if an incorrect answer from part a) is used and the
calculations are done correctly.

Page 28
Revision Questions

2) $a = (v - u) \div t$,
so $t = (v - u) \div a$
= (2.7 − 0) ÷ 0.5 = **5.4 s**

9) Weight = mass × gravity
= 60 × 1.6 = **96 N**

16) Resultant force = 19 000 − 13 500 = **5500 N**

20) Mass = momentum ÷ velocity
= 14 700 ÷ 15 = **980 kg**

21) Change in momentum = force × time
= 230 × 10
= **2300 kg m/s**

23) Moment = force × perpendicular distance
= 5 × 1.3 = **6.5 Nm**

25) The cable closest to the mass / the left-hand cable.

Section 2 — Electricity

Pages 34-35
Warm-Up Questions

1) The current in the circuit increases.
2) False
3) $V = I \times R$
= 1.5 × 6 = **9 V**
4) As the temperature increases, the resistance
of the thermistor decreases.

Exam Questions

1 a) A *[1 mark]*
b) Direct current *[1 mark]*. This means that the current
keeps flowing in the same direction *[1 mark]*.

2 a)
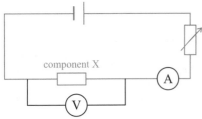

[1 mark for adding the ammeter in line with component X,
1 mark for adding the voltmeter across component X.]

b) It will decrease *[1 mark]*.
c) E.g. start with the resistance of the variable resistor fixed
at a high level. Take a reading of current from the ammeter
[1 mark] and voltage from the voltmeter *[1 mark]*.
Decrease the resistance of the variable resistor in equal
steps and take another pair of readings each time *[1 mark]*.

3 a) If the LED is lit up, current is flowing in the circuit
[1 mark].

b) The resistance increases *[1 mark]* because the resistance
of a light-dependent resistor increases with decreasing
light intensity *[1 mark]*.

4 a) (resistor) D *[1 mark]*
The graph with the shallowest slope corresponds to the component
with the highest resistance.

b) i) Voltage = current × resistance / $V = I \times R$
[1 mark — accept any rearranged version of the
same equation.]

ii) Choose a point on the line and use the values of I and V for
that point to find R using $V = I \times R$.
For example, at $I = 4$ A and $V = 2$ V, so:
$R = V \div I = 2 \div 4 = $ **0.5 Ω**
[3 marks for correct answer, otherwise 1 mark for
correct rearrangement of the formula and 1 mark for
correct substitution.]

The gradient of an I-V graph is equal to resistance. The graph for
component B is a straight line, so you could have found the resistance
of component B here by finding the gradient of the line using the formula:
gradient = change in y ÷ change in x.
You'd get the marks for using this method too.

iii) $V = I \times R$
So $I = V \div R = 15 \div 0.75 = $ **20 A**
[3 marks for correct answer, otherwise 1 mark for correct
rearrangement and 1 mark for correct substitution.]

5 a) i) C *[1 mark]*
ii) A *[1 mark]*

b) i) E.g.

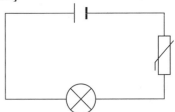

[3 marks available for a circuit diagram showing a circuit
that will work containing just a thermistor, a power source
and a lamp. Otherwise 1 mark for drawing a complete
circuit including a lamp, and 1 mark for drawing a
complete circuit including a thermistor.]

ii) The current increases *[1 mark]*. As the temperature in
the room increases, the resistance of the thermistor
(and so the circuit) will decrease *[1 mark]*.

Page 40
Warm-Up Questions

1) Voltage of power supply
= voltage across lamp + voltage across motor
= 1.5 + 3.0 = **4.5 V**
2) True

Exam Questions

1 a) E.g. if one bulb breaks, the other still lights up *[1 mark]*.
b) $V = I \times R$, so:
$R = V \div I = 12 \div 0.5 = $ **24 Ω**
[3 marks for correct answer, otherwise 1 mark for correct
rearrangement and 1 mark for correct substitution.]
c) It would decrease *[1 mark]*.

2 a) $V_1 = 4.20$ V and $V_2 = 4.20$ V *[1 mark]*
In parallel circuits, the potential difference is the same across all branches.

b) The current through a component depends on the total
potential difference and the total resistance across all the
components in series with it.
Total resistance across branch = $R_1 + R_2$
= 2.00 + 2.00 = 4.00 Ω
$I = V \div R = 4.20 \div 4.00 = $ **1.05 A**
[4 marks for correct answer, otherwise 1 mark for
calculating resistance, 1 mark for correct rearrangement
and 1 mark for correct substitution.]

3 a) electrons *[1 mark]*

b) i) Charge = current × time / $Q = I × t$
[1 mark — accept any rearranged version of the same equation.]

ii) Convert time to seconds: $t = 20 × 60 = 1200$ s
$Q = I × t = 5 × 1200 =$ **6000 C**
[3 marks for correct answer, otherwise 1 mark for changing time to seconds and 1 mark for correct substitution.]

c) **3 J** *[1 mark]*. Energy transferred per unit charge is equal to voltage, and the battery has a voltage of 3 V or 3 J/C *[1 mark]*.

d) $I = Q ÷ t = 12 ÷ 3.0 = 4.0$ A
$E = Q × V$ and $V = I × R$, so $E = Q × I × R$.
$R = \dfrac{E}{Q × I} = \dfrac{36}{12 × 4.0} =$ **0.75 Ω**
[4 marks for the correct answer, otherwise 1 mark for calculating the current, 1 mark for writing a correct formula to find resistance and 1 mark for correct substitution of values into the formula.]

Page 44
Warm-Up Questions
1) Live wire, earth wire and neutral wire.
2) Energy is transferred to the resistor, which heats the resistor. Toasters contain a coil of wire with a high resistance. When a current passes through the coil, its temperature increases so much that it glows and gives off infrared (heat) radiation, which cooks the bread.

Exam Questions
1 a) To stop people from getting electric shocks / protect the wiring of the house / prevent fires in the event of a fault *[1 mark]*.

b) Because pennies won't melt like a fuse wire in the event of a current surge, so the circuit won't be broken *[1 mark]*.

2 a) When current flows through the wire, the charges do work against the resistance and energy is transferred to thermal energy stores *[1 mark]*. The higher the resistance, the more energy is transferred *[1 mark]*.

b) i) Power = current × voltage / $P = I × V$
[1 mark — accept any rearranged version of the same equation.]

ii) Convert power to W, $P = 2.8 × 1000 = 2800$ W
$I = P ÷ V = 2800 ÷ 230$
$= 12.17... $ A = **12 A (to 2 s.f.)**
[3 marks for correct answer, otherwise 1 mark for correctly converting power to W and 1 mark for correctly substituting into a correctly rearranged equation.]

iii) She should choose kettle B because it has the higher power rating *[1 mark]*. This means that it transfers more energy per unit time, so it will boil the water faster *[1 mark]*.

Page 49
Warm-Up Questions
1) A material that can conduct electric charge easily, e.g. copper, silver.
2) A material that doesn't conduct electric charge very well, e.g. plastic, rubber.

Exam Questions
1 a) Electrons are removed from the dusting cloth *[1 mark]* and transferred to the polythene rod *[1 mark]*.

b) Bring the object with unknown charge near to the suspended polythene rod *[1 mark]*. If the rod moves away from / is repelled by the object, the object is negatively charged *[1 mark]*. If the rod moves towards / is attracted by the rod, the object is positively charged *[1 mark]*.

2 a) Inside the printer are two metal plates that can have a voltage applied to them *[1 mark]*. The voltage gives the plates opposite charges, which causes the droplets passing between them to be deflected, as they are attracted by one and repelled by the other *[1 mark]*. The amount and direction of deflection can be controlled by changing the size and direction of the voltage *[1 mark]*.

b) i) Light reflected off some parts (the white parts) of the original document onto the image plate *[1 mark]*.

ii) The black parts of the document don't reflect light on to the plate, so the image plate keeps its positive charge in those places *[1 mark]*. A negatively-charged black powder *[1 mark]* is brought close to the plate. It is attracted to the positively-charged parts of it *[1 mark]*. Then a positively-charged piece of paper *[1 mark]* is brought close to the plate and the negatively-charged black powder is attracted to the paper *[1 mark]*.

Page 50
Revision Questions
4) $V = I × R$, so $R = V ÷ I = 12 ÷ 2.5 =$ **4.8 Ω**
9) $Q = I × t$, so $I = Q ÷ t = 80 ÷ 2 =$ **40 A**
16) a) $P = I × V$, so $I = P ÷ V = 1100 ÷ 230 = 4.782...$ A
A **5 A** fuse would be appropriate.
b) $P = I × V$, so $I = P ÷ V = 2000 ÷ 230 = 8.695...$ A
A **13 A** fuse would be appropriate.

Section 3 — Waves

Page 54
Warm-Up Questions
1) a) The distance from one peak to the next.
You didn't have to say "peak" here — you could have said the distance between any two matching points on next-door waves.
b) The time it takes (in s) for one complete wave to pass a point.
2) $λ = v ÷ f$
$= (3 × 10^8$ m/s$) ÷ (6 × 10^6$ Hz$) =$ **50 m**
3) In transverse waves, the vibrations are at 90° to the direction energy that is transferred by the wave. In longitudinal waves, the vibrations are along the same direction as the wave transfers energy.
4) false
Remember, waves transfer energy and information, but not matter.
5) A wavefront is an imaginary plane that cuts across multiple waves that are moving together in the same direction, and connects the points on adjacent waves which are vibrating together.

Exam Questions
1 a) The height of the wave from the rest position of the wave to a crest *[1 mark]*.
b) C *[1 mark]*
2 a) The Doppler effect is the change in the frequency and wavelength of a wave *[1 mark]* due to the wave source moving towards or away from the observer *[1 mark]*.
b) Wave speed is constant, so a moving source can 'catch up' to the waves produced in front of it *[1 mark]*. This causes the wavefronts in front of the source to bunch up, so the frequency of the waves gets higher and their wavelength gets shorter *[1 mark]*. The wavefronts behind the source spread out, so the frequency of the waves gets lower and their wavelength gets longer *[1 mark]*.
c) The distant star is moving away from the Earth *[1 mark]*. The Doppler effect causes frequencies emitted by a source moving away from a detector to be lower than expected *[1 mark]*.

208

Pages 59-60

Warm-Up Questions

1) radio waves
2) False
All EM waves travel at the same speed through free space (a vacuum).
3) Infrared radiation
4) Gamma rays are a form of ionising radiation that penetrate far into the human body. There they can cause cell mutation or destruction, leading to tissue damage or cancer. To reduce the risk when using them, e.g. exposure should be kept to a minimum / sources should be kept in lead-lined boxes.

Exam Questions

1 a) gamma radiation *[1 mark]*.
b) Treating the fruit with radiation kills the microbes in it *[1 mark]*, so it will stay fresh for longer *[1 mark]*.
2 a) B *[1 mark]*
b) Data is carried as pulses of light *[1 mark]*. A pulse of light enters the narrow core of a fibre at a certain angle at one end and is reflected from the sides again and again until it emerges at the other end *[1 mark]*.
c) E.g. telephone and broadband internet cables / to see inside the body *[1 mark]*.
3 a) E.g. microwaves can cause internal heating of human body tissue *[1 mark]*.
b) E.g. infrared also has a heating effect *[1 mark]*, but it has a higher frequency than microwaves and carries more energy (so it will have a greater heating effect) *[1 mark]*.
4 a) The long-wave radio signals bend round the surface of the Earth to reach the house *[1 mark]*. The short-wave radio signals reflect off the ionosphere to reach the house *[1 mark]*.
b) i) microwave radiation *[1 mark]*
ii) They are transmitted through the atmosphere into space, where they are picked up by a satellite receiver orbiting Earth *[1 mark]*. The satellite transmits the signal back to Earth in a different direction, where it is received by a satellite dish connected to the house *[1 mark]*.
5 The fox is hotter than its surroundings, so it gives off more infrared radiation *[1 mark]*. The night-vision camera detects how much infrared radiation objects give off and uses this to form an image *[1 mark]*.
6 a) A detector is placed behind the truck *[1 mark]*. The X-rays are absorbed by some objects *[1 mark]*, but are transmitted by others *[1 mark]*. A negative image is formed with brighter areas where fewer X-rays get through, indicating the objects that absorbed the X-rays *[1 mark]*.
b) Exposure to X-rays can be harmful *[1 mark]*, so the driver and passengers should step outside the truck while it is exposed to X-rays to minimise their exposure *[1 mark]*.
7 a) They are not harmful. Almost all of the ultraviolet radiation is absorbed *[1 mark]* by a (phosphor) coating on the inside of the glass, which then emits visible light instead *[1 mark]*.
b) A camera focuses light onto a light-sensitive film or an electronic sensor *[1 mark]*. The photographer can control how much light enters it by controlling how big the aperture is *[1 mark]*. The photographer can control how long the film or sensor is exposed to the light by changing the shutter speed *[1 mark]*.

Pages 67-68

Warm-Up Questions

1) a transverse wave
2) 2 times
3) When an incident ray passes into a material, $n = \dfrac{\sin i}{\sin r}$ (where n = the refractive index of the material, i = the angle of incidence and r = the angle of refraction).

4) E.g. draw around a rectangular glass block on a piece of paper and direct a ray of light through it at an angle. Trace the incident and emergent rays. Remove the block, then draw in the refracted ray between them. Draw the normal at 90° to the edge of the block, at the point where the ray enters the block. Use a protractor to measure the angle of incidence (i) and the angle of refraction (r). Calculate the refractive index using Snell's law.

Exam Questions

1 a) The angle of incidence is equal to the angle of reflection *[1 mark]*.
b) E.g.

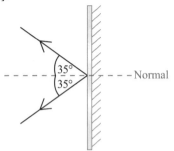

[1 mark for correctly drawn incident ray with an angle of incidence of 35°, 1 mark for correctly drawn reflected ray with an angle of reflection of 35°.]
c) Waves travel at different speeds in materials with different densities *[1 mark]*. When a wave crosses a boundary into another medium at an angle, it changes speed and direction *[1 mark]*. This is refraction *[1 mark]*.
2 a) $\sin C = \dfrac{1}{n}$, so $C = \sin^{-1}\left(\dfrac{1}{n}\right) = \sin^{-1}\left(\dfrac{1}{1.54}\right) = 40.492...$
$= \mathbf{40.5° \ (to \ 3 \ s.f.)}$
[3 marks for correct answer, otherwise 1 mark for correct substitution and 1 mark for correct rearrangement.]
b) If you bend an optical fibre sharply, some light will meet the boundary at an angle smaller than or equal to the critical angle *[1 mark]*. Some light will escape the optical fibre, so less light will be used to make the image *[1 mark]*.
3 a) E.g. the angle of incidence for which the angle of refraction is 90° *[1 mark]*.
b) It will be reflected back into the acrylic / it will be totally internally reflected *[1 mark]*.
c) $n = \dfrac{1}{\sin C} = \dfrac{1}{\sin 41.8°} = 1.5003... = \mathbf{1.50 \ (to \ 3 \ s.f.)}$
[3 marks for correct answer, otherwise 1 mark for using the correct equation and 1 mark for substituting correct values into the equation. Deduct 1 mark for giving units.]
4 a) $i = 45°$
$n = \dfrac{\sin i}{\sin r}$ so $\sin r = \dfrac{\sin i}{n} = \dfrac{\sin 45.00°}{1.514} = 0.467...$
So $r = \sin^{-1}(0.467...) = 27.842... = \mathbf{27.84° \ (to \ 4 \ s.f.)}$
[4 marks for correct answer, otherwise 1 mark for using correct equation, 1 mark for correct substitution and 1 mark for correct rearrangement.]
b) The separation happens when different colours refract by different amounts *[1 mark]*, but light doesn't refract when it crosses a boundary along the normal *[1 mark]*.
c) Angle of incidence for violet light $= i = 45°$
$\sin r = \dfrac{\sin i}{n} = \dfrac{\sin 45.00°}{1.528} = 0.4627...$
So, $r = \sin^{-1}(0.4627...) = 27.565...°$
Subtract this angle from the angle of refraction of red light:
$\theta = 27.842... - 27.565... = 0.27692... = \mathbf{0.2769° \ (to \ 4 \ s.f.)}$
[4 marks for correct answer, otherwise 1 mark for correct rearrangement of the equation to find r, 1 mark for correct angle of refraction of violet light and 1 mark for correctly subtracting one angle from the other. Allow the marks if an incorrect answer from part a) is used correctly. Do not deduct marks for using an incorrect number of significant figures in calculations.]

Page 72

Warm-Up Questions

1) longitudinal
2) 20-20 000 Hz
3) The louder a sound, the greater the amplitude of the sound wave.

Exam Question

1 a) i)

Statements	Order
Measure the distance between the microphones. This is the wavelength.	4
Stop moving microphone 2 when the traces line up.	3
Use the measured distance and the frequency of the signal generator to find the wave speed.	5
Begin with both microphones at an equal distance from the speaker.	1
Keeping microphone 1 fixed, slowly move microphone 2 away from the speaker (keeping it in line with microphone 1), causing trace 2 to move.	2

[3 marks for all entries correct, 2 marks if two entries correct, and 1 mark if one entry correct.]

ii) $v = f \times \lambda = 50 \times 6.8 =$ **340 m/s**
[2 marks for correct answer, otherwise 1 mark for substituting correct values into the equation.]

b) i) D *[1 mark]*

ii) One time cycle is 8 divisions long, so T = 0.005 × 8 = 0.04 s
$f = \frac{1}{T} = \frac{1}{0.04} =$ **25 Hz**
[2 marks for correct answer, otherwise 1 mark for substituting correctly into correct equation.]

Page 73

Revision Questions

3) $f = v \div \lambda = 150 \div 0.3 =$ **500 Hz**
10) 10°
12) $n = \sin i \div \sin r = \sin 30° \div \sin 20°$
  $= 0.5 \div 0.342... = 1.461... =$ **1.5 (to 2 s.f.)**
13) A = yes, B = no, C = no and D = yes.

Section 4 — Energy Resources and Energy Transfer

Pages 79-80

Warm-Up Questions

1) chemical energy store
2) Energy can be stored, transferred between stores, and dissipated — but it can never be created or destroyed. The total energy of a closed system has no net change.
3) Energy is (usefully) transferred from the kinetic energy store of the bat to the kinetic energy store of the ball. Some energy is also transferred from the kinetic energy store of the bat to the thermal energy stores of the bat, the ball and their surroundings, and transferred away from the kinetic energy store of the bat by sound.

Exam Questions

1

Scenario	Energy Transferred From...
A skydiver falling from an aeroplane.	gravitational potential energy store
A substance undergoing a nuclear reaction.	nuclear energy store
A stretched spring returning to its original shape.	elastic potential energy store
A piece of burning coal.	chemical energy store

[3 marks for all correct, otherwise 2 marks for 2 correct or 1 mark for 1 correct]

2 a) kinetic energy store *[1 mark]*

b) i) efficiency = $\frac{\text{useful energy output}}{\text{total energy output}} \times 100$ *[1 mark]*

ii) efficiency = $\frac{\text{useful energy output}}{\text{total energy output}} \times 100$
total energy output = total energy input = 20 J
efficiency = (8 ÷ 20) × 100 = **40%**
[2 marks if answer correct, otherwise 1 mark for correct substitution of values into the formula.]

c) efficiency = $\frac{\text{useful energy output}}{\text{total energy output}} \times 100$

total energy output = $\frac{\text{useful energy output} \times 100}{\text{efficiency}}$

total energy output = total energy input

So, energy supplied to fan B = $\frac{10 \times 100}{55}$
= 18.181... = **18 J (to 2 s.f.)**
[3 marks if answer correct, otherwise 1 mark for correct rearrangement of the formula and 1 mark for correct substitution of values into the formula.]

d) Disagree — fan B has a lower energy input than fan A / transfers less energy per second than fan A. *[1 mark]*
You get the mark here if you got the answer to part c) wrong, but used your answer correctly in part d).

3 a) 10 J *[1 mark]*
You know the total input energy is 200 J. The input energy arrow is 20 squares wide, so the value of each square must be 200 J ÷ 20 = 10 J.

b) 50 J *[1 mark]*
The useful energy arrow is 5 squares wide, and each square represents 10 J. So the amount of energy that's usefully transferred = 5 × 10 J = 50 J

4 a) E.g. thermal energy store/sound energy store *[1 mark]*

b) Energy transferred to weight = 100 − 50 − 20
  = **30 kJ** *[1 mark]*

c) E.g.

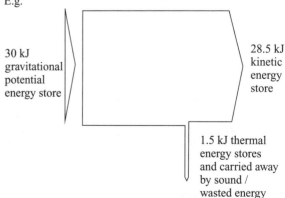

30 kJ gravitational potential energy store

28.5 kJ kinetic energy store

1.5 kJ thermal energy stores and carried away by sound / wasted energy

[1 mark for drawing a recognisable Sankey diagram, 1 mark for all of the arrows being drawn in roughly the correct proportions, 1 mark for all of the arrows being correctly labelled.]

Pages 86-87
Warm-Up Questions
1) false
Thermal radiation can also be called infrared radiation.
2) Vibrating particles transfer extra energy from their kinetic energy stores to the kinetic energy stores of neighbouring particles. Gradually the energy is passed all the way through the solid, causing a rise in temperature at the other side.
3) Because the particles in solids can't move from their fixed positions. (They can only vibrate.)
4) Heat energy is transferred from the heater coils to the water by conduction. The particles near the coils get more energy, so they start moving around faster. This means there's more distance between them, i.e. the water expands and becomes less dense. This reduction in density means that hotter water tends to rise above the denser, cooler water. As the hot water rises, the colder water sinks towards the heater coils. This cold water is then heated by the coils and rises — and so it goes on. You end up with convection currents going up, round and down, circulating the heat energy through the water.

Exam Questions
1 a) Conduction *[1 mark]* and radiation *[1 mark]*
  b) Flask C *[1 mark]*.
     There is a larger temperature difference between flask C and the surrounding gel *[1 mark]*.
     You receive no marks for part b) if you answered A or B.
2 a) conduction *[1 mark]*.
  b) E.g. it will trap pockets of air, so it will stop convection currents being set up in the air gap *[1 mark]*.
3 a) Solid *[1 mark]* because the particles are not free to move *[1 mark]*.
  b) i) E.g.

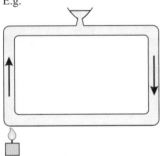

     [1 mark for 2 arrows drawn anywhere inside the glass tube showing the correct flow of water]
     ii) The water particles near the heater gain energy (and get further apart) *[1 mark]*. This causes the water near the heater to expand and become less dense, so it rises up the pipe *[1 mark]*. Colder, denser water elsewhere in the pipe sinks down and replaces this heated water *[1 mark]*.
  c) C *[1 mark]*.
4 a) matt black *[1 mark]*
  b) shiny white *[1 mark]*
  c) E.g. he could use an infrared detector to measure the emitted radiation / he could use a ruler to make sure he measures the radiation emitted from each side from the same distance *[1 mark for any sensible suggestion]*.

Page 91
Warm-Up Questions
1) The energy transferred when a force moves an object.
2) Power = $\dfrac{\text{work done}}{\text{time taken}}$
3) kinetic energy = ½ × mass × speed² / $KE = \frac{1}{2} \times m \times v^2$

Exam Questions
1 B *[1 mark]*
2 a) i) Work done = force applied × distance moved in the direction of the force / $W = Fd$ *[1 mark]*
    ii) $W = Fd$
        $= 50 \times 15 = $ **750 J**
    [2 marks for correct answer, otherwise 1 mark for correct substitution of the variables into the formula.]
  b) The temperature of the wheel increases *[1 mark]* because doing work causes some energy to be transferred to the thermal energy store of the wheel *[1 mark]*.
3 a) $KE = \frac{1}{2} \times m \times v^2$
     $KE = \frac{1}{2} \times 105 \times 2.39^2$
        $= 299.8852... $ J = **300 J (to 3 s.f.)**
     [3 marks for correct answer, otherwise 1 mark for correct formula and 1 mark for correct substitution of the variables into the formula.]
  b) i) $GPE = m \times g \times h$, so:
     energy lost from g.p.e. store $= 105 \times 10 \times 20.2$
                                  $= 21\ 210$ J
                                  $= $ **21 200 J (to 3 s.f.)**
     [3 marks for correct answer, otherwise 1 mark for correct formula and 1 mark for correct substitution of the variables into the formula.]
    ii) It is transferred to the cart's kinetic energy store *[1 mark]*.

Pages 98-99
Warm-Up Questions
1) Burning coal releases sulfur dioxide, which causes acid rain. Acid rain can e.g. harm trees / damage soils / have an impact on wildlife.
2) Any two from: e.g. it doesn't produce greenhouse gases which contribute to global warming / it doesn't produce pollution / energy from the Sun won't run out (for 5 billion years) / energy from the Sun doesn't cost anything.
3) A renewable energy resource is an energy resource that won't run out.

Exam Questions
1 C *[1 mark]*
2 a) i) thermal *[1 mark]*, thermal *[1 mark]*, kinetic *[1 mark]*
    ii) Advantage — e.g. geothermal power is a renewable resource / no fuel is required so there are low running costs / geothermal power stations have very little impact on the environment once set up. *[1 mark for any sensible answer.]*
       Disadvantage — e.g. there are high initial costs in drilling down several km / the cost of building a power station is often high compared to the amount of energy obtained / the possible locations for power stations are very limited. *[1 mark for any sensible answer.]*
  b) Advantage — e.g. wind farms have low running costs (as there are no fuel costs) / wind is a renewable resource (it won't run out) / wind farms cause no atmospheric pollution. *[1 mark for any sensible answer.]*
     Disadvantage — e.g. some people think wind farms spoil the view/make too much noise / a lot of wind farms are needed to generate the same amount of electricity as a fossil fuel power station / wind speed varies, so they're not particularly reliable / wind farms usually require specific (remote) locations, so building and maintenance work is expensive / you can't increase the supply of electricity when demand is high. *[1 mark for any sensible answer.]*
3 a) D *[1 mark]*
  b) Energy is transferred from the kinetic energy store of the waves to the kinetic energy stores of the turbine and generator *[1 mark]*.
4 a) Energy is transferred from the nuclear energy store of the atoms in the fuel to the thermal energy store of the water/steam *[1 mark]*.

b) i) Nuclear fuels don't release any greenhouse gases (e.g. carbon dioxide) that contribute to global warming *[1 mark]*.

ii) Any two from: e.g. mining the fuel can harm the environment in the area it is mined. / Mining, processing and transporting the nuclear fuel before it is used causes atmospheric pollution/releases greenhouse gases. / Nuclear power stations carry the risk of major catastrophes, which have a huge impact on the environment. / Radioactive waste is difficult to dispose of safely and is harmful to the environment (and sometimes to humans). *[2 marks — 1 mark for each correct answer.]*

5 a) E.g. a solar cell *[1 mark]*

b) E.g. solar water heating panels *[1 mark]* — they absorb energy from the Sun to heat water inside them *[1 mark]*.

c) E.g. the cost of connecting solar cells to the national grid is high compared to the amount of electricity they generate *[1 mark]*. It is often not practical to connect them to the national grid *[1 mark]*.

6 a) Energy is transferred from the gravitational potential energy store of the water to the kinetic energy store of the water *[1 mark]*, then to the kinetic energy stores of the turbines and the generator *[1 mark]*. Electricity is generated and the energy is transferred electrically from the generator to the national grid *[1 mark]*.

b) Any two from: e.g. they can cause the loss or destruction of habitats / rotting vegetation in flooded areas releases methane/CO_2/greenhouse gases / they can change the landscape drastically. *[2 marks — 1 mark for each correct answer.]*

c) Pumped storage *[1 mark]*.

d) Any two from: e.g. they cause no atmospheric pollution / they use a renewable energy source / there are no fuel costs / maintenance and running costs are low / tides are regular and predictable, so this is a fairly reliable energy source. *[2 marks — 1 mark for each correct answer.]*

Page 100
Revision Questions

2) efficiency = $\dfrac{\text{useful energy output}}{\text{total energy output}} \times 100$

total energy output = total energy input = 120 J
efficiency = (90 ÷ 120) × 100 = **75%**

4) a) 10 squares = 100 J, so 1 square = 10 J
Energy transferred to kinetic energy store
= 8 squares = 8 × 10 = **80 J**

b) 10 squares = 100 J, so 1 square = 10 J
Energy wasted = energy transferred to thermal energy store
= 2 squares = 2 × 10 = **20 J**

c) efficiency = $\dfrac{\text{useful energy output}}{\text{total energy output}} \times 100$

total energy output = total energy input = 100 J
efficiency = (80 ÷ 100) × 100 = **80%**

8) $W = F \times d = 535 \times 12 =$ **6420 J**

9) $P = W \div t$
$W = 540$ kJ = 540 000 J and $t = 4.5$ minutes = 270 s
$P = 540\ 000 \div 270 =$ **2000 W**

10) $KE = \frac{1}{2} \times m \times v^2 = \frac{1}{2} \times 78 \times 2.3^2$
$= 206.31 =$ **210 m/s (to 2 s.f.)**

Section 5 — Solids, Liquids and Gases

Page 105
Warm-Up Questions

1) Submerge the object in a eureka can filled with water. Use a measuring cylinder to measure the volume of water displaced by the object. This is the volume of the object.

2) pascals/Pa

3) It is held in the kinetic energy stores of its particles.

4) The particles must be travelling in the right direction, and must be travelling fast enough to overcome the attractive forces of the other particles in the liquid.

Exam Questions

1 a) $\dfrac{\text{pressure}}{\text{difference}} = \text{height} \times \text{density} \times \dfrac{\text{gravitational}}{\text{field strength}}$ /
$p = h \times \rho \times g$ *[1 mark]*

b) i) $\rho = \dfrac{m}{V} = \dfrac{514.0}{0.5000} =$ **1028 kg/m³**
[2 marks if answer correct, otherwise 1 mark for correct substitution of values into the formula.]

ii) 245 kPa = 245 000 Pa
$p = h \times \rho \times g$
$h = \dfrac{p}{\rho \times g} = \dfrac{245\ 000}{1028 \times 10} = 23.83... =$ **24 m (to 2 s.f.)**
[3 marks if answer correct, otherwise 1 mark for correct rearrangement of the equation and 1 mark for correct substitution of values into the equation.]

You still get the marks for part ii) if the density you found in part i) was incorrect.

2 a) i) Particles are held close together in a fixed, regular pattern *[1 mark]*. They vibrate about fixed positions *[1 mark]*.

ii) gas *[1 mark]*

b) i) melting *[1 mark]*

ii) When the substance is changing state, the energy provided when it is heated is used to break the bond between particles bonds *[1 mark]* rather than raise the temperature, so the substance stays at a constant temperature *[1 mark]*.

c) i) Evaporation *[1 mark]*. A liquid can evaporate at temperatures that are lower than the liquid's boiling point, whereas boiling happens only at the boiling point *[1 mark]*. Particles in the liquid can only evaporate if they are travelling in the right direction, fast enough to overcome the attractive forces of the other particles in the liquid, whereas when a liquid boils, all of the particles have enough energy to escape *[1 mark]*.

ii) When a liquid evaporates the fastest particles are most likely to escape the liquid *[1 mark]*. When they do, the average speed/energy in the kinetic energy stores of the remaining particles in the liquid decreases *[1 mark]*. The drop in average speed/energy causes a drop in temperature *[1 mark]*.

Pages 112-113
Warm-Up Questions

1) The average kinetic energy will increase by a factor of three (it will triple).

2) As gas particles move about, they randomly bang into each other or anything that gets in the way. When they collide with something they exert a force on it and their momentum and direction change. In a sealed container, gas particles smash into the container walls and create an outward pressure.

3) The specific heat capacity of a substance is the energy required to change the temperature of the substance by 1 °C per kilogram of mass.

Exam Questions

1 a) i) The average speed decreases *[1 mark]*.

ii) The energy of the particles in a substance decreases with decreasing temperature *[1 mark]*. There is a minimum energy that the particles can have, so there is a minimum temperature *[1 mark]*.

iii) –273 °C *[1 mark]*

b) i) –263 °C *[1 mark]*

ii) 904 K *[1 mark]*

To convert from the Kelvin scale to the Celsius scale just subtract 273, and to convert from the Celsius scale to the Kelvin scale add 273.

2 a) The substance is melting *[1 mark]*.

b) Melting point = –7 °C *[1 mark]*
Boiling point = 58 °C *[1 mark]*

3 $\frac{p_1}{T_1} = \frac{p_2}{T_2}$

$p_2 = \frac{p_1 \times T_2}{T_1} = \frac{107 \times 405}{288} =$ **150 kPa (to 3 s.f.)**

[3 marks if answer correct, otherwise 1 mark for correct rearrangement of the equation and 1 mark for correct substitution of values into the equation.]

4 a) i) The pressure increases *[1 mark]*. The volume decrease leads to the number of collisions in a given time on a given area between particles and the walls of the cylinder increasing *[1 mark]* and so the force applied by the particles to the cylinder walls increases *[1 mark]*.

ii) $p_1V_1 = p_2V_2$

$p_2 = \frac{p_1 V_1}{V_2} = \frac{98 \times 0.014}{0.013} = 105.53... =$ **110 kPa (to 2 s.f.)**

[3 marks if answer correct, otherwise 1 mark for correct rearrangement of the equation and 1 mark for correct substitution of values into the equation.]

b) As the gas is heated, the average energy in the kinetic energy stores of the particles increases *[1 mark]*. This means they move faster and collide with the walls more often in a given time *[1 mark]*, increasing the outwards force/pressure on the walls of the cylinder *[1 mark]*.

5 E.g. measure the mass of the empty insulated flask and then fill it with the liquid you are testing. Measure the mass of the flask again to find the mass of the liquid *[1 mark]*. Connect the power supply to the joulemeter and the immersion heater and place the immersion heater into the liquid *[1 mark]*. Measure the temperature of the liquid using the thermometer *[1 mark]* and then turn on the immersion heater. Turn off the immersion heater once the temperature of the liquid has increased by 10 °C *[1 mark]*. Read the energy shown on the joulemeter and use $\Delta Q = m \times c \times \Delta T$ to calculate the specific heat capacity *[1 mark]*.

Page 114
Revision Questions

2) $\rho = m \div V$
$V = m \div \rho = 2 \div 1000 =$ **0.002 m³**

5) $F = p \div A$
$A = 5 \text{ cm}^2 = 0.0005 \text{ m}^2$
$F = 600 \div 0.0005 =$ **1 200 000 Pa** (or **1200 kPa**)

12) $p_1V_1 = p_2V_2$
$p_2 = (p_1V_1) \div V_2 = (50 \times 500) \div 100 =$ **250 kPa**

13) $\frac{p_1}{T_1} = \frac{p_2}{T_2}$
$p_2 = \frac{p_1 \times T_2}{T_1} = \frac{50 \times 300}{290} = 51.724... =$ **52 kPa (to 2 s.f.)**

15) $\Delta Q = m \times c \times \Delta T$
$c = \Delta Q \div (m \times \Delta T)$
$\Delta T = 45 - 21 = 24 \text{ °C}$
$c = 110 \div (0.25 \times 24) = 18.333... =$ **18 J/kg °C (to 2 s.f.)**

Section 6 — Magnetism and Electromagnetism

Pages 119-120
Warm-Up Questions

1)

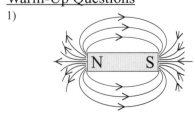

2) False
3) It means it loses its induced magnetism quickly.
4) In the direction of the current.

Exam Questions

1 a) The field is uniform / The field lines are straight, parallel and evenly spaced *[1 mark]*.
b) Attraction *[1 mark]* — opposite poles attract *[1 mark]*.

2 E.g. put the magnets on a piece of paper and place many compasses in different places between the magnets to show the magnetic field at those points *[1 mark]*. The compasses will line up with the magnetic field lines *[1 mark]*.
You could also have described how to use iron filings to shown the pattern — that would get you the marks too.

3 a) A coil of wire *[1 mark]*.
b)

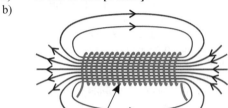

coil of wire   magnetic field

Inside the coil, the field is uniform. Outside the coil, the field is the same as that of a bar magnet.
[1 mark for showing by sketch or for saying that the field is uniform inside the coil and 1 mark for showing by sketch or saying that the field is like that of a bar magnet outside the coil.]

c) When the electromagnet is turned on, current flows through the coil of wire and produces a magnetic field *[1 mark]*. Iron is a magnetic material, so magnetism is induced in it and the bar is attracted to the electromagnet *[1 mark]*. When the current stops, there is no longer a magnetic field around the electromagnet *[1 mark]*. Magnetism is no longer induced in the bar, so it is no longer attracted to the electromagnet and drops *[1 mark]*.

d) Magnetically hard materials don't lose their magnetism quickly *[1 mark]*, so when the electromagnet is turned off the core will stay magnetic for a while and still attract iron and steel, meaning the crane won't drop the metal *[1 mark]*.

4 a) E.g.

N   S

[1 mark for any indication that the current goes anticlockwise.]

b) After 90° the force on the top arm will act upwards and the force on the bottom arm will act downwards, so the forces will oppose the rotation of the loop *[1 mark]*.

c) By swapping the direction of the current/contacts every half turn (using a split-ring commutator) *[1 mark]* so the forces on the loop always act in a way that keeps the loop rotating *[1 mark]*.

d) E.g. increase the current. / Increase the number of turns on the loop. / Increase the strength of the magnetic field. *[1 mark]*

5 When the a.c. current flows through the coil of wire in the magnetic field of the permanent magnet, the coil of wire experiences a force *[1 mark]*. The force causes the coil, and so the cone, to move *[1 mark]*. The a.c. current is constantly changing direction, so the force on the coil is constantly changing. This causes the cone to vibrate back and forth *[1 mark]*. The vibrations cause the air to vibrate, producing sound waves *[1 mark]*.

Page 125

Warm-Up Questions

1) Electromagnetic induction is the creation of a voltage (and maybe a current) in a wire which is experiencing a change in magnetic field.

2) False

It's motors that have split-ring commutators — a.c. generators use slip rings and brushes instead.

3) A step-up transformer increases the voltage of an alternating current. They have more turns on their secondary coil than their primary coil.
A step-down transformer decreases the voltage. They have more turns on their primary coil.

Exam Questions

1   C *[1 mark]*

2 a) As the wheel rotates, the magnet rotates inside the coil of wire *[1 mark]*. This creates a changing magnetic field in the coil of wire which induces a voltage *[1 mark]*.

   b) Any two from: e.g. increase the strength of the magnet. / Increase the number of turns on the coil of wire. / Increase the speed of rotation of the magnet.
[2 marks — 1 mark for each correct answer.]

3 a) A step-up transformer is used to increase the voltage of electricity supplied by the power stations to be very high *[1 mark]*. A higher voltage means less current for a given power (as $P = I \times V$) and so less energy lost as heat *[1 mark]*. Step-down transformers are then used to bring the voltage of the supply back down to a safe level to be supplied to the consumer *[1 mark]*.

   b) i) $$\frac{\text{input (primary) voltage}}{\text{output (secondary) voltage}} = \frac{\text{number of turns on primary}}{\text{number of turns on secondary}}$$
or $\frac{V_p}{V_s} = \frac{n_p}{n_s}$ *[1 mark]*

     ii) $\frac{V_p}{V_s} = \frac{n_p}{n_s}$, so $V_s = \frac{n_s}{n_p} \times V_p$
$\frac{n_s}{n_p} = 16$ and $V_p = 25\,000$ V
So $V_s = 16 \times 25\,000 = $ **400 000 V**
[4 marks for correct answer, otherwise, 1 mark for rearranging the equation correctly, 1 mark for saying that $n_s \div n_p = 16$ (separately or as part of the equation), and 1 mark for substituting the numbers correctly into the equation.]

Page 126

Revision Questions

18) $\frac{V_p}{V_s} = \frac{n_p}{n_s}$ so $V_s = \frac{n_s}{n_p} \times V_p = (50 \div 10) \times 30 = $ **150 V**

19) $V_p I_p = V_s I_s$ so $V_p I_p = 6000$. $I_p = 6000 \div 30\,000 = $ **0.2 A**

Section 7 — Radioactivity and Particles

Pages 132-133

Warm-Up Questions

1) The total number of protons and neutrons in the nucleus.

2) an ion

3) Alpha particles are large and heavy, so they collide with lots of atoms, causing ionisation.

4) beta (particles)

5) gamma (rays)

Exam Questions

1 a) i)

Particle	Charge	Number present in an atom of iodine-131
Proton	positive	53
Neutron	zero	78
Electron	negative	53

[3 marks — 1 mark for each correct answer]

     ii) protons and neutrons *[1 mark]*

   b) A *[1 mark]*

Isotopes have the same number of protons but a different number of neutrons, so they have the same atomic number (no. of protons) but a different mass number (no. of protons and neutrons). The number of protons always equals the number of electrons in a neutral atom.

   c) i) background radiation *[1 mark]*

     ii) Any two from: e.g. air / food / building materials / soils / rocks / radiation from space (cosmic rays) / living things *[2 marks — 1 mark for each correct answer]*.

   d) gamma (rays) *[1 mark]*, alpha (particles) *[1 mark]*, beta (particles) *[1 mark]*, neutron radiation *[1 mark]*

2 a) Beta (particles) *[1 mark]*, because it passes through the paper, but not the aluminium (so it is moderately penetrating) *[1 mark]*.

   b) photographic film *[1 mark]*

   c) Background radiation is not due to the sources the student is using in the experiment *[1 mark]*. The student needs to subtract the background count rate so that her results only include the radiation emitted by the source *[1 mark]*.

3 a) $^{1}_{0}\text{n}$ *[1 mark]*

   b) $^{199}_{84}\text{Po} \rightarrow {}^{195}_{82}\text{Pb} + {}^{4}_{2}\alpha + {}^{0}_{0}\gamma$

[4 marks — 1 mark for the α atomic and mass numbers correct, 1 mark for the γ atomic and mass numbers correct, and 1 mark each for the mass and atomic numbers of Po.]

4 a) The atomic number doesn't change *[1 mark]* and neither does the mass number *[1 mark]*.

   b) 208 *[1 mark]*. Alpha decay reduces the mass number by 4 as 2 neutrons and 2 protons are emitted as an alpha particle *[1 mark]*. Beta decay doesn't affect the mass number as a neutron turns into a proton in the nucleus *[1 mark]*. Gamma decay doesn't affect the mass number (or the atomic number) *[1 mark]*.

Pages 141-142

Warm-Up Questions

1) becquerels (Bq)

2) gamma (rays) and beta (particles)

3) Squirt a gamma source into the pipe, let it flow along, and go along the outside with a detector. If there's a crack in the pipe, the gamma source will collect outside the pipe, and your detector will show extra-high radioactivity at that point.

4) Because big movements in the ground could disturb the canisters the radioactive material is buried in and allow it to leak out. If this material gets into the groundwater it could contaminate the soil, plants, rivers, etc. and get into our drinking water.

Exam Questions

1 a) i) $2 \times 60 = 120$ seconds
$120 \div 40 = 3$ half-lives
$8000 \div 2 = 4000$, $4000 \div 2 = 2000$, $2000 \div 2 = $ **1000 Bq**
[2 marks for the correct answer, otherwise 1 mark for calculating the number of half-lives.]

ii) 8000 ÷ 2 = 4000, 4000 ÷ 2 = 2000, 2000 ÷ 2 = 1000,
1000 ÷ 2 = 500, 500 ÷ 2 = 250, 250 ÷ 2 = 125.
So it takes 6 half-lives to drop to less than 200 Bq.
6 × 40 = 240 seconds
240 ÷ 60 = **4 mins**
*[3 marks for the correct answer, otherwise 1 mark
for calculating the number of half-lives and 1 mark
for calculating the number of seconds.]*

b) A *[1 mark]*

2 a) Contamination is when unwanted radioactive
particles get onto an object *[1 mark]*.

b) Irradiation: Any one of: e.g. use shielding/stand behind
barriers / work in a different room to the source / store the
sample in a lead-lined box *[1 mark]*.
Contamination: Any one of: e.g. wear gloves / handle the
source with tongs / wear a protective suit or mask *[1 mark]*.

3 a) The iodine-123 is absorbed in the same way that the
patient's body normally absorbs iodine, but gives out
radiation which can be detected outside the body *[1 mark]*.
The patient is given iodine-123 and the amount of
radiation emitted from the thyroid gland is monitored to
check whether it is absorbing iodine properly *[1 mark]*.

b) Alpha particles can't penetrate tissue/would be blocked
by the body *[1 mark]*, so you couldn't detect them
outside of the body *[1 mark]*. Alpha particles are also
strongly ionising *[1 mark]* so they're dangerous
to use as medical tracers *[1 mark]*.

c) Technetium-99m because it's got a short half-life
[1 mark], which means it's easier to detect because
its activity is higher/it won't be very radioactive
inside the patient for long *[1 mark]*.

4 a) E.g. Uranium-235/U-235 *[1 mark]*

b) i) A slow-moving neutron gets absorbed by a uranium-235
nucleus causing it to split *[1 mark]*. The uranium nucleus
will split to form two daughter nuclei *[1 mark]*,
a small number of neutrons *[1 mark]* and a large amount
of energy *[1 mark]*.

ii) In a nuclear reactor, the neutrons released from each
fission event collide with other uranium nuclei causing
other fission events that release more neutrons *[1 mark]*.
This is known as a chain reaction *[1 mark]*.
The nuclear reactor contains a moderator that slows
down the neutrons released from fission so that they
can successfully collide with uranium nuclei *[1 mark]*.

c) They limit the rate of fission by absorbing excess neutrons
[1 mark].

5 A high temperature and pressure are needed for the
reaction to take place *[1 mark]*. This is because
the protons are positive, so they repel each other *[1 mark]*.
To get close enough to fuse together, they need to overcome
this electrostatic repulsion. This means they need lots
of energy in their kinetic energy stores *[1 mark]*.

Section 8 — Astrophysics

Page 147
Warm-Up Questions
1) The Milky Way
2) E.g. the mass of the planet and the distance of the object
from the planet.
3) Convert the orbital radius to m:
$r = 55\ 000\ 000 \times 1000 = 55\ 000\ 000\ 000 = 5.5 \times 10^{10}$ m
Convert the time period to seconds:
$T = 1800 \times 60 \times 60 = 6\ 480\ 000$ s
Put the numbers into the formula for orbital speed:
$$v = \frac{2 \times \pi \times r}{T} = \frac{2 \times \pi \times (5.5 \times 10^{10})}{6\ 480\ 000}$$
$= 53\ 329.50... = $ **53 000 m/s (to 2 s.f.)**

Exam Questions
1 a) B *[1 mark]*.
2 a) C *[1 mark]* — Comets usually have highly elliptical
orbits with the Sun not at the centre *[1 mark]*.

b) 1.2 km/s, e.g. because orbital speed only depends on
the orbital radius and the time period. *[1 mark]*

c) Convert time period to s, $T = 24 \times 60 \times 60 = 86\ 400$ s
Convert radius to m, $r = 42\ 000 \times 1000 = 42\ 000\ 000$ m
$$v = \frac{2 \times \pi \times r}{T} = \frac{2 \times \pi \times 42\ 000\ 000}{86\ 400}$$
$= 3054.326... = $ **3100 m/s (to 2 s.f.)**
*[3 marks if answer correct, otherwise 1 mark for
correct conversion of units and 1 mark for correct
substitution of values into the equation.]*

3 a) time period = $72.0 \times 365 \times 24 \times 60 \times 60$
$= 2\ 270\ 592\ 000$ s
$= $ **2.27 × 10⁹ s (to 3 s.f.)** *[1 mark]*

*There are 365 days in a year, 24 hours in a day, 60 minutes in an hour
and 60 seconds in a minute — that's where all these numbers come from.*

b) At the point where the comet is at its closest point to
the star *[1 mark]* because that's where the gravitational
force on the comet from the star is strongest *[1 mark]*.

c) Convert km/s to m/s: $v = 7.4 \times 1000 = 7400$ m/s
Rearrange $v = \frac{2 \times \pi \times r}{T}$ to make r (orbital radius) the subject:
$$r = \frac{v \times T}{2 \times \pi} = \frac{7400 \times 2\ 270\ 592\ 000}{2 \times \pi}$$
$= 2.6741... \times 10^{12}$ m $= $ **2.67 × 10¹² m (to 3 s.f.)**
*[3 marks if answer correct, otherwise 1 mark for
correct rearrangement of the equation and 1 mark for
correct substitution of values into the equation.]*

*If you used 7.4 km/s in the formula to give an answer in km and then
converted that to m instead, that's fine too.*

Pages 153-154
Warm-Up Questions
1) False
2) Very hot stars emit more high frequency light than
lower frequency light, and so they appear blue.
3) E.g. how bright a star is when seen from Earth depends
on its distance from Earth — so a dim star may look
the same as a bright one if it is nearer to the Earth.
4) That distant galaxies are moving away from us at high speed.

Exam Questions
1 a) B *[1 mark]*
b) A cloud of dust and gas in space *[1 mark]*.
c) gravitational force / gravity *[1 mark]*
2 a) D *[1 mark]*
b) Alkaid is the brightest star *[1 mark]* as it has the
lowest absolute magnitude (and the lower the absolute
magnitude, the brighter the star) *[1 mark]*.
3 a) Tadpole Galaxy *[1 mark]*. It is the furthest away *[1 mark]*,
so it is likely to be travelling away fastest *[1 mark]*.
b) Measurements of red-shift show all the distant galaxies,
(whichever direction you look in) are moving away
from us *[1 mark]*, and that the more distant a galaxy,
the faster it's moving away *[1 mark]*. This suggests
that the universe is expanding from a single point
[1 mark]. Something must have initially started the
expansion, which we think was the Big Bang *[1 mark]*.
4 The star initially forms from a nebula (a cloud of dust and
gas) that is drawn together by gravity (to form a protostar)
[1 mark]. As the dust and gas are drawn together, the star
gets denser and hotter (and the particles of dust and gas
collide more). Eventually, the temperature gets hot enough
for hydrogen nuclei to undergo nuclear fusion to form
helium, and the star becomes a main sequence star *[1 mark]*.
When the star's core runs out of hydrogen, the star expands
and turns red and forms a red supergiant *[1 mark]*.

The red supergiant eventually explodes in a supernova *[1 mark]*. The supernova throws the outer layer of dust and gas into space, leaving behind either a very dense neutron star *[1 mark]*, or an even denser black hole, depending on its size *[1 mark]*.

5 a) $\Delta\lambda = (612.5 \times 10^{-9}) - (587.5 \times 10^{-9}) = 25 \times 10^{-9}$ m

$$\frac{\Delta\lambda}{\lambda_0} = \frac{v}{c}$$

Rearrange to find velocity:

$$v = \frac{\Delta\lambda \times c}{\lambda_0} = \frac{(25 \times 10^{-9}) \times (3.0 \times 10^{8})}{587.5 \times 10^{-9}}$$

$= 1.27659... \times 10^7$ m/s $= \mathbf{1.277 \times 10^7}$ **m/s (to 4 s.f.)**

[3 marks for correct answer, otherwise 1 mark for correct calculation of $\Delta\lambda$ and 1 mark for correct rearrangement and substitution.]

b) $$\frac{\Delta\lambda}{\lambda_0} = \frac{v}{c}$$

Rearrange to find $\Delta\lambda$:

$$\Delta\lambda = \frac{v \times \lambda_0}{c} = \frac{(1.27659... \times 10^7) \times (686.7 \times 10^{-9})}{3.0 \times 10^8}$$

$= 29.221... \times 10^{-9}$ m

$\lambda = \lambda_0 + \Delta\lambda = (686.7 \times 10^{-9}) + (29.221... \times 10^{-9})$

$= 715.921... \times 10^{-9}$

$= \mathbf{715.9 \times 10^{-9}}$ **m** or $\mathbf{7.159 \times 10^{-7}}$ **m (to 4 s.f.)**

[3 marks for correct answer, otherwise 1 mark for correct rearrangement and substitution and 1 mark for correct calculation of $\Delta\lambda$.]

You'd still get all the marks for part b) if you got the answer to part a) wrong, as long as your method in b) was correct.

Page 155
Revision Questions

14) Rearrange $\dfrac{\Delta\lambda}{\lambda_0} = \dfrac{v}{c}$ to find λ_0:

$$\lambda_0 = \frac{\Delta\lambda \times c}{v} = \frac{(15 \times 10^{-9}) \times (3.0 \times 10^8)}{7.8 \times 10^6}$$

$= 5.769... \times 10^{-7}$ m $= \mathbf{5.8 \times 10^{-7}}$ **m (to 2 s.f.)**

Practice Paper 1P

1 a) i) B *[1 mark]*

  ii) B *[1 mark]*

b) i) Gravitational potential energy = mass × gravitational field strength × height / GPE = $m \times g \times h$ *[1 mark]*

  ii) GPE = $m \times g \times h$ = 1500 × 10 × 40 = 600 000 J = **600 kJ**
  [2 marks for correct answer in kJ, otherwise 1 mark for substituting the correct values into the correct equation.]

c) i) elastic potential energy store (of the spring) *[1 mark]*

  ii) efficiency = $\dfrac{\text{useful energy output}}{\text{total energy output}} \times 100\%$ *[1 mark]*

  iii) useful energy output = 18.0 kJ
  total energy output = useful energy output + wasted energy
  $= 18.0 + 41.5 = 59.5$ kJ
  So efficiency = $\dfrac{\text{useful energy output}}{\text{total energy output}} \times 100\% = \dfrac{18.0}{59.5} \times 100\%$
  $= \mathbf{30.3\%}$ **(to 3 s.f.)**
  [3 marks available for correct answer, otherwise 1 mark for calculating the total energy output (and input) and 1 mark for substituting correctly into correct equation.]

2 a) 27 s *[1 mark]*

b) i) The gradient tells you the speed, so the speed is constant when the graph is linear. The graph is linear between 15 s and 27 s, so: $27 - 15 = \mathbf{12}$ **s** *[1 mark]*

  ii) 0 N *[1 mark]*
  When an object is travelling at a constant speed in a fixed direction, all the forces are balanced and so the resultant force will be zero.

c) B *[1 mark]*.
  The swimmer is travelling fastest when the gradient of the graph is steepest. Of the options given, the graph is steepest between 9 m and 10 m. You can draw a tangent to see this more clearly.

d) i) (average) speed = $\dfrac{\text{distance moved}}{\text{time taken}}$ / $v = \dfrac{s}{t}$ *[1 mark]*

  ii) $v = \dfrac{s}{t} = \dfrac{20}{25} = \mathbf{0.8}$ **m/s**
  [2 marks for correct answer, otherwise 1 mark for correct substitution.]

  iii)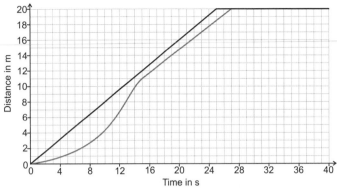

  [1 mark for the first section of the line being a straight upwards slope, 1 mark for the sloped section having the correct start and end points.]

e) Yes, the camera will be able to film the swimmer for the whole length because its distance-time graph is always above the swimmer's *[1 mark]*, and so the camera is always ahead of the swimmer (or level at $t = 0$) *[1 mark]*.

3 a) The thickness of the cotton wool jacket *[1 mark]*.

b) E.g. starting temperature of the water / length of time water is left to cool / volume of water used *[1 mark]*.

c) The pockets of air cannot move *[1 mark]*, which prevents convection currents from forming around the outside of the beaker *[1 mark]*.

d) i) Calculate the mean (average) of her data for each cotton wool jacket thickness *[1 mark]*.

  ii) E.g. the graph shows that for this beaker of water, the final temperature of the water increases with the thickness of the cotton wool jacket *[1 mark]*.

4 a) Stopping distance = thinking distance + braking distance
  $= 9 + 14 = \mathbf{23}$ **m** *[1 mark]*

b) E.g. so that an average value can be calculated *[1 mark]*. This makes the data more reliable because any individual vehicle may have an extreme value of braking distance / because any individual driver may have an extreme value of thinking distance *[1 mark]*.

c) Any three from: e.g. the thinking distance is increased if the driver is tired / under the influence of drugs/alcohol / elderly / inexperienced.
  The braking distance is increased in poor weather conditions / if the surface of the road is slippery / if the car is heavier / if the brakes/tyres are worn/faulty.
  [5 marks available — 1 mark for each correct factor (up to 3 total) and 2 marks for all correctly linked to braking or thinking distance, otherwise 1 mark for only two correctly linked to braking or thinking distance.]

5 a) gravity *[1 mark]*

b) $v = \dfrac{2 \times \pi \times r}{T}$ where r is the distance from the satellite to the centre of the Earth.
  Convert T to seconds, $T = 24 \times 60 \times 60 = 86\ 400$ s
  so $r = \dfrac{v \times T}{2 \times \pi} = \dfrac{3080 \times 86\ 400}{2 \times \pi}$
  $= 42\ 353\ 040.2... $ m $= \mathbf{42\ 400\ 000}$ **m (to 3 s.f.)**
  [3 marks for correct answer, otherwise 1 mark for converting the time period to seconds, 1 mark for correctly rearranging and substituting into the equation.]

c) The object will weigh less on Venus than on Earth *[1 mark]* as the gravitational field strength on Venus is lower than on Earth (and weight is proportional to gravitational field strength) *[1 mark]*.

d) red giant (star) *[1 mark]*

6 a) Any two from: e.g. it can cause cell/tissue damage *[1 mark]* / cell death *[1 mark]* / cell mutations/cancer *[1 mark]* / radiation sickness *[1 mark]*.

b) Geiger-Müller detector *[1 mark]*

c) i)

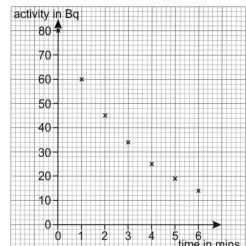

[3 marks available — 1 mark for suitable scales chosen (more than half of the graph paper is used), 1 mark for the axes correctly labelled with variables and units, 1 mark for all the points plotted correctly to within half a square. Deduct 1 mark if 2 or more points are plotted incorrectly.]

ii)

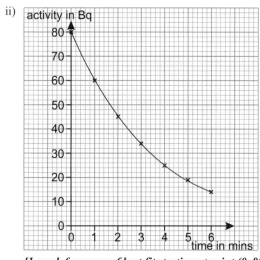

[1 mark for curve of best fit starting at point (0, 80), 1 mark for suitable curve of best fit.]

iii) Half-life = **2.4 mins** (accept any value between 2.3-2.5)
[2 marks for correct answer, otherwise 1 mark for attempting to use the graph correctly to find the half-life.]

To find this, you needed to draw a horizontal line from 40 Bq (half of the initial activity) on the activity axis across to the curve. Then you draw a vertical line down to the time axis to find the value of the half-life.

d) Any one from: e.g. some substances on Earth, such as air/food/building materials/soil/rocks *[1 mark]*. / Radiation from space/cosmic rays *[1 mark]*. / All living things contain radioactive material *[1 mark]*. / Nuclear waste *[1 mark]*. / Radioactive material released from past nuclear explosions *[1 mark]*.

e) i) $^{226}_{88}$Ra → $^{222}_{86}$Rn + $^{4}_{2}\alpha$ *[1 mark]*

ii) C *[1 mark]*

7 a) current *[1 mark]*

b) i) E.g. he has not ignored the anomalous point *[1 mark]*.

ii) Voltage = current × resistance / $V = I \times R$ *[1 mark]*

iii) $V = 5$ V, $I = 1.4$ A

$V = I \times R$ so $R = \dfrac{V}{I} = \dfrac{5}{1.4} = $ **3.6 Ω (to 2 s.f.)**

[3 marks for the correct answer, otherwise 1 mark for correctly substituting into the equation and 1 mark for the correct unit.]

c) i) The graph of the fixed resistor will be a straight line (through the origin), while the graph for the lamp is a curve *[1 mark]*.

ii) The shapes of the graphs are different because the resistance of the fixed resistor is constant (so current is directly proportional to voltage) *[1 mark]*, while the resistance of the lamp increases with current *[1 mark]*.

8 a) clockwise *[1 mark]*

Use Fleming's left-hand rule and remember the magnetic field goes from north to south.

b) A current-carrying wire in a magnetic field experiences a force due to the motor effect *[1 mark]*. The force causes one side of the coil to move upwards and one side to move downwards, causing it to rotate *[1 mark]*.

c) Any two from: e.g. increase the number of turns on the coil *[1 mark]*. / Increase the current in the wire *[1 mark]*. / Increase the magnetic field strength *[1 mark]*.

9 a) $P = \dfrac{F}{A} = \dfrac{25}{0.01} = $ **2500 Pa**

[2 marks for correct answer, otherwise 1 mark for correct substitution.]

b) The force on piston A causes a pressure in the liquid *[1 mark]*. This pressure in the liquid is transmitted equally through the liquid in all directions *[1 mark]*. The pressure of the liquid at piston B causes a force on piston B *[1 mark]*.

c) The pressure on piston B is equal to the pressure on the liquid from piston A: $P_A = P_B$.
So the pressure on piston B = P_B = 2500 Pa
Force on piston B = F_B
$F_B = P_B \times$ Area of piston B = 2500 × 0.15 = 375 N
[2 marks available — 1 mark for stating the pressures on pistons A and B are equal, 1 mark for substituting into the correctly rearranged equation to find the force on piston B.]

10 a) The angle of incidence when a ray hits the outer layer of a fibre is greater than the critical angle *[1 mark]*, so the ray is totally internally reflected and almost none 'escapes' *[1 mark]*.

b) i) E.g. shine a light ray at the block on a piece of paper, at an angle to the block's surface, and trace the block and the incident and emergent rays *[1 mark]*. Remove the block and draw in the refracted ray by connecting the incident and emerging rays. Draw in the normals, and measure the angle of incidence *[1 mark]* and the angle of refraction *[1 mark]* at the air-material boundary. Use the equation

$n = \dfrac{\sin i}{\sin r}$ to calculate the refractive index *[1 mark]*.

You could say lots of other things here. For example, you could say that you'll repeat the experiment for different values of i, or that you'll take several measurements at each value of i.

ii) E.g. laser beams can cause blindness if they shine in your eyes *[1 mark]*, so the student should wear special goggles/ensure that the laser beam is never pointed towards a person/make sure no one stands in front of the laser beam *[1 mark]*.

c) θ = critical angle (c).

$\sin c = \dfrac{1}{n}$ so,

$\theta = \sin^{-1}\left(\dfrac{1}{n}\right) = \sin^{-1}\left(\dfrac{1}{1.5}\right) = 41.81...°$
$= $ **42° (to 2 s.f.)**

[4 marks for correct answer, otherwise 1 mark for stating the equation for sin c, 1 mark for rearranging the equation correctly and 1 mark for correctly substituting into the equation.]

11 a) i) Total distance travelled = total area under the graph.
Splitting it into a rectangle (0-19 s) and a triangle (19-26 s):
Area under the graph = (19 × 15) + ((7 × 15) ÷ 2)
$= $ **337.5 m**
[2 marks for the correct answer, otherwise 1 mark for indicating that the distance is represented by the area under the graph and showing working to calculate the area under the entire graph.]

ii) gradient of velocity-time graph = acceleration

so acceleration = $\frac{\text{change in } y}{\text{change in } x} = \frac{0-15}{26-19} = \frac{-15}{7}$

$= -2.14285...$ m/s^2

$F = m \times a$, and since the question only asks for the size of the force, you can ignore the minus sign:

So, $F = 1000 \times 2.142... = 2142.85... N = $ **2140 N (to 3 s.f.)**

[4 marks for correct answer, otherwise 1 mark for correct calculation of the gradient of sloped section of v-t graph, 1 mark for equating this to the acceleration, and 1 mark for correct substitution into F = m × a.]

You could also have done this by finding the change in speed from the graph, and using force = change in momentum ÷ time. You'd still get all the marks if you did it correctly this way.

b) i) E.g. at point A when the skydiver first jumps, the downwards force of his weight due to gravity is pulling him down and there are no resistive forces (drag) acting upwards *[1 mark]*. As the skydiver's velocity increases, the resistive forces acting upwards increase *[1 mark]*. When the resistive forces acting upwards balance the force of his weight acting downwards *[1 mark]*, he reaches his terminal velocity and remains at a steady speed until point B *[1 mark]*.

ii) E.g. opening the parachute causes the surface area to increase *[1 mark]*. This causes the resistive forces on the skydiver to increase (while the downwards force of his weight remains unchanged), causing deceleration *[1 mark]*.

12 a) The microwave oven emits microwaves *[1 mark]*. The microwaves penetrate a few centimetres into the food before being absorbed by the water molecules in the food *[1 mark]*. The energy is then conducted or convected to other parts of the food *[1 mark]*.

b) i) speed = frequency × wavelength / $v = f \times \lambda$ *[1 mark]*

ii) $v = f \times \lambda$ so $\lambda = \frac{v}{f} = \frac{3.0 \times 10^8}{2.5 \times 10^9} = $ **0.12 m**

[2 marks for correct answer, otherwise 1 mark for substituting into the correctly rearranged equation.]

c) i) Some microwaves are absorbed by molecules in the body and can heat human body tissue internally *[1 mark]*. Some people are worried that this might damage health *[1 mark]*.

ii) Radio waves have fewer harmful effects than microwaves because they have a lower frequency *[1 mark]* and so transfer less energy *[1 mark]*.

Practice Paper 2P

1 a) i) D *[1 mark]*

ii) The paint drops all have the same negative charge and so repel each other, forming a fine spray *[1 mark]*. The drops are attracted to the (positively-charged) body panel *[1 mark]*, and so spread out across the panel, including to parts that are not directly facing the spray gun *[1 mark]*.

b) i) E.g. during refuelling, friction causes electrons to be transferred between the fuel and the metal tanker *[1 mark]*. If the tank was made of an insulator, electrons transferred would be unable to move / to be conducted away, and so a charge would build up on the tank *[1 mark]*.

ii) A build-up of charge can cause a spark, and since the fuel and its vapours are flammable, this could cause a fire or an explosion *[1 mark]*.

2 a) momentum = mass × velocity / $p = m \times v$ *[1 mark]*

b) Skater A: $p = m \times v = 70 \times 9.0 = $ **630 kg m/s** *[1 mark]*
Skater B: $p = m \times v = 50 \times 6.6 = $ **330 kg m/s** *[1 mark]*

c) $p = m \times v \Rightarrow v = \frac{p}{m} = \frac{630+330}{70+50} = $ **8 m/s**

[2 marks if answer correct, otherwise 1 mark for correct rearrangement of the equation and correct substitution of values into the equation.]

You'll still get the marks in part c) if either of your answers from part b) were wrong, as long as you used the correct method.

d) i) Skater B exerts a force of 100 N in the opposite direction to the original force *[1 mark]*.

ii) (Unbalanced) force = mass × acceleration / $F = m \times a$ *[1 mark]*

iii) $F = m \times a$
$a = F \div m = 100 \div 50 = $ **2 m/s^2**

[3 marks if answer correct, otherwise 1 mark for correct rearrangement of the equation and correct substitution of values into the equation and 1 mark for the correct unit.]

3 a) i) Biofuels = 6×10^9 kWh *[1 mark]*
Hydroelectric = 1×10^9 kWh *[1 mark]*

Allow 1 mark only if the answers are 6 kWh and 1 kWh and the × 10^9 is omitted.

ii) Wind power *[1 mark]*

iii) E.g. there are more hours of daylight in summer than in winter, so more electricity can be generated from solar power / there are generally more clear days during summer so more electricity can be generated from solar power *[1 mark]*.

b) Advantage: e.g. non-renewables are reliable / we can easily alter energy output to meet demand *[1 mark]*. Disadvantage: e.g. non-renewables will eventually run out / burning some non-renewables, e.g. fossil fuels, produces pollutants / burning some non-renewables, e.g. fossil fuels, can cause global warming *[1 mark]*.

c) $100 - 59.2 - 23.9 = $ **16.9%** *[1 mark]*

d) Advantages — any two from: e.g. the reaction in the nuclear reactor doesn't produce any carbon dioxide emissions (it doesn't contribute to global warming/air pollution). / There is still a lot of nuclear fuel left in the ground. / Nuclear reactions release more energy for the amount of fuel used compared to burning fossil fuels.
[2 marks — 1 mark for each correct advantage.]
Disadvantages — any two from: e.g. it takes longer/costs more to start up nuclear power stations than fossil fuel power stations. / There's a risk with nuclear power of leaks of radioactive material or major catastrophe. / Radioactive waste from nuclear power stations is very dangerous and difficult to dispose of safely. / Decommissioning nuclear power stations is very expensive.
[2 marks — 1 mark for each correct disadvantage.]

4 a) i) E.g. room temperature/power supplied to heater *[1 mark]*.

ii) Control variables need to be kept constant to make sure that any observed changes are due to just one variable (the independent variable) being changed *[1 mark]*.

b) i)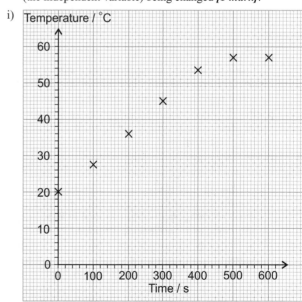

[3 marks — 1 mark for suitable scales chosen (more than half of the graph paper is used), 1 mark for the axes correctly labelled with quantities and units, 1 mark for all the points plotted correctly to within half a square. Deduct 1 mark if 2 or more points are plotted incorrectly.]

ii)

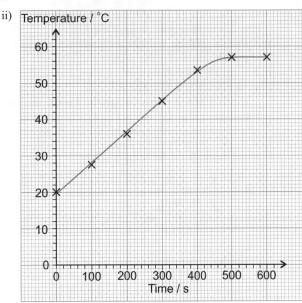

[2 marks — 1 mark for line of best fit drawn straight until 350 s, 1 mark for line of best fit curving to flat at 500 s.]

c) i) gas *[1 mark]*

ii) C *[1 mark]*

iii) The line is flat because a change of state is occurring *[1 mark]* and all energy transferred to the substance is being used to break intermolecular bonds and change the state of the substance, not increase its temperature *[1 mark]*.

d) i) As temperature increases, the volume of the gas increases / volume is proportional to temperature *[1 mark]*.

ii) Temperature = 25 + 273 = 298 K *[1 mark]*
Reading from the graph, volume at 298 K = **6.1 cm³**
[1 mark, allow for error in calculation of temperature carried forward].

To convert from degrees Celsius to kelvins just add 273.
To go from kelvins to Celsius, subtract 273.

5 a) It is a step-up transformer. The voltage increases across it / it has more turns on the secondary coil than the primary coil *[1 mark]*.

b) i) $\dfrac{\text{input (primary) voltage}}{\text{output (secondary) voltage}} = \dfrac{\text{number of turns on primary}}{\text{number of turns on secondary}}$

/ $\dfrac{V_p}{V_s} = \dfrac{N_p}{N_s}$ *[1 mark]*

ii) $\dfrac{V_p}{V_s} = \dfrac{N_p}{N_s}$

$\Rightarrow N_s = \dfrac{N_p \times V_s}{V_p} = \dfrac{5000 \times 400\,000}{25\,000} = \mathbf{80\,000 \text{ turns}}$

[3 marks if answer correct, otherwise 1 mark for correct rearrangement of the equation and 1 mark for correct substitution of values into the equation.]

c) i) input (primary) voltage × input (primary) current = output (secondary) voltage × output (secondary) current
/ $V_p I_p = V_s I_s$ *[1 mark]*

ii) $V_p I_p = V_s I_s$, so:

$I_p = \dfrac{V_s I_s}{V_p} = \dfrac{400\,000 \times 250}{25\,000} = \mathbf{4000\ A}$

[2 marks if answer correct, otherwise 1 mark for correct rearrangement of the equation and correct substitution of values into the equation.]

d) The electricity produced at power stations has too high a current to be transmitted efficiently. Step-up transformers are needed to increase the voltage and so decrease the current before the electricity is distributed *[1 mark]*. This reduces heating in the wires (the higher the current, the larger the heating effect) *[1 mark]*.

6 a) An electromagnet is a coil of wire connected to a voltage supply which produces a magnetic field when a current flows through it *[1 mark]*.

b) i) E.g.

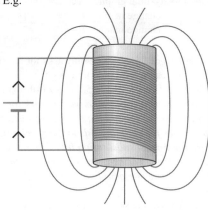

[1 mark]

ii) A magnetically soft core means the core quickly stops being magnetic after the electromagnet is turned off (and so a metal load/object can be dropped) *[1 mark]*.

c) i) moment = force × perpendicular distance from the line of action of the force to the pivot ($M = F \times d$) *[1 mark]*

ii) moment = force × perpendicular distance from the line of action of the force to the pivot
total clockwise moment = 5 × 28 000
total anticlockwise moment = 10 × weight of anvil
total clockwise moment = total anticlockwise moment
5 × 28 000 = 10 × weight of anvil

$\Rightarrow$ weight of anvil = $\dfrac{5 \times 28\,000}{10}$ = **14 000 N**

[3 marks if answer correct, otherwise 1 mark for calculating the clockwise moment and 1 mark for correct rearrangement of the equation and correct substitution of values into the equation.]

7 a) The specific heat capacity of a substance is the energy required to raise the temperature of 1 kg of that substance by 1 °C *[1 mark]*.

b) The results will be more accurate *[1 mark]*, because less of the energy supplied by the coils will be lost from the liquids *[1 mark]*.

c) The change in temperature of a heated substance is dependent on the mass of the substance *[1 mark]*. By keeping both masses the same, any differences in temperature between the two liquids are dependent only on their respective specific heat capacities *[1 mark]*.

d) $\Delta Q = mc\Delta T$
So, $c = \Delta Q \div m\Delta T$
$\Delta T = 93 - 18 = 75$
$c = 126\,000 \div (1 \times 75)$
= **1680 J/kg°C**

[4 marks for correct answer, otherwise 1 mark for correct rearrangement, 1 mark for correct calculation of change in temperature and 1 mark for correct substitution.]

e) Water has a higher specific heat capacity than oil *[1 mark]* so it transfers more energy to the surroundings compared to oil, for the same decrease in temperature *[1 mark]*.

Index